VICTORIAN ASPIRATIONS

VICTORIAN ASPIRATIONS

The Life and Labour
of Charles and Mary Booth

———◦◉◦———

BELINDA NORMAN-BUTLER

London
GEORGE ALLEN & UNWIN LTD
RUSKIN HOUSE   MUSEUM STREET

First published in 1972

© George Allen & Unwin Ltd 1972

ISBN 0 04 923059 X

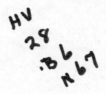

Printed in Great Britain
in 11 point Barbou type
by W & J Mackay Limited, Chatham

*This book has always belonged to my mother
and is dedicated to my two sisters with whom
three is company*

PREFACE

My reasons for writing about my grandparents, Charles and Mary Booth, are three. I knew and loved her for thirty years. I remember him clearly. While Charles Booth's place in social history is well established, very little is known of that working relationship with his wife which puts their marriage into the Curie class, except that the Curies were never apart and the Booths seldom together.

Charles James Booth, a fair, spare, travelled individualist from the provinces, persuaded Mary Macaulay, a brilliant, brown-eyed, vehement London-Scottish girl, to marry him against the stream of her traditional instinct. His original mind was hidden under great reserve. She brimmed over with passionate likes and dislikes. These two totally opposite characters found great happiness and opportunity in their life together. Charles provided for his family by founding the Booth Steamship Company and incorporating it with his brother's leather business. Mary cherished her husband during several years of disturbing ill-health and shouldered the major responsibility of bringing up their six children. Once financially established Charles turned to urgent social problems and applied his own methods of scientific measurement to human need. From 1878 to 1914 he was away from England for at least three months of every year, and whether in the United States or in this country, he was seldom in one place for more than three nights at a stretch. He worked a weekly circuit between London, Liverpool and the Midlands, allowing himself a little more latitude between New York, Boston and Philadelphia. During these absences he consulted his wife daily, by letter, on every aspect of his business and his Inquiry. She entered into the details and decisions of both. She worked on all his manuscripts, rephrasing, regrouping, excising and condensing. Each year, for seventeen years, she saw one volume and several pamphlets through the press.

In her *Memoir* to her husband my grandmother characteristically does not mention her own contribution to his work. In Professor and Mrs Simey's book *Charles Booth: Social Scientist*, a remarkable picture is given of a new science and the man who initiated it, but from this angle only a part of Charles and scarcely anything of Mary can be seen.

I felt therefore than an attempt should be made to set a family conversation piece in the Booth gallery beside the Simeys' half-length portrait and Mary's sketch of her husband.

My uncle, George Macaulay Booth, sent me the family papers and from these another enchanting personality emerged, that of Charles Macaulay, Mary's father. He was as much himself on paper as in person, whereas she was more herself in conversation and action. One of the difficulties of writing this story is that all the main characters in three generations are called Thomas, Charles or Mary. Another is Charles Booth's power of withdrawing himself deliberately behind the scenes he describes with such vividness. Even so the two deepest impulses of his heart are unmistakable: he loved her and he loved his work. In the dedication of the final volume of *Life and Labour in London* his feeling for both are expressed:

> My work now completed has been from first to last dedicated to my wife without whose constant sympathy it could never have been begun, continued, or ended at all.

It is in the light of these words that this story of Charles and Mary Booth's life and labour and love has been written.

St Alban's Grove   B.N.B.
1961–2
1965–6
1969–71

ACKNOWLEDGEMENTS

I wish to put on record the unparalleled assistance given me by my mother, Mrs William Thackeray Ritchie; the vital information and support from my uncles, Colonel Thomas Macaulay Booth and Mr George Macaulay Booth, and from my aunt, Lady Gore-Browne; and the expert advice and personal encouragement of Dr John Pafford and Mr Handasyde Buchanan, without which this book would never have been completed.

I wish to thank the Librarian of the British Library of Political and Economic Science at the London School of Economics for permission to quote the writings and papers of Beatrice Webb; the Goldsmith Librarian for permission to quote from the Booth and Macaulay papers now in the keeping of London University Library; and Mr Timothy Rodgers and Miss Pamela Baker for their help and co-operation in the Palaeography Room.

My thanks are also due to my mother's dearest friends, Miss Ruth Darwin and Lady Barlow, for permission to quote from one of Lady Darwin's letters; to Mr A. W. E. Fletcher for permission to quote from Mr Thomas Fletcher's essay on universal suffrage and from one of his letters to Charles Booth; to Mr John Macaulay Booth for permission to reproduce some family photographs; to the late Judge Felix Frankfurter who in his lifetime gave me permission to quote from *Felix Frankfurter Reminisces*, by Harlan B. Phillips, published by William Morrow and Company, Inc. (copyright Harlan B. Phillips 1960); to Rachel, Lady Clay, for her reminiscences; to Sir James Butler and Mr H. D. Ziman for pruning the first draft; and to all those who have helped me in so many ways.

Finally I must congratulate Miss Stella Brown and Mrs David De Vile on their skill in deciphering my handwriting over many years and express admiration for the judgement and stamina shown by Mrs Henrietta Gatehouse during the last few months.

CONTENTS

ILLUSTRATIONS

I
MACAULAYS AND POTTERS
1768–1867

My grandmother, Mary Catherine Macaulay, was born small, dark and vital on 4 November 1847, and lived in that mould for over ninety-one years. Her father, Charles Zachary Macaulay, a grandson of the manse, was a member of a Highland clan which had gradually migrated from the Outer Isles to London. Her mother belonged to the redoubtable Potter family of Manchester Liberals who had moved to Gloucestershire. Mary was the only daughter and second child of her parents, Tom being four years older and Charles two years younger. Both parents adored the delightful elder boy, while Charles was his mother's favourite. The special link between Mary and her father lasted his lifetime and hers, and lives on now, not only in letters and legends, but in well-remembered references and snatches of talk. 'M'father liked scarlet,' Mary used to say, joining the two words into one, 'and I like scarlet'. In a softer, more intimate voice she called him 'Papa' and would look round about, as if expecting to see him. She spoke of her mother with detachment, but not pity, as of one who had failed in her job as a woman. Nevertheless, Mary inherited as much from the Potters as from the Macaulays and both strands crossed in childhood and formed her character to an unusual extent.[1]

For centuries the McAulays, a branch of the great MacGregor clan, lived in the Western Highlands. Ardincaple on the mainland was their chieftain's home but a younger branch moved to the island of Lewis where neighbour fought neighbour with reciprocal barbarity and scratched a bare living from sea-shore and croft. My grandmother told us that Donald Cam McAulay and his son the Man of Brenish were

---

[1] Those readers to whom ancestry is anathema should turn to page 23 immediately, returning perhaps later on to find out why Mary was such a traditionalist.

famed for courage and endurance but she never mentioned the cunning of Aulay McAulay of Ardincaple, who when the MacGregors were proscribed quickly changed sides and took up with the Protestant Campbells. Influenced no doubt by this example John, son of the Man of Brenish, became a Presbyterian clergyman in Harris, and all his five sons followed him into the Church. When Prince Charlie was hiding in Skye, after his disastrous defeat in the Forty-five, it was one of these sons of the Reverend John McAulay who got wind of his presence and alerted the local representatives of the law, only to be outwitted by Flora Macdonald. Two hundred years later I was disgusted when I learnt of his activities; but at the time the Duke of Argyll, head of the Campbell clan, was evidently pleased by such Protestant zeal, and appointed the young man as his chaplain at Inverary Castle. John McAulay responded by marrying a Campbell and anglicising the spelling of his name.

The third son of his large family, Zachary, was born in 1768 and when he was seventeen became a manager on a sugar estate in Jamaica. Zachary came to loathe his position and thankfully grasped at the first chance of returning to Britain, bringing with him an intense and lasting hatred of slavery. While he had been away his sister, Jean, had married Thomas Babington of Rothley Temple, a wealthy Leicestershire land-owner of great spiritual depth and sweetness, who subsequently became MP for Leicester. In 1787, the year of his marriage, he joined that small group of men who formed the Anti-Slavery Committee under the parliamentary leadership of Wilberforce. The parlour at Rothley became a favourite venue for their deliberations and to this attentive audience Zachary described the tasks of an overseer of slave labour in the sugar-cane fields; the cruelties and indignities suffered by the slaves; the callousness that imperceptibly overcame the man with the whip; and the inevitable degradation of both master and slave. At first his literary ability and first-hand experience were used for propaganda purposes. Later he became governor of the settlement in Sierra Leone which had been established for those slaves who had won their freedom by remaining loyal to Britain during the War of American Independence. After five years' intense responsibility out there Zachary returned to England in 1799 and married a Bristol Quaker, Selina Mills. Their eldest son was born at Rothley Temple the following year and christened Thomas Babington after his uncle. When they left and wherever they moved, in good and bad times, the link with Rothley was never broken. Aunt Jean, with ten children of her own, always had a welcome for her nine Macaulay nieces and nephews. The youngest of all, Charles Zachary,[1] was born in Clapham in 1816, and became in due course the father of the heroine of this story.

Owing to Zachary's concentration on the slave trade controversy money was always short in the Macaulay household but there was a lot of happiness. Charles went daily to his lectures at University College, now the University of London; won a prize of five pounds for rhetoric —not a surprising feat in his family—and studied chemistry and natural science as well as classics and mathematics. Tom, the future historian, who was earning his living by his pen in London at this time, light-heartedly described their youngest brother's behaviour at a dance for his sister Hannah's amusement:

> . . . while I was suffering under a boring conversationalist a smart independent-looking young man dressed like a sailor in a blue jacket and check shirt marched up and asked a Jewish-looking damsel near me to dance with him. I thought I had seen the fellow before; and after a little looking I perceived that it was Charles; and most know-ingly I assure you did he perform a quadrille with Miss Hilpah Manasses. . . . I bade him goodnight. 'What,' said the young hope-ful, 'are you going yet?' It was near one o'clock, but this joyous tar seemed to think it impossible that anybody should dream of leav-ing such delightful enjoyment till daybreak. . . . There is a fancy-dress ball for you. If Charles writes his story of it, tell me which of us does it best.
>
> Ever yours,
> T.B.M.

It is no wonder that the young student turned to his eldest brother as to a heroic friend and mentor. Their relationship thrived as much on paper as in person and was intensified when their mother died suddenly. At this juncture it was decided that Charles should study medicine and surgery in Paris. His French must have been more than adequate al-ready and soon became as fluent as the letters he sent home describing his adventures. In one long budget of news, the mud and cobbles of the road to the capital, the squalor of the inns and villages, the uncurtained windows of Paris itself are contrasted with the glittering splendour of the Palais-Royal, 'where people of all nations and languages . . . are

[1] See the Macaulay family tree p. 232.

talking with an energy and rapidity which to a Macaulay are perfectly confounding'. This is praise indeed!

T. B.'s friend and patron, Lord Holland,[1] had given Charles an introduction to the British Ambassador, who made the young man welcome, as did the Duchesse de Broglie, Madame de Stael's daughter and an ardent Abolitionist. At the very first Embassy soirée he attended, Charles was introduced to Mrs Norton, one of the three beautiful Miss Sheridans, whose divorced husband refused to give her access to her children and actually claimed, as was legally possible at that time, the money she earned by her pen. Both these injustices were set right by her experiences and efforts. Charles quoted the phrase Burke used about Marie-Antoinette—'surely never lighted on this orb, which she scarcely seemed to touch, a more delightful vision'—when describing such radiance to those at home.

Meanwhile Thomas Babington Macaulay, who could have paid his way in Parliament on his literary earnings, had he not been responsible for making a home for his adored sisters, decided that something drastic had to be done to replenish the family purse. Kind Lord Holland put his young protégé's name forward at a time when the British Government had the power of nominating one member of the Indian Legislature but the East India Company directors had the power of veto. As soon as his nomination was approved the reluctant T. B. M. resigned his seat in the House and implored Hannah to join him in his self-imposed exile. In 1834 they set out and within the year she married Charles Trevelyan,[2] his able assistant. Even this happy and likely event, hardly a displacement because the trio formed a joint ménage, caused T. B. considerable pain until the children began to arrive. Then he changed his mind. But his opinion of the disadvantages of colonial service was reinforced by four years' personal experience. In one of the many letters which flowed from him to his brother Charles during this period is a brilliant description of life in Calcutta which had more effect on the young man than he would have wished later on.

In 1838 T. B. Macaulay returned to England, too late to see his father alive, but in time to be present at the dedication of Zachary Macaulay's memorial plaque in Westminster Abbey. The warmth of family welcome

---

[1] Lord and Lady Holland welcomed young men of literary ability and liberal sympathies to Holland House and exerted great political power in this way.
[2] Later Sir Charles Trevelyan, Bt. See the Macaulay family tree, p. 232.

was matched by a wider recognition of his work in India. Although Lord Melbourne said he would prefer to sit in a room with 'a chime of bells, ten parrots and one Lady Westmoreland', he was persuaded to ask T. B. to join the Cabinet as Secretary for War and a seat was found for him in the House of Commons. Looking about for a Private Secretary T. B. could think of no one better than his brother Charles. Deep affection and a singular lack of adventurousness led the young man to accept the position and abandon a promising career as a surgeon.[1]

Thus, in 1839, Charles Macaulay was sent to Manchester on political business, and met a remarkable personality, Richard Potter, known as 'Radical Dick'. He had been the Liberal Member for Wigan since 1832, was a founder member of the *Manchester Guardian*, and had made both a name and a fortune for himself in the north. His wife, Mary Seddon from Leicester, gypsy-like in appearance, was a natural musician and linguist, with a passionate, jealous temperament. After the birth of the fourth baby she lost her reason for some years, and never entirely regained stability of mind, although she retained a great interest in her children and grandchildren. The four young Potters, Richard, Mary, Sarah and Kitty, lived at home with their father, and Charles dined with them all several times. No doubt he enjoyed being the hub and not the rim of the wheel for once—anyone living constantly with the historian would enjoy an occasional chance of hearing his own voice. The two young men became fast friends and Charles found Mary handsome, agreeable and placid.

One evening when Charles was with some friends a laughing reference was made to Miss Mary having lost her heart to the visitor from London. The next morning Charles, feeling that he had committed himself, asked to see her, and offered her his hand in marriage. Amazed, she rejected him at once. Much relieved, the young man walked back to the inn, packed his bag, and went off to the Square to wait for the coach. Unfortunately, Mary had run off at once to tell her governess what had happened. The governess said that she would be very unlikely to get such a good offer again and hurriedly sent a messenger with a note to catch the suitor before he left for London. Charles Macaulay was actually pulled off the coach at the very last minute and, while his luggage went safely on to London, the young man went back

---

[1] Charles Macaulay had become by this time assistant to Sir Benjamin Brodie, Sergeant Surgeon to George IV, William IV and Queen Victoria.

to be accepted. It would have been happier for both of them if he had gone back on his word.

The Potters welcomed the marriage and always valued Charles, but the Macaulay clan was horrified by the idea of an alliance with a merchant's daughter. They looked on themselves as Gown and Sword, not Town and Ploughshare, and their almost absurd veneration for the historian was reinforced by Hannah's county connections. Both she and Fanny were particularly incensed. T. B. himself, whose famous pen had financed the entire family, was more concerned than censorious. He loved Charles and never failed him in the years to come, when Mary's continuing obstinate childishness made reconciliation with his sisters almost impossible. Their snobbery was matched by her stupidity. They never admitted her to their family circle nor did she ever attempt to earn her entry by sharing her husband's tastes and trials.

Obviously Charles needed a new career before he could marry. T. B. knew that a commissioner was needed to superintend the change from French to English in both the practice and the language of the Law Courts in Mauritius. He managed to get his brother appointed, incidentally providing the island with an excellent commissioner. The young couple were married in October 1841 and sailed immediately for Mauritius. Their elder son was born the following year and christened Thomas after his uncle.

Unfortunately only a tiny proportion of what must have been an extensive correspondence between the brothers has survived, because Charles's wife, on a tidying spree in the early fifties, found a trunk of old letters in the attic and burnt the lot. Her husband came home from the office and wept when he found the ashes in the grate. It may have been an unconscious expedient for getting her own back on the Macaulay family—but she certainly had no inkling of the wider interest that T. B.'s letters would have commanded, or of the bitter blow she had dealt her husband. One of the few that remain written in November 1848, describes how he had been working intensely on his history, 'rising at day break and sometimes sitting at my desk for twelve hours . . . Hannah and Longman predict complete success and say that it is as entertaining as a novel'.[1] In another letter of 3 March 1849[2] he mentioned with pride that 'none of Sir Walter's novels went faster', and

[1] G. O. Trevelyan, *Life and Letters of Lord Macaulay*.
[2] Hitherto unpublished.

urged Charles to accept the post of Colonial Secretary in Mauritius, which Lord Grey was about to offer him. It is amusing to see that T. B. took exactly the opposite point of view to the one he had expounded in 1836, and touching to find that he showed unexpected consideration for his brother's problems. The answer proved to be a decided negative. Charles knew that his wife's character was unsuited to a pro-consular position and that it would be almost impossible to work in Mauritius and maintain a home in England even with the help of his brother-in-law. Richard Potter did in fact watch over the inadequate Mary who had already returned home. Mary Catherine Macaulay was born in her father's absence on 4 November 1847. 'You were the only one of my children I did not welcome into the world', Charles wrote long after to his daughter, but he loved her more dearly than anyone else in it.

Great changes had taken place in England during Charles's stay in Mauritius. The Corn Laws were repealed in 1846, the Factory Act passed in 1847, and a terrible return of cholera hastened the passing of the Public Health Act in 1848. The old Poor Law Commissioners were merged with many national and local bodies to form the Board of Health, under parliamentary control. This new agency opened up a real opportunity for improving the condition of the people of England and a young surgeon, already versed in administration, with some knowledge of the law, was obviously in the running for such a service. Charles Macaulay became Secretary to the newly formed Board of Health until it was abolished in 1858, when he was transferred to the Audit Office.

The reunited family moved to Eastbourne Terrace in Bayswater, where the third child, called Charles after his father, was born in 1849. Here Mary learnt her letters upside down, by watching her brother, Tom, at his books, and at the age of three she was reading Plutarch's *Lives*, and found it 'such a relief', as she told me, 'when the search for something to play with was ended by the solace of books.' For the rest of her life she read as naturally as she breathed.

Aged four, Mary was taken across the Park to the Great Exhibition in 1851. Eighty years later, in 1931, she visited the Royal Academy's commemorative soirée with the select number of people who had actually attended the original Exhibition, and commented scathingly on the number of bath-chairs and ear-trumpets among the guests. She herself was independent of such aids, and enjoyed an energetic afternoon, looking again at the statue of the slave girl which had made such an impact on her as a little girl in 1851. No doubt the Macaulay antislave trade tradition fixed the subject firmly in her memory. My grandmother also liked to recall how she looked over the banisters and saw her father and his friend Colonel Reithmuller in the hall below, the latter in full dress uniform with a cocked hat covered with feathers, as they left early in the morning to attend the Duke of Wellington's funeral. The date was 18 November 1852 and Mary was just five. Less pleasantly she remembered watching her dark wayward Potter grandmother walking restlessly to and fro across a large London drawing-room, lighted by windows at either end, in which were two grand pianos. The child was often left alone for a day at a time in this strange, frightening atmosphere. The psychological effect in later life was to make Mary more, not less, rational. She disliked unnecessary exhibitions of emotion, and her detestation of abnormality must have come from these encounters with a grandmother who was not sane, and a mother who was not altogether adult.

She went to Hyde Park College[1] nearby where her intellectual capacity and ardent temperament were given full rein. She made it all so vivid for me seventy years later that I remember the names of her two school companions, Agnes Cowie and Marian Fraser. Sybil Romilly, the daughter of another prominent Liberal family, was Mary's closest friend. Both of them attended Monsieur d'Egville's dancing-class in regulation white boots. It was typical of Mrs Macaulay that in spite of many protests and tears she sent her daughter to the dancing-class for a second year in the same pair of white boots. The child, crying with pain, was seen at last by her father hobbling up the stairs on her return. He immediately questioned her, took off the boots, and saw the damage that had been done. Of course new boots were bought, but she retained all her life what she called her 'riding toe': one big toe which turned across the others.

These small misfortunes were soon forgotten because of her father, whose courage rose to the task of creating happiness in a handicapped home. His talent for inventing jingle verse to suit any occasion was a joy to his children and he shared with them his interest in books,

[1] The Miss Harrisons not only ran Hyde Park College but with their slender means bought one house after another in unfashionable Holland Park and installed elderly people at reasonable rents. Harrison Homes form a very big, well-established venture nowadays and are needed more than ever.

politics, games and gossip. No man ever did more to earn the devotion of a very unusual daughter and he found in her company the affection and understanding he so badly needed.

Unlike his brother the historian, Charles never monopolised the conversation and he became a notable host to a small circle of chosen friends and favourite uncle to a large number of nephews and nieces. Dinner-time was earlier in those days at 4 or 5 p.m., and tea was taken at 9 or 10 p.m. Whether there was a dinner-party or no, Mary, at an early age, always came down for 'dessert', which was served after the meat course in the dining-room. Wearing a white muslin frock with a sash, she sat beside her father and listened to the conversation. On one occasion she remembered the guests blaming the inadequacy of the Army commissariat for all the horrors and the setbacks of the Crimean War. The date was 1854, and Mary was seven. She had no idea of what a 'commissariat' was, and decided to look it up in the dictionary. She dared not interrupt a conversation with a question.

Years later her own children also came down in pretty frocks and clean shirts, at about 5 o'clock, to the drawing-room, not the dining-room, where tea—with a great paraphernalia of silver kettle, tea-caddy, tea-pot, sugar-bowl and sandwiches—had just been removed from a round, fold-up table. She read to them, built castles with bricks, set out toy animals and toy soldiers, and played dance tunes for musical bumps. The emphasis had changed. It may be that in the long run she got more from these early contacts with the grown-up world as it really was than her own children did from a make-believe one. She did however always understand children's feelings better than her father.

My grandmother told me how she went into his study one afternoon, just before Christmas 1855, and found on the table *The Rose and the Ring* by W. M. Thackeray, in its original pink covers. The attractive pictures outside and in caught her eye, and in a moment she was deep in the story. Perhaps a quarter of an hour later, 'Uncle Tom' (the historian) and 'Aunt Hannah' (Lady Trevelyan) came to call, and sat for some time talking to her father. The standard of children's behaviour in those days was such that she had to put the book back on the table and listen to grown-up conversation. At last the visitors got up to leave, and just as they reached the door her father's eye fell on *The Rose and the Ring*. He picked it up and said, 'Have you seen this latest thing of Thackeray's? A bit of Christmas nonsense.' Uncle Tom said, 'No', and his brother tossed it to him, saying, 'Do look at it. It will amuse you.'

Eight-year-old Mary, scarlet in the face but silent, watched her fairy treasure being taken out of the house. Since I am a great-granddaughter of Thackeray as well as of Charles Macaulay, I always found this story particularly poignant.

Five years later Lord Macaulay died exactly as he would have chosen to die, of a heart attack while reading in his accustomed place. 'The last book he read was the first number of the *Cornhill Magazine*. It was open at Thackeray's story on the table by the side of the chair in which he died,' wrote Charles Macaulay to a mutual friend, confident that the information would be passed on to the author, and adding that the 'noble article' about his dear brother in the February issue of the *Cornhill* 'had touched us all so nearly'. Thackeray, who was editor of the *Cornhill*, answered that he was thankful if he had given Lord Macaulay's family pleasure and added: 'My daughter will never forget your brother's great friendliness and courtesy one day when I took her to see him at Holly Lodge.' Charles, in a personal reply, went one better and wrote of 'hearts bound together by links of iron'.

There was a stiff entrance examination into the East India Company in those days, as so many penniless boys wished to brave the dangers and share the rewards of Indian service. Tom, having won his place, set off at the age of seventeen, on a voyage from which he never returned. Mary, aged twelve, developed a heart condition, possibly a reaction to his absence, which made it necessary for her to leave the school life she enjoyed so much, and spend several months of absolute quiet. This led in turn to Miss Marshall's boarding school in Stanford Road, Kensington. Miss Marshall's dictum was 'Backs first', and one hour a day was spent in walking up and down the schoolroom with a back-board. The food was plentiful and dull, as was the conversation. Translation from German into French, French into English, and back again, was unending. Every night for twenty minutes the girls brushed their hair with dry brushes, and once a week the brushes were dipped in water in lieu of a shampoo.

One day Mary's mother visited the school, dressed as usual very untidily. Mary was much embarrassed to find that the parlourmaid had mistaken Mrs Macaulay for the new cook, whose arrival was awaited. This is a touching contretemps—the untidy, unselfconscious, usually self-centred mother trying in vain to get in touch with her pent-up, brilliant, bored little girl.

During the two years Mary was away from home she not only grew up, but she grew strong, and her returning health vindicated her parents' decision. She never lost the magnificent carriage with which Miss Marshall's backboards invested her, but while acknowledging her debt to that lady she never quite forgave the boredom of her regime. 'If ever I learnt patience,' she used to say, 'it was at Miss Marshall's.'

Holidays, on the other hand, were the greatest fun because kind Uncle Richard and Aunt Laurencina invited her to spend them with their ever-growing family of girls at Standish in Gloucestershire. There is something overpowering in the thought of nine dark-eyed, warm-hearted and talented Potter daughters.[1] Laurencina, the eldest, and Kate, next in age, were particular friends of Mary's at this time; later on she became closest of all to Beatrice, the eighth daughter. Just to get into the train for Standish was happiness itself for Mary. To walk across green fields, through woods, over hillsides; to brave wind and rain or bask in sunshine; to meet country people and hear unexpected turns of phrase; to watch cows pushing through a gate, or a cart-horse pulling a load; all these were an elixir to her. Even in old age, when she seldom left her Leicestershire home, she never lost her first instinctive enchantment with country life.

In addition, life was very free at Standish. The girls argued and laughed while they danced and rode out hunting. There was a generosity about the whole family to which Mary responded with her ardent nature, and it was from her Potter blood that she inherited a power of conviction and argument which, allied to the Macaulay intellect, led Kate Potter to say, 'Mary is absolutely unbeatable except in the hunting field.' Riding, of course, was no part of London life, where Mary had already learnt when to hold her tongue, if not how to hold her reins. Much restraint was needed to avoid arousing her mother's jealousy. 'Old Woman' often chose to withdraw into herself but sometimes, irked by family gaiety, she would crush it with the words, 'That will be enough, Charlie.' Her husband, rather than argue with his wife in front of the children, would immediately fall silent.

At the age of sixteen Mary left school for good. She took over the housekeeping, and divided the rest of the day into so many hours for history, so many hours for Euclid, and so many hours for distraction. Applying her mind to the piano, she taught herself to play competently,

---

[1] See Potter family tree, p. 232.

but she was no musician. Her mother, with an inherited feeling for real music, could not abide her daughter's playing, so the hour set aside for the piano only added to the disharmony of the household.

Mary's progress with Euclid, on the other hand, was unnoticed, and therefore uncriticised. After a year's solitary concentration, she went with her father to a dinner-party and sat next to Mr Arthur Cohen, known as 'the beautiful Jew', and the first member of Anglo-Jewry to be made a Q.C. He asked her kindly and perhaps even condescendingly, what she did with herself. She told him with customary truthfulness. He made it evident in a smiling way that he did not believe her. She offered to put the whole thing to proof, and he asked her to prove Pythagoras' Theorem. Drawing with her spoon on the white linen table-cloth, she came out of this ordeal with flying colours. After dinner Mr Cohen introduced her to his wife, and a friendship grew up between the Cohens and this dark, glowing little person, whose simplicity of appearance was belied by the fire of her conversation.

Mary's adored elder brother had served for five years in the East India Company's Regiment of the 15th Sikhs. His furlough was due, and he took ship for home. A dispatch from Gibraltar gave warning that Tom was critically ill with typhoid; and he died as the ship came up past the Isle of Wight. The poor father, who had eagerly awaited his chance to board her, hardly recognised the tall bearded young man who now lay dead on his bunk as the boy he had known and loved so well. Mary never forgot the tragic death of her brother, and spoke of him all her life with pride and love. Such a welcome, and so much hope, had been stored up for this lovable young man that Mary and her father needed a great deal of courage to rebuild family life again upon smaller foundations.

In such a quiet family backwater, dances were rare and precious events. My grandmother told me that, when invited at 9 p.m., her mother always ordered the carriage round at 8 p.m. Oblivious of the difficulties of the host and hostess, she would sit and talk in the empty drawing-room for half an hour with Mary at her side, silent and distressed. About the time when other guests began to arrive, this impossible lady would rise to her feet, say how much she had enjoyed the visit, explain that she liked to go to bed regularly at 9 p.m., and depart, taking Mary with her, just as the music was striking up.

In some ways her father's attitude to his daughter's future was as curious as her mother's, and although he was critical of how little his sister, Hannah Trevelyan, had done for her niece, he seems to have been perfectly content for his 'heart's darling' to remain penned in a tiny family circle. For instance Colonel and Mrs Fraser, parents of one of her schoolfriends, invited Mary to go with them to Scotland, and though the Frasers were particular friends, and Mary had a passion for Scott's novels and longed to see for herself the wild, sad country which she had so often visited in imagination, her father dismissed the idea with a few words: 'It would cost twenty pound,' he said. Long afterwards, when describing to me her life at home, Mary used to say how very much things had changed. 'My father,' she said, 'though never a rich man, always kept five hundred pounds on call at Williams Deacons for an emergency.' When one thinks of five hundred pounds in the bank, of Mary's brown eyes sparkling at the thought of going to Edinburgh, and of her father's adoration for his daughter, one is struck by his blindness. Unconsciously, no doubt, he could not bear to be left even for a fortnight without her companionship. As well as his intellectual capacity she fortunately inherited her father's natural spirits, without which it would have been difficult to endure such an irksome situation at home. They read and talked and laughed together and went on ten- and twelve-mile expeditions. Neither the walks nor the talks were the solace to her which they seemed to be for her father. Like many daughters Mary felt imprisoned.

Naturally enough, Mary found the key to her future at Standish. When Laurencina Potter, nicknamed Lally, became engaged to Robert Holt of the Liverpool shipping family, she asked Mary to be one of her bridesmaids. Lally, as befitted the eldest of a big family, was a kind-hearted and managing young woman. On a June morning in 1867 she did all the bridesmaids' hair herself, and arranged the wreaths on their heads, before she set off for the church. Mary was among this well-groomed bevy and at the wedding party she met a young man called Charles James Booth. He was twenty-eight years old and she was twenty-one.

II

THE BOOTHS OF LIVERPOOL

1749–1871

The turnpikes of Great Britain in the eighteenth century must have been crowded with eager young men walking, riding or driving, according to the length of their purses, from the country to the city. Seeking greater opportunities than those open to them as younger sons on family farms, they needed training for professional careers or apprenticeships in trades. When the Booths and Potters left Lancashire's still lovely valleys and uplands for Liverpool and Manchester, the Macaulays were sailing away from the Outer Isles to Glasgow, London, Jamaica and India.

Thomas Booth left his father's farm near Warrington when he was eighteen years old and in less than a decade had established himself as a corn factor in Liverpool. He married Esther Noble, a farmer's daughter; gave her name to one of his grain ships; and had a large family. Always a Nonconformist, he was gradually drawn into Unitarianism and became a founder member of the new chapel in Renshaw Street. By the time he was forty, in 1789, he was held in such repute by his fellow citizens that he became their spokesman with the Board of Trade on matters concerning the Corn Laws. James, his eldest son, went to Cambridge, and became Permanent Under-Secretary at the Board of Trade. Henry, the second son, aided Stephenson in the commercial development of traction engines, contributing some inventive ideas of his own. His statue stands among others commemorating Liverpool's outstanding citizens in St George's Hall, which was not built until 1854 and now towers classically above the docks and the Mersey tunnel.

Charles,[1] the third son, joined his father as a corn merchant and married Emily Fletcher,[2] the third daughter of another prominent and

---

[1] See the Booth family tree, p. 232.
[2] See the Fletcher family tree, p. 232.

philanthropic Unitarian. She was devoted to her brothers and sisters, one of whom married Henry Roscoe, whose son became the distinguished chemist of that name; another married a young barrister who was later to become Mr Justice Crompton; and the third was forgiven for marrying an Anglican clergyman, John Llewelyn-Davies. This united and talented cousinhood grew up together very happily in what was then an exceptionally beautiful city, set on rising ground above the Mersey, within reach of North Wales and the Lakes. John Wood's Georgian town hall, opened in 1797, gave pleasing dignity to civic functions, and clubs such as the Athenaeum, built in the following year, provided an elegant Grecian library for the leisure hours of energetic businessmen. On Sundays they all drove in their carriages to the Unitarian chapel in Renshaw Street, thereby fostering earthly as well as heavenly associations. Music, literature and the arts flourished in an unsophisticated yet cultivated society, which glows in retrospect with an innocent belief in progress and plenty. Painting in water-colour was practised even more than the piano, and Emily, the least good-looking of the handsome Fletchers, possessed a special gift in this respect. She transmitted it to her five children: Anna, Alfred, Tom, Charles and Emily Booth.

Charles James, the fourth of this family quintet, was born on 30 March 1840 and inherited from his mother's side a wide brow, an aquiline nose and a striking pair of blue eyes. Like his father, he had a spare figure, a receding chin, a quiet manner, and an even temper. Always rapid of gait, with little sense of balance, Charles's gaiety and curiosity gave him considerable powers of endurance. When he was thirteen his mother died and he turned to his father with unusual confidence and intimacy. Nor did this diminish when several years later the widower married the friendly, sensible woman who as governess to the girls had already helped to maintain a very happy home in Croxteth Lane, overlooking Prince's Park.

At the age of ten Charles left a small dame-school to which he had been going, for the Royal Liverpool Institution, following in the footsteps of his brothers. Closer to him in age and friendship than Alfred, Tom was the 'clever one of the family' who went on to become a Wrangler at Cambridge. However, when the whole school was set an arithmetic paper, it was Charles—aged fifteen—who came first. This was his only distinction but it was a significant one, and it added to his father's conviction that he had better go into business. After a month or two in London and Heidelberg, at the age of sixteen Charles was apprenticed to Lamport and Holt, a trading concern, where he was kindly treated and given a sound business training. Of all his recreations, sketching came first and could be conveniently combined with walking expeditions to the Lakes, one of which he took with his employers and described in a buoyant letter to his brother Alfred. 'Charley' became quite a dandy as he grew up and was a general favourite at informal neighbourly parties. Tom Fletcher and Francis Prange, both school friends, followed his lead. When she was old enough Antonia Prange joined her brother and his friends in their acting and dancing and surpassed them in painting. She was 'singularly interesting and charming'[1] and in the most natural way Charles's affection for her as a schoolgirl changed into adoring love for the young woman to whom he gave his whole heart.

The death of his father in 1860 drew Charles and Antonia still closer, but at twenty and eighteen they were still far too young to think of marrying. Mr Booth left his children £20,000 each, great wealth in those days, and as Charles had finished his apprenticeship he was free to see something of the world before settling down to a business career. Just before his twenty-first birthday he set off overland to the Near East, taking his time to see and do all he wished, never apparently feeling lonely or ill at ease. His sketches have a Lear-like quality and show a receptive and appreciative eye. The diaries are alive with selective detail about sights, travels and companions, but except for a Lancashire lad's determination not to be fooled they are disappointingly non-introspective. Once or twice something of the brusque objectivity of his character comes through. When describing the stone on which Christ's body was supposedly washed as 'a soapy-looking slab', he states roundly, 'I write as if I believed all this rubbish.' Then he adds, 'It was a strange sight to see pilgrims of several sects and many nations agreeing in the eagerness of superstition, kneeling and kissing with such devout fervour.' In a later and less forthright mood he has added under these lines the phrase, 'Perhaps they are better than I.'

He was equally unconvinced by the displays of physical endurance under suffering given by the dervishes of Scutari as they pushed swords into their stomachs. He wondered how much was acting and how much was genuine 'in the frightful state they got themselves into'. However,

---

[1] Quotation from Mary Booth's *Memoir* of Charles Booth.

Charles Booth 1863

Mary Macaulay 1873

Charles Booth 1906

Mary Booth 1890

PLATE I

PLATE 2 Mary Booth with her father, Charles Macaulay, and her son Tom 1878

he admitted to being wrong in his estimate of an adventurous young woman of twenty-four, who was 'not T—'s mistress' but merely travelling abroad by herself. They went on an expedition together and 'had great fun and talked about every mortal thing'. In Venice the letters he had longed for arrived with bad news. For the first time he mentions 'Tonie', whose health, never robust, was now giving grave concern. The Pranges had decided to seek a cure abroad and Charles at once altered his plans in order to meet Francis Prange in Dresden, a city which Charles would have enjoyed so much more but for his anxiety. Presumably Tonie had consumption, and the two young men were discussing the length of her convalescence when a telegram told them that she had mistakenly swallowed an overdose of medicine which had 'aggravated a bilious fever'. 'A more miserable day' Charles never spent, but when Francis left him to rejoin the Prange family he 'could not but hope'. The diary which began on 3 March 1862 with the breezy words 'Up this morning at 5.30 a.m. as soon as I heard the Pilot's voice' ended on 16 September with the flat sentence: 'I heard last night that she had died.' Packing up his grief, his aspirations and his chattels he returned immediately to the shelter of Tom's comfort and companionship in Liverpool. Unfortunately, Tom was so taken with Charles's sketches of the Near East that not a year after Antonia's death he set off also for Constantinople, only to die there shortly afterwards of fever.

This, the third tragedy of Charles's early manhood, was the most dreadful blow of all. His father's death seemed not unnatural; the loss of Antonia was the end of a romantic dream; but the death of the brilliant brother whose promise and friendship were woven into Charles's own life was reality at its sharpest and bitterest. Courage and a decided independence of ordinary human contact, verging on coldness, came to his aid. Grief only accentuated a characteristic already present in this unusual young man, who gave his heart very seldom and then with 'an intensity all his own'.[1]

Ambition, hitherto harnessed to Tom's career, now became a driving force in his own. The least academic of his family, he was determined to establish himself as a businessman of repute. His old firm, Lamport and Holt, offered him a partnership, but he decided instead to ship to New York and have a look at the leather business in which his brother, Alfred, had already invested some money, with a view to taking part in

[1] Mary Booth, *Charles Booth: A Memoir*.

it himself. He had hardly arrived before Alfred's partner became seriously deranged and the brothers found themselves entirely responsible for a small agency which sold skins on commission. Alfred, who was already conversant with the New York scene, remained there, but after a period of reconstruction Charles decided to return and open an agency in Liverpool. At the same time he had in mind a far grander scheme. He wanted to build up a shipping line to carry not only Alfred's skins but other merchandise to and fro across the Atlantic.

At home again he spent a great deal of time discussing this idea with Philip Holt, who had married his sister Anna, and with Alfred, Philip's brother, who was a brilliant marine engineer. They were all agog with the possibilities of steamships, but Charles had to find the necessary trade to make his ideas viable. Philip, it is said, told him that as long as he left the China Seas to Alfred Holt and Company he could steam and trade where he pleased. Nineteenth-century Mersey princes spoke like this! Charles urged his brother Alfred to send him every detail of South American imports and exports, and when these had been agonisingly digested he decided to send the first Booth merchant steamship to northern Brazil. The Booth Steamship Company and the construction of Manaos harbour grew from this decision. Charles's name, however, never headed the firm which owed so much to him. It began as Alfred Booth and Company, a tiny commission business, and so it remained.

The next problem was to 'raise the wind', as Charles put it, to build two steamships, the *Augustine* and the *Jerome*, in which the entire family fortune was to be invested. Charles worked ten and eleven hours a day from his one-man-and-a-boy leather agency, supervised the work at Hart and Synott's shipyards, and spent much time in Alfred Holt's drawing-office as well.

However, the intensity of Charles's interest in shipyards and leather sales did not entirely absorb his energies. He made the most of his opportunities for fun and debate, taking for himself the advice he sent his very quiet brother in New York: 'Knock all the pleasure you can out of existence and damn the expense!' 'What a fellow Charley is,' wrote his sister Emily, and indeed, fresh from eighteen months in New York he took the lead at home with renewed zest and spirit.

The Booths and their neighbourly friends and relatives lived either in dignified eighteenth-century red brick streets which still exist, unpainted and unloved, rising about the Mersey in the vicinity of Gilbert Scott's twentieth-century cathedral; or in the attractive early Victorian stucco houses with leafy gardens on still higher ground, leading to Prince's Park and Sefton Park. The cousinhood made the most of their talents, painting and writing for each other's critical eye, and collaborating in a magazine called *The Colony*. It reflects the high standards and social conscience of a comfortable, settled, hitherto self-satisfied society, just becoming aware of immense problems ahead. One of these was the question of universal suffrage. Tom Fletcher in one essay wrote that he disbelieved equally in Bright's ideal working man and in the traditional intelligence of the upper classes, but felt it 'fair that all people should have a chance of taking care of their own'. Naturally enough he and Charles and Francis Prange campaigned enthusiastically and unsuccessfully in the Liberal interest in the General Election of 1865. The three school friends tried to persuade illiterate Irish immigrants in the Toxteth slums to oust the sitting Tory MP whose jovial *laissez-faire* attitude and free beer had a greater appeal than their reasoned approach. However, house-to-house visits laid bare ignorance, poverty and squalor on a scale hitherto neither seen nor imagined and Charles was deeply shocked. He invented two comic characters called Lady Christina Compassion and the Reverend Ebenezer Fanatic who appeared in family charades. Jokes sometimes show more clearly than anything else the sombre avenues of a man's thought. Brought up as Unitarians, the cousinhood discussed new religious and philosophic ideas with great freedom. Uncle James Booth was known to have said that 'Dissent was a mistake' when he opted for co-operation with the Established Church. Charles dissented from dissent and felt that neither the disestablished values of thrift, continence and modesty nor the mystical ritual of the Church of England threw any light on how to help those in desperate need. Charity on the necessary scale was out of the question. Where did the answer lie? Truth, not faith, became the goal. Albert and Henry Crompton, enthusiastic followers of Auguste Comte,[1] carried Charles along with them for some time in their ardour for Positivism. They attended services in a beautiful circular temple in Liverpool, surrounded by statues of great and good men. He found much that appealed to him in Comte's writings, particularly in the catechism of Positivism which came out in 1852 stating: 'It is only thro' the more marked influence of the reason over the general conduct

---

[1] August Comte (1798-1857) was originally a disciple of Saint-Simon. He published his *Philosophie positive* in 1826, and *Catéchisme positiviste* in 1852.

of man or of society that the gradual march of our race has attained
. . . that persevering continuity which distinguishes it from. . . the
barren expansion of even the highest animal orders.' But there was an
element of absurdity about the cult of Comte which led him to dis-
associate himself from the movement and look elsewhere for what he
described as a 'natural' law, a balance between traditional morality and
the overthrow of all restraint, a *modus vivendi* to include every aspect
of life.

Darwin brought out the *Origin of Species* in 1859. Its impact was all
the greater because of the quiet manner in which it was written, and
the religious ferment of the time. Charles, who would dearly have
loved to go on believing in the Almighty he had been brought up to
revere, felt that science had as clearly disproved His existence as
Galileo had demonstrated the correct solar system. If this were the case,
men, instead of saying 'God's will be done' and resigning themselves to
intolerable conditions, must accept resonsibility for the mess they had
made of the world and strive themselves to better it.

Education, therefore, was vital, and education for all, free of cost and
free of sectarian influence. Charles joined the Birmingham Education
League founded by Joseph Chamberlain to promote secular education.
This initial link between the two men is interesting, and it led to the
first survey Charles ever made. He estimated that 25,000 children in
Liverpool 'were neither at school nor at work'[1] and that this was a
double waste. He also helped to establish the Liverpool Trades Hall
where working men could meet in decent surroundings. He enjoyed his
contacts, joined in the discussions, and did his best to help over rates of
pay and working conditions, but there was insufficient support and the
scheme withered away. In the municipal elections of the following
year, he and Tom Fletcher returned to the political fray with Francis
Prange as Liberal candidate, and a whole programme of local improve-
ments. Once again the reformers were trounced by 'beerocracy', and
the very people who would have benefited most from a change of
policy refused to vote against the Tory *status quo*. Charles turned away
in disgust and never again sought help through political channels. Nor
did he consider that his work for the Education League had been ultimately any more successful. Forster's Education Act of 1870 ensured a
patchwork compromise of Church and State schools throughout

[1] T. S. and M. B. Simey, *Charles Booth: Social Scientist.*

England, and those pressing for secular education felt that they had been out-manoeuvred by the Established and Nonconformist Churches. Charles described the result of this double defeat as 'a depression which takes effect at once in my head and prevents me from working, being past fighting against'.

Whatever else ended in disappointment and bitterness, ships and trade never failed in all his long life to bring him interest, excitement, worry and satisfaction. The first of the Booth steamships, the *Augustine*, was launched on her maiden voyage by Emily in February 1866 with Charles aboard. The engines gave endless trouble and the 25-year-old young man was diverted from his personal problems by concentrating on those of his very first ship.

A year later Robert Holt's wedding to Lally Potter took place and the spirited young bridesmaid from London became a serious rival to the *Augustine*. Charles asked Mary Macaulay, in his capacity as editor, to contribute to the *Colony*, and she responded with a broadside: 'You are all running mad over business and I can only say in conclusion that if I am asked here again I shall beg to put off the visit until my hair turns grey and life ceases to be an enjoyment.' This was direct and accurate criticism of Charles, but it was also tantamount to a pressing wish for another invitation, and in August 1868 kind Lally Holt, probably urged on by Charles, asked Mary to stay.

He looked again at her oval face, perfect teeth, bright eyes and the dark hair which was brushed straight up and plaited into a crown on the top of her head. As she played the piano to him, he wondered whether her upright back would be too much for him, but it was this positive quality in her character for which he thirsted. He decided she must be his wife. He told her that the S.S. *Augustine* on her maiden voyage bore a flying bee on her flag, and that when the captain returned he told Charles, 'It won't do, Sir. We shall be known as the "Bug Line".' He asked her to choose between the large letter 'B' and the bumble-bee as an emblem for his ships; she chose the letter 'B', thereby endorsing the captain's advice. It was her first contribution to the Booth Steamship Company, and certainly the simplest.

Unfortunately another contribution to the *Colony* was both tactless and ill advised. Critical of the self-satisfaction induced by suburban good works, she drove a Highland onslaught into the pleasant precincts of Prince's Park and Sefton Park: 'Covered by the sense of charity and the fluff of flannel, what poisoned darts of gossip may not be flung, what

37

inanities uttered without exciting comment. As Blucher survives to posterity in his boots, and Garibaldi will in his shirts, so poor Dorcas lives in these societies for circulating gossip.' The hyperbole of the last sentence, which does not quite come off, was a Macaulay way of life, their form of fun and exercise, like fencing or playing tennis. However the ladies of the *Colony* were understandably piqued, particularly as Mary, who was staying with Lally Holt, had headed her essay 'Dullasever Villa' and signed it 'Frivolity'. One man's joke is another man's poison. As far as the Booths went, she had written and signed her own epitaph: frivolous and worldly.

My grandmother always respected the trading aspects of the great port but to her dying day disliked Liverpool's social scene. Its outlook was necessarily different from that to which she was accustomed. At home in London, money was scarce among her father's friends, and yet newspapers, periodicals and books strewed their tables, and literary and political anecdotes added salt to their conversation. Charles's cousinhood commanded far ampler means, but life in Liverpool was more constricted; local loyalty and local interest were very strong, as they still are. The *Colony* was read and discussed more than the *Quarterly*; controversy was less lively, agreement less gracious; jokes were heartier but fewer; the very climate itself was more equable, but darker and damper than that of London. These first impressions became fixtures. The respect never softened the criticism and the criticism never vitiated the respect.

When Mary's second visit came to end, Charles asked his sisters to help him with his courtship, which they instinctively refused to do, so he relieved his feelings by sending her quantities of flowers without signing his name on the card, and only told her the truth of the mystery after their marriage. As soon as another wedding gave him an excuse, he went up to London, hoping to see the girl he had set his heart on marrying. There his favourite first cousin, Caroline Crompton,[1] whose father, the judge, now lived in London, agreed to help him. Together they called at Gloucester Terrace, only to hear that Mary had been ill and had gone to Brighton with her father to recuperate. It says much for Charles's determination, and Caroline's kindness, that even though they did not know the address at which Mary and her father were staying, they set out in pursuit. Caroline went to stay with a friend while

---

[1] See the Fletcher family tree, p. 232.

Charles put up at an inn. By pure chance he came across Mr Macaulay, as he must now be called, walking along the Brighton front. They had met before at Lally's wedding. The suitor made himself as agreeable as possible, and announced that he would call. Mary's father went home much upset to tell her how this extraordinary young man had forced himself upon their acquaintance.

The same afternoon Charles and Caroline came to pay their respects and Mary, with her customary directness, decided that the cousins were probably engaged. The next day the four of them, Mr Macaulay in attendance as watchdog, went for a walk, and rain—that constant accompaniment of English courtship—began to fall heavily. Charles held his umbrella over Mary, saying what an honour it was for the umbrella, and at last it dawned on Mary that she was being wooed. On their return, Charles asked Mr Macaulay for his daughter's hand in marriage; after consulting Mary he told Charles that she refused to consider the offer. Many a man would have given up and gone back to Liverpool at this moment, but Charles showed his mettle, and said that he had not been treated fairly. If Mary was to refuse him, she must refuse him to his face; he must be allowed to try for himself.

In the drawing-room he proceeded to do this at length. Half way through the interview Aunt Fanny Macaulay entered, and endeavoured to sit him out; but Charles would not go. He spoke with a north country accent, saying 'castle' and 'grass' as southerners say 'lass'. To some of the Macaulays, who had shed their Highland way of speaking, this was another factor for disapproval, although Lady Holland had always feared that T. B. Macaulay's middle-class manner of address might stand in his way! Basically the two families came from identical social backgrounds, but the fame of the historian and the civil and military prowess of the Macaulays made them look down on commerce and the provinces. Put down on paper a hundred years later, this narrow prejudice looks ridiculous; but at that time it was a particularly difficult barrier for Mary to cross. Finally, she said she could not possibly love anyone as much as Papa, and Charles said that that would do nicely, and escorted the generous Caroline back to London. Her reward was a lifetime's affection.

The following day, 22 January 1871, Emily Booth noted bleakly in her diary: 'Charley became engaged to Mary Macaulay, having gone to London the day before—he came home on Tuesday 24th.' Mary was just twenty-three and Charles almost thirty-one, but personality not seniority had won the day. She could not withstand the conviction and poetry of his love, although she often told me with what a pang she gave up the name of Mary Macaulay, which certainly has a ring to it! She never liked the name Booth, but she always loved Charles, the name her father and her husband shared, and which she gave to her youngest son.

Mr Macaulay's character comes out strongly at this time. 'He wouldn't suit me but I think he will suit you,' was one of his remarks. Once the die was cast he stood by the young couple through thick and thin. Not only that, but a rare affection grew up between the two men. Aunt Hannah Trevelyan, who had made no attempt to introduce those suitors she considered eligible to her niece, now deplored this engagement, and felt that the marriage would be as great a come-down as that of her brother with Mary Potter long ago. However, her husband, Sir Charles Trevelyan, having passed Charles Booth on the doorstep of Gloucester Terrace, went in to ask who it was who had brushed past him. 'I've never seen such a beautiful fellow in my life,' he said.

Mary never lost a real appreciation of good looks. It certainly gave those who possessed them an unfair advantage with her, and helped Charles more than he knew to overcome the distance that lay between Liverpool and London.

III
CHARLES AND MARY
1871–1879

On 29 April 1871, Charles and Mary were married at East Teignmouth. Mary wore an old green frock, because her fiancé did not like her bridal gown, but her mother put on a new bonnet covered with pink roses and on walking up to the church was cheered by some little boys, who thought she was the bride.

The Booths drove off westward in the afternoon with Mary's maid sitting behind them in the dog-cart. After 'putting all to rights', in her own phrase, my grandmother came down to a little sitting-room, and sat by the fire quite alone. The restless young husband had already set off for a long walk. She described this hour as being the strangest she had ever spent. What was she doing in this country inn, all alone, waiting for a man she scarcely knew? The honeymoon was spent driving about Cornwall in the dog-cart, arguing about everything. 'It was sometimes very hot,' said Charles; he did not allude to the weather.

Immensely attracted to each other despite or because of divergent personalities, they began on their honeymoon a marriage-long dialogue, often argumentative, always complementary. Had they taken to the Law, Mary might have made the better advocate in a murder trial, but Charles would have been elevated to the Bench. She had a way, as I remember, of pressing her case and thinking better of her companion if total agreement was expressed. Charles always preferred asking questions to answering them and sought his own solutions within a quiet mind, wishing to convince himself more than others. This pattern of partisan eloquence on her part and cooler comment on his became a settled habit, the backbone of their lives. In this way they hammered out the aspirations which ennobled their marriage.

They read a great deal together, but Mary read *Clarissa* on her own. Her father had forbidden her to do so at home, and when the time came she bought a copy and took it on her honeymoon.

After the wedding, the poor man wrote his daughter two heart-broken letters, in which he described the whole thing as 'A bad business. . . . Oh my dearie illie Gal.' A month later he was confirmed, drawn to this step as much by the vicar's understanding of unorthodox views as by his own desperate need of support. Meanwhile he welcomed the honeymoon couple's return with a proper paean—'Joy! Joy for ever! Hurrah, oh my eye! We shall give you such a reception as will make you wish to spend your lives coming to us.' After the visit he wrote: 'To see you looking so well and so happy has acted like a strong cordial, bracing me up with renewed courage. . . . It is all very well for Charley to compare himself to a substantial burgher but I object to your being likened to the daughter of a mountain robber. . . . It is well that we have been so much thrown together for now I can imagine you gossiping, discussing and criticising. Oh, what a gift the imagination is! It seems to me sometimes as if death itself can never deprive me of the constant companionship of my heart's darling.'

Beginning at this point a remarkable series of letters between Mary and her father run on uninterruptedly until his death in 1886. They give a concentrated picture of the young couple's life and his own devotion and wisdom. As to himself, there is no breath of complaint, but the facts show through the jokes. The Audit Office was being absorbed into the Treasury and although offered another secretaryship Mr Macaulay refused it on the grounds that it was a sinecure. Mary said she would have gone down on her knees to beg him to take it had she been at home. Sinecure or no, she knew what his life would be without a job. A London house would have been hard to maintain without Mary's help, so this unselfish man packed up a case of favourite books, sold almost everything else that had made a settled home for twenty-five years, and moved to a series of small seaside lodging-houses. What made matters worse was that as soon as his charm had won him friends in Teignmouth, Ramsgate or Southsea, Old Woman found out that she did not like the place after all and they moved elsewhere. She spent her time throwing sticks into the sea for her dog, who was too stout and bored to retrieve them. Like mistress, like dog.

The master occupied himself by writing a book on the validity of the Christian faith which was well received and vanished without trace. It had done its job. The author's spirit was never again disturbed. Living continually with two people who were not quite normal, for his younger son had inherited an uneven development, Charles Macaulay's radiant enjoyment of everyday life shines through all his letters. His perceptive sympathy was remarkable and after an initial visit to Liverpool he told his son-in-law that he was 'conscious of something which contrasts strangely with the brightness of the picture'. This is the first hint of the shadow that engulfed Charles for nearly five years.

Nor was Mary particularly happy in the first months of marriage and she longed for her father's support. Although she was deeply in love with her husband, his intellectual destruction of her simpler religious faith was as much a cause for uncertainty as the difficulties of adjustment to the Booth family. Her warm heart flew out of its cage to love and succour Tom Fletcher's young French wife, but otherwise she was as reserved in her homesickness as the Booths were entrenched in their disapproval. Deceived by her air of pride they did not see how lonely and vulnerable she was. Jealous also of her brains, her charm and the dash of Macaulay certainty, they liked to correct her behaviour as if she were a little girl. On one occasion she told me she picked up the *Spectator* and said, 'What does old Baa Baa think today?', merely quoting her father's phrase. This led to a long lecture about respecting those who were older and cleverer. Why must she be always so cocksure and impertinent? All this would have melted away with time had the Booths not blamed Mary for Charles's increased withdrawal from his family, which hurt and perplexed them.

In June 1884 he wrote a memorandum on this subject which began with these words: 'It was before my marriage that my ways of thought ran in different channels from those of my brother and my sisters.' It closes with an involved but intelligible sentence: 'What I have to reproach myself with is the way in which I have allowed Mary to bear the brunt of the difficulties which have from time to time arisen between me and my family of which she has been in no manner the cause, but which they have been as ready to visit upon her as I have been negligent in defending her.'

The entire family fortune was invested in Alfred Booth and Company, and everything depended on acute, painstaking judgement. Charles, the younger but more forceful brother, had to lead from behind, and his concentrated efforts irritated his more easy-going partners. Implied criticism is always rebutted with interest. Natural reserve became a habitual safeguard at the office: at home the very frankness of Charles's relationship with his wife let loose all the dogs of doubt which had gnawed at his peace of mind for many a year. His health deteriorated alarmingly. Mr Macaulay recommended

. . . a good year of idleness, a life of wandering dilettantism in Switzerland and Italy for a year at least. What would suit you would also suit Polly. You might lose some of the chances of 'turning your zeros into sixes and nines.' 'Is not life more than meat and the body more than raiment.' I would gladly give up the hope of seeing you a millionaire for the prospect of having you both sound in wind and limb. . . .

Yours very affectionately
C. MACAULAY.

In February 1873, the far from 'millionaires' had a baby who was called Antonia after Charles's first love, and Mary after his generous-minded wife! Mary was always moving furniture around, knocking two rooms into one, or enlarging a window. Her father teased her about the energetic alterations she would make when she was out and about again. 'Lord, what a commotion there will be amongst the things. They have had rather a sleepy time of it for some weeks and will require an extra shaking to wake them up.'

But no shaking up and rearrangement altered the basic difficulties of their life. Charles's nervous indigestion had increased to such an extent that he could barely eat anything at all. My grandparents therefore avoided dining out whenever possible, and this was construed as 'giving themselves airs'. Finally Charles decided to leave Liverpool for good and live on 5 per cent of his capital per annum until he could take up ordinary work again. 'Mary was relieved,' he commented later on, when he told her of his decision. It was not hers.

Taking the baby, now always called Dodo, and a nursemaid, the little family party journeyed to Geneva in search of health and serenity. Both eluded them. Various regimes were tried out and various doctors consulted. Charles continued to lose weight. Links with home, such as books and journals, so welcome to Mary, had to be hidden from Charles because they proved too disturbing for his state of mind. What had begun probably with those early tragedies combined with hasty meals, over-exertion, and that ardent search for truth, had developed into a general breakdown.

They heard of a new cure and went to look for its help in the hills above Bex in the canton of Vaud, a district of supreme beauty. As soon as the fruit season began, Charles was to roam about eating only what he could pick, taking his time. In the experience of watching the seasons come and go, feeling the thrust of new growth against hard ground, sharing the easy flowering of summer and the golden crown of autumn, Charles found emotional and physical release. Whenever sickness laid him low in the future, his life-long love of shape and colour came to his rescue, but it was at this crucial period that he sought and found the answer to destructive inner disturbance. Long afterwards in 1891 his 12-year-old daughter Meg, perplexed by differing attitudes to religion expressed in drawing-room and schoolroom, asked him what he thought about it all. Looking at her intently he said, 'I think I believe in a Purpose.'

My grandmother's sympathy and courage throughout this ordeal were exceptional. She made friends with the village women and particularly admired their beautiful hair and the intricate braiding which crowned their heads. She sorrowed when shining plaits had to be sold for ready money. Few women would have chosen to have their second child in a primitive wooden chalet high above Bex. What her father must have feared is his own secret. Snow still lay thick on the ground in mid-April when the innkeeper set out to fetch medical help. Charles gazed anxiously out of the window and at last, seeing the doctor and midwife struggling up the hill, he rushed out to help them. Tom was born in his absence and my grandmother told me how, weak and alone, she tried to wrap up her baby boy in a blanket to protect him from the intense cold. Her gesture, as her curved arm brought the sofa cushion into her side, remains in my mind. She never knew when she made an indelible mark.

The doctor was much perturbed. '*Quel père de famille!*' he exclaimed. How could he have guessed that this out-of-health, out-of-work young couple would have seven children, most of whom have worn their ninety years lightly, and that a work of more than national importance would be achieved by the emaciated husband with the help of his delicate little wife.

Although Charles was still far from strong the Booths returned to England in the late autumn of 1874 and set off on the voyage to Manaos which was to complete Charles's cure, leaving Dodo and Tom behind in Liverpool. Charles wanted to investigate the behaviour of a newly designed high pressure boiler, which might have proved to be very economical in fuel in cases where speed was immaterial. The experiment was not successful, but it was a restful way of re-entering business life. The voyage took three months and Mary used to describe it in a dreamy voice, very unlike her usual brisk accents. She sat on deck all day, neither reading nor writing. No doubt the strain of Charles's illness had taxed her vitality. 'I forgot myself,' she used to say, pronouncing the word 'Meself', as she always did. She gazed at the stars by night, and by day at the tremendous expanse of water. On one occasion, after a storm, she looked up and saw by the stars that the ship was off course. The compass had failed. It was like her to have had such an accurate, as well as such an appreciative, eye for beauty.

In Brazil Mary found the ladies living an almost harem life, whispering and gossiping in shady secluded quarters, wearing the tightest of stays under black satin, with their hair exquisitely dressed and pomaded and their fingers covered with diamonds. They sat all day in darkened rooms while little black boys waited on them and fanned them; they never read; they sometimes stitched at a little bit of embroidery; and they ate enormously. What must they have thought of their visitor, dressed always in white loose muslin clothes; her hair coiled simply on the top of her head; her skin almost as brown as her eyes, because of walking about with her husband on his business errands?

At last came the voyage home. 'If it had not been for Dodo,' said Mary, fifty years later, 'I could have hardly borne to steam into Liverpool Docks.' It had been arranged that if all was well with the children, a blue scarf would be waved on the quay. The whole crew cheered when they saw the reassuring sign. While Mary had been star-gazing, Charles had made up his mind as to the future.

He told his partners of his decision to set up an office in London to deal with the merchandise side of Alfred Booth and Company. This was the final break. Although they knew vaguely of his wish to secede, they had not believed he would actually cut the painter. His elder sister, Anna, never forgave him for leaving Liverpool. She felt it was a betrayal of all that the Booth family held dear. Philip Holt would not speak to him for some years. As Emily lived with the Holts her position was not easy. She had loved Charley dearly and when the worst of the trouble was over she tried to revive their friendship, but it was too late. He had grown away from her. There is only one direct reference to Charles after his marriage in all the many pages of her private journal. It was essential to maintain a steady business footing between the two brothers and Mary remembered that never a week-end went by in the seventies without her helping Charles to compose a 'careful letter to

Alfred'. Charles, who could not understand such passionate anger, made no attempt to bridge the gap, believing that it would close naturally one day. He felt no animus against his family, but did not need his home ties. It was this which hurt them so deeply that the wound never healed. Having gained a measure of health during his year of independence, he was determined to re-establish his wife and children in freedom, cost what it might in family disapproval.

While Charles set up his office in London with all his old dispatch, Mary took a fifteen-year lease of a large and hideous house in Grenville Place, South Kensington. It had no through draught, and almost no sun, but at least it was not far from Kensington Gardens. Nowadays the London County Council's round, blue plaque of honour records that Charles Booth, social scientist, 1841–1916, lived at No. 6. How solid and settled it looks. Yet at the time Charles had not settled anything! If he had not been able to sustain his recovery in health, get along with his partners and make a success of the London agency, Charles would have had to follow his father-in-law into some backwater. In battling for his family's security, however, he found great happiness, and when he came to inquire into poverty on other levels he never wished to relieve anyone of the responsibility of earning the family living which he considered to be the root and fruit of a man's life.

This return from exile to her father's companionship and a well-known context was a wonderful moment for Mary. Never again would she let herself be banished from home! The Potter family was always welcoming; Sybil Romilly, now Mrs Douglas Nicholson, and Caroline Crompton, now Mrs George Robertson, came to talk and laugh, but the Booths led a very quiet life. It was enough for Charles to do his daily stint, whether in London or Liverpool, and to read and reflect in the evenings.

Dodo with her gaiety and gifts was the princess of the nursery party. Tom was a handsome, sweet-natured, unusually sensitive boy. Mary, straining for perfection, taught the children herself, supported Charles's flickering vitality and won back the old intimacy with her father. All this and the imminent arrival of a new baby taxed her strength.

In September 1876 her father wrote, 'It is a great comfort to think that though you may have twelve children and perhaps twelve husbands, you can only have one Old Paw!' On 9 October 1876 the new baby, Paulina Mary, was born and, as after Dodo's birth, Mary was once again knocking holes through walls, painting them green, choosing a Morris wallpaper, and achieving an unexpectedly quiet, dark and rather grand interior to the Grenville Place drawing-room. In a December letter, Mr Macaulay teased his daughter about her 'Alhambra Palace', and added a comment which shows the morbid side of the intense Macaulay feelings for their nearest and dearest: 'When we come to die there is nothing which is at once so comforting and so sad as the sight of those we love best. Extremes meet, and there is always a suggestion of pain in the climax of pleasure.'

Pain followed hard on the heels of Mary's happiness. Only a few months after her birth, brown-eyed Polly died very suddenly of croup. The tragedy brought intense grief. Fifty and sixty years later Mary never spoke of this loss without tears, blaming herself for having trusted a foolish nurse. Her father sought to answer her confusion and sorrow with sensitive and solid advice. 'I am becoming more and more an advocate of an Established Church; not that I believe, as you know, in the thirty-nine Articles,' he wrote, and as the years went on Mary's reaction to life with all its beauty, failure and uncertainty conformed to her father's belief in 'the necessity of expressing gratitude even without the certainty of a Universal Recipient'. On 22 September 1877, George Macaulay Booth made his appearance, with the same brown eyes as Paulina. His charm and vitality increasingly consoled Mary for her loss. Another cause for rejoicing was the first-rate news of Charles's health which Mary could at last send her father. He wrote back: 'I shall not be surprised if after teaching us all upon how little a human animal can live, he will begin to give an example of how much a human animal can eat without busting up.'

This human animal was entirely occupied with Alfred Booth and Company. One of the few letters he kept besides Mary's was written by Tom Fletcher from Liverpool at this time, and describes the peculiarities of Alfred, who 'comes in two or three times a week, a silent indecisive presence. Really Alfred is a puzzle to sail shipmate with. I can never get anything out of him, I never know whether he is coming to the office or when he has left. It is like going partners with a sphinx.' It was the sphinx's end of the business which was in trouble. Although in 1875 and 1876 overall profits had risen slightly, in 1877 they dropped to nil because of losses in America. Charles decided that he must take the skin business of Alfred Booth and Company in hand personally, and arranged to visit New York early in 1878. The pattern of nine months at home, divided between London and Liverpool, and three months in

PLATE 3 Family group at Gracedieu 1888. Charles Booth stands behind Beatrice Potter, Mary Booth behind Alfred Booth

PLATE 4 Charles Booth and Mary, at her desk, in the drawing-room
Gracedieu 1890

America, became a settled thing for the rest of his working life, and led incidentally to a remarkable exchange of letters between husband and wife. They wrote to each other every day. She was a partner in the business in all but name, weighing every decision, and giving sensible advice. Just a few extracts must be given here as they set the pattern for the years to come.

The first of many sea letters, written on board the S.S. *Algeria*, reached her in March 1878:

. . . As I lie in bed thinking over all the mistakes and blunders I have made, [the phrase] comes continually to my lips, 'Bless my wife, bless my dear wife.' I then think of all she has done for me and all she is ever doing for me, and I am grateful. And then behind all that, and bigger than all that, comes up my love for her. There is wonder, and there is admiration, and there is some fear sometimes, I know, but the big thing is the love and trust I have in her. Surely never man needed the help of a wife more than I did, or was so slow to admit it and take advantage of the wife by his side, but though wisdom has been forced forward by these years, you are always wise by the side of me. I cannot say that I wish I had more confidence in myself, for I evidently have plenty, but I wish it were of a firmer, better-grounded kind. What have I done that I, lying here seasick, should believe that I can pick up the disordered skein of a business and set it right? At any rate, my best chance of success lies in not under-rating the difficulties, and being very moderate in my expectations of success, and—above all— in holding fast to the central and achieved success of house and home and future for my children, such as will make them, and you, and me happy, even if it has to be something smaller than 6 Grenville Place.

Meanwhile Mary was writing:

How funny it is that people seem to think that one will be so miserable alone and that one would prefer company of any sort to an evening by oneself. Now what I want is you, not company, and the idea of the value of you to me being degraded into your being just company I don't like at all. . . . It is curious after all the excitement of last week to be in the dead silence of this. No news of course from you, none from New York, all vague wonders and a feeling of resting on one's oars and gathering up one's strength and courage to meet the good or bad that may come. European affairs look as black as thunder, Germany already grumbling at Austria's preparations, Russia utterly defiant and we not yet united. The mob however behaved like Balaam the other day, refused to curse the Government and instead smashed Gladstone's windows.

At this time the Queen and the populace were all for war with Russia. They sang, and she would have liked to join in, 'We don't want to fight but by jingo if we do' outside Gladstone's house before hurling stones. When Disraeli, after hovering on 'the Dizzy Bank', succeeded in agreeing on a conference in Berlin under Bismarck's chairmanship, the Queen—forgetting that this was not what she had hoped for—gave a dance, and waltzed for the first time since 'He' died [1].

References by both Charles and Mary to 'der alte Jude', as Bismarck called Disraeli with great respect, contain unstinting praise, and for Mary, as for the Queen, Gladstone could never do anything right. Over home policy Charles and Mary were sometimes at variance, but on the position of England abroad they were as one. 'That scoundrel Bismarck' comes in for much adverse comment, but Russia 'is the real threat'. 'I quite agree with you,' wrote Mary to Charles about Disraeli, 'He has played his game admirably. One is so much struck too with the dignity of his position, dealing only with the larger issues, never descending into personalities, or taking any notice of the storm of really disgusting abuse which is always being heaped upon him by the hotheads of the other side, whilst Gladstone talks eternally of himself and keeps the House of Commons up for hours whilst he explains the purity of his motives and the extreme pain that it costs him to assume the part of an agitator.'

When Charles's long packet of news arrived, Mary welcomed it warmly, and wrote back: 'Oh my precious one. . . . You make too much of me. I love you and could work for you and help you with whatever brains and strength I have. I bring a good will and a set purpose to bear on everything that has the remotest connection with our welfare but I am so often wrong, over-punctilious, red-tapist, starched in my ideas. . . . I think that, after all, my greatest safety may lie in the buoyant high spirits that are coming back to me with my strength.'

Charles found on arrival in New York that the business was in an almost total state of collapse, and that his brother and other colleagues seemed incapable of creative responsibility. The next few weeks were, therefore, a time of tremendous personal pressure, and perhaps because

[1] 'He' and 'His' in the Queen's diary always means Prince Albert.

of this he wrote a character sketch of himself which is devastatingly piercing and prophetic. He knows he can deal with a mass of detail. He knows he is persistent. He acknowledges a certain coldness in his heart. In spite of what other people think of him he says, 'I am no fool'.[1] The more foolishness Charles found in the administration of his partners, the more they found to distrust in him. Nor did Mary's conviction that the Macaulay family was worth all other families put together help to soothe ruffled feelings. In response to one of his letters she promised to write to Aunt Roscoe 'with all imaginable graciousness. I shan't give myself airs'. This was one of the complaints of her in-laws and there was just enough truth in it to make Mary self-conscious and overdo her graciousness. 'But', as she once said to me, 'a certain combination of adequate looks and brains always leads to jealousy on the part of those with either, but not both, and then one can do nothing right!'

In fact at this time Mary was less unpopular than Charles, and Anna Holt even wrote to say that she and Philip hoped to see her when they came to London. Mary's comment to Charles was that she did not like the way they were civil to her the moment his back was turned, but she couldn't stop them coming to call. This attempt at reconciliation went fairly well and led to still better things when on the following day Philip met Mary by chance in Kensington Gardens. Surrounded by children she found that 'her nerve held' and that she could talk quite naturally to the man who had not spoken to her for years.

Charles, momentarily vulnerable, needed every possible support and actually protested once about Mary's 'cold formal letters', a ridiculous criticism considering the outpouring of love, stories of the children, chronicles of defective drains, smoking chimneys, and worries about finding wet-nurses which topped up the holds of westward-bound steamships. On the anniversary of their wedding day, Dodo was reported as saying, ' "Mama, you like everything your own way and so do I, but I don't get it." Oh these chicks of yours, they are so very sweet. If I had known you would have had such chicks I would have said, "Yes, Yes Boy" the first time you asked me straight off. . . . Seven years ago today since that strange eventful morning when we two knowing so little of each other . . . stood together to say the words "till death us do part". How different our life seems now to what we then expected; for me unspeakably happier; my love for you a hundred times deeper. I hold out my hand across the sea and say all my promises again.'

[1] See Appendix A, p. 215

In holding out her hand to her husband Mary was also reaching out at home towards the social ideas which specially interested both of them. Her first visit to the Barnetts at Whitechapel, where Kate Potter, Mary's cousin, was working, took place in the spring of 1878. She told Charles that she had seen and heard horrible things. 'Boy, Boy, I must do something, put out a hand to help in all this misery. I do so long for strength and health.' Obviously Canon Barnett advised her to concentrate for the moment on her family and keep her powder dry. 'Most interesting long talk with Mr Barnett about work and waiting and enthusiasm,' she wrote in her diary. Samuel Barnett was born in 1844, the son of a rich Bristol businessman. After reading law at Oxford, he travelled for a while and then entered the Church in 1867. The Booths may have met him when he was a curate in Marylebone, and they certainly knew of his collaboration with Miss Octavia Hill in founding the Charity Organisation Society. He had married Henrietta Rowland in 1873, and these two delightful, good-looking do-gooders went to live in the vicarage of St Jude's in Whitechapel. In 1877 they founded the Children's Country Holiday Fund, and in 1884 Toynbee Hall. The Whitechapel Art Gallery was the outcome of their determination to bring art and music to the East End. Canon Barnett and Dame Henrietta, as they became, were household names in thousands of homes, rich and poor. The parallel between Charles and Samuel Barnett is obvious. Born and dying within three years of each other, they came from the same comfortable, provincial background, married wives of tremendous energy, and wielded great influence in the social field. It is easy now to realise the worth of the Barnetts' 'work and waiting and enthusiasm', but Mary discovered and valued its importance at first sight.

She did not guess, however, the importance of a young cousin who called on her in Grenville Place while Charles was still away.

IV
MARY AND BEATRICE
1879–1885

Beatrice Potter was eleven years younger than her first cousin Mary and had been one of the babies at Standish in the old days. This difference in age gave Mary the certainty of greater experience which also contributed ultimately to the rift in their intimacy. Beautiful throughout her life, youth and vulnerability must have given Beatrice an overwhelming attraction at this moment. Together with complete purity of intention, she possessed two other qualities hard to analyse. Perhaps it was innate force and a certain capacity for manoeuvre which aroused such intense admiration, such fierce antagonism. Yet on this first occasion she gave Mary the impression of uncertainty and unhappiness. 'Beatrice Potter came to see me this afternoon and we had a long talk. She is as odd as ever she can be, but a good sort of girl. She is dreadfully bothered with the "Weltschmerz", the uselessness of life, etc. etc. I sympathised and comforted as well as I could. Then she went off, after the manner of the Potters, into a dissertation on the characters of all her sisters, praising Maggie to the skies and roundly abusing Lally, as they all do, denying even her claim to brains which Teresa admits.'

At the very outset of the relationship between Mary and Beatrice, two contradictory facets are visible: a basic affection and a basic lack of understanding. Had Mary still been living with her parents, unmarried and unsettled, at the age of twenty-five, she too would have been wondering about the purpose of life, but she would not have poured out her soul at the first opportunity to anyone sympathetic enough to listen. Beatrice confided in Mary because she felt sure she was talking to another rebel within the family circle but in a sense she was ten years too late. Mary had gone through too much in Charles's wilderness of doubt not to value the fields and fences of traditional thought and to yearn for their peace and shelter. She responded, however, to Beatrice's beauty, eloquence and distress, and for the time both thought their roads were leading in the same direction.

Beatrice tells how her acquaintance with Mary and Charles ripened into friendship in *My Apprenticeship*:

Charles Booth married the attractive and accomplished daughter of Charles Macaulay, who happened to be my cousin, and who had met him for the first time at the house of my eldest sister, the wife of R. D. Holt. Meanwhile his multifarious activities, carried out from early morning to late at night, whether in the ship-owning venture which he started with his brother, or in political propaganda or continuous reading, caused a severe breakdown in health, which necessitated some years abroad, and a long period of inability to work or even to read.

It was during the period of his convalescence, I think in the late 'seventies', that my cousin brought her husband for the first time to stay with us. I recall with some amusement the impression made on a girl's mind by this interesting new relative. Nearing forty years of age, tall, abnormally thin, garments hanging as if on pegs, the complexion of a consumptive girl, and the slight stoop of the sedentary worker, a prominent aquiline nose, with moustache and pointed beard barely hiding a noticeable Adam's apple, the whole countenance dominated by a finely moulded brow and large, observant grey eyes, Charles Booth was an attractive but distinctly queer figure of a man.[1] One quaint sight stays in my mind; Cousin Charlie sitting through the family meals 'like patience on a monument smiling at'—other people eating, whilst, as a concession to good manners, he occasionally picked at a potato with his fork or nibbled a dry biscuit. Fascinating was his unselfconscious manner and eager curiosity to know what you thought and why you thought it; what you knew and how you had learnt it. And there was the additional interest of trying to place this strange individual in the general scheme of things. No longer young, he had neither failed nor succeeded in life, and one was left in doubt whether the striking unconventionality betokened an initiating brain or a futile eccentricity. Observed by a stranger, he might have passed for a self-educated, idealistic compositor or engineering draughtsman; or as the wayward member of an aristocratic family of the Auberon Herbert type; or as a University professor; or, clean shaven and with the appropriate collar, as an ascetic priest, Roman or Angli-

---

[1] The photograph on the jacket was taken at this time.

can; with another change of attire, he would have 'made up' as an artist in the Quartier Latin. The one vocation which seemed ruled out, alike by his appearance and by his idealistic temperament, was that of a great Captain of Industry pushing his way, by sheer will-power and methodical industry . . . into new countries, new processes and new business connections. And yet this kind of adventurous and, as it turned out, successful, profit-making enterprise proved to be his destiny, bringing in its train the personal power and free initiative due to a large income generously spent. . . . Charles Booth had also the scientific impulse, in his case directed towards the structure and working of society . . . and over-powering curiosity about the nature of things; originality in designing ways and means of research; and above all, a splendid courage and persistency in the pursuit of knowledge. Further, Charles Booth was singularly appreciative . . . of any suggestions from fellow-workers and sub-ordinates.

On 26 July 1879, Margaret Paulina was born, a solemn, fat baby, very unlike the fairy creature she later became. Mary found it difficult to be thrilled with her fifth child, and wrote of her rather caustically. Perhaps the thought of the first Paulina deflected her tenderness, and certainly—like many Victorian women—she was worn out with childbirth. Real danger and prolonged pain attended accouchements in those days. Mary's greatest friend, Sybil Nicholson, died in childbirth and so did my great-aunt Minnie Thackeray.

Meanwhile Charles was working more and more in Liverpool and in 1880 Alfred Booth finally handed him complete command of the business. When he returned to New York that summer, Charles wrote to Mary: 'I find that my rôle of "senior partner" and successful man has cost me a few dollars this week, but it is wise expenditure as I am not extravagantly inclined. As to your expenditure, do not forget that there are to be no accounts or calculations or looking forward until I come. Never mind how much you spend. I know we are well able to afford an extra hundred or two hundred pounds this year.'

This was just as well, for Mary's love for pretty things had once again led her into extravagance, and she owned up to Charles that she paid six pounds for two beautiful little tables for the drawing-room and bought two coloured vases for the niches on the staircase. She hoped he would forgive her as she could not withstand this sort of temptation.

Charles's ideas about how to spend money and time were quite different. On one visit to Liverpool he wrote: 'I have studied the ways of the people this evening having supped at a Coffee Palace which was next to the Mission Hall, with a door through. . . . It is bedizened with texts. . . . Good food might excuse texts but texts don't excuse bad food.' However, 'Nothing could equal the atrocity of the beer' at the Music Hall to which Charles later adjourned, where there were no texts.

Mary was already showing that taste for occasional solitude which when she was an old woman became a predilection. It gave her the chance which she openly avowed to Charles to be free of his influence: 'I think the Roman Catholics are right in their ideas of what a Retreat should be; that one should be a good deal alone, left to face one's own mind and not too much under the influence of another.'

Later that summer when Charles was once again away in America, Mary took her children down to Ramsgate to see their grandparents and there was an orgy of photographing. She 'gave Papa a copy all for himself of my photograph, which he likes though he says it is the face of a priest, not a woman—an odd criticism. . . . He sends you his blessing and [says] he forgives you, for marrying me I suppose. He is the dearest Old Paw. I really never saw anyone so good. It is sad work though here; it weighs upon one's spirits.'

Meanwhile, in New York during gruelling days of heat and work, Charles used to get up at 6.30 a.m. and run his bath while writing in his night-shirt to his wife. In one letter he wondered whether it was right that he should sacrifice everything to his work, and concluded that it was his 'nature to and no wife could be better to me about it than my wife, at least unless she was thankful to be rid of me'. He urges her not to be anxious for the future, but to attend to the present with an easy heart: 'Your health and the children's health and their manners and the rest will come all right. Your greatest anxiety is your father and to that you must school yourself. He may live for years yet, but you are sure to be often anxious about him and you must do all you can not to let your anxiety get the upper hand and make you ill. You want to be strong and well to do what lies to you to make the years smooth for him.'

The person who smoothed the years for Mary was Charlotte Garforth, who came as parlourmaid soon after Polly's death and, such was her character, soon shared the household responsibility. A remarkable friendship grew up between employer and employed. In the years to come when Mary was coping with holidays in the country, Charlotte would be spring-cleaning the town house and looking after the master who came and went for a night or even an hour or two in the course of his constant travelling. Charles always sent messages to Charlotte when he was abroad, and in return for her humour and affection he took under his wing Charlotte's inadequate family. When she married a policeman, the wedding party was held at Grenville Place, and the link with 'Mrs Rumbold' was never broken. Her husband proved as improvident as the Garforths, so that after many attempts to set them up in small shops, the Booths finally pensioned the Garforths and when Mrs Rumbold was widowed she returned to their service.

In reply to a long letter from Charles about a 'Methodist religious watering place called Ocean Row',[1] Mary described her own rising faith in a very different watering-place.

I was exceedingly interested in your account of the curious American religious dissipation; strange and unwholesome it all seems to me, and that, though I am more religiously disposed than ever. I wonder now how I could ever have lived without it and am ashamed of myself and my doubts when I look back, yet I think I can understand your position and feelings better than I used to do. At any rate, I do not think that you and I will clash, I don't think you would have seriously disliked our religious observance yesterday. We went to the Garrison Church, Tom, Dodo and I, and saw the soldiers troop in to the sound of fife and drum. Then Prince Edward of Saxe-Weimar, the Commandant here, with his Staff amidst galaxies of under-Officers and men stationed to keep order. Then we, with others following, had to find seats where we could. I looked round at the soldiers and the little brasses let in everywhere so thickly under the painted windows: 'To the Memory of Captain D . . . killed at A . . ., the Officers of the 44th, etc. etc.' Above was hung the old, worn Colours that had seen many fights, suspended now, tattered and faded, from the capitals of the pillars. I liked it all and to be in the midst of it, and to kneel and stand and hear the dear words of our Church Service. Oh, I do love it very much! To have ever left it as much as I have once seems strange to me, a sort of treason, rebellion, certainly ingratitude.

Charles replied on 26 August: 'Your letters seem more peaceful and if peace brings religion and religion brings peace, why at any rate I bless both.'

[1] See Appendix B, p. 218.

During the early days of marriage, it was her father who had urged Mary to write and later on her husband took up the plea. He felt she would be happier if she could use her pen for a definite aim instead of squandering her ability on her family. Thus encouraged she completed and submitted the manuscript of a novel to a publisher, who refused it. She burnt it immediately, and the episode cost her acute humiliation, followed shortly by a heart-attack which may have been a physical reaction to mental stress. The truth was that like many highly intellectual people she lacked imagination, and the liveliness of her conversation never reached the page. So she put all thought of writing behind her.

However, as she told Charles, there was a happy side to her acceptance of reality: 'I think I have never found my powers of enjoyment keener or my head more clear. In fact, the gritty stage of my early womanhood seems to be left behind. For how long, who knows? I could almost pray that if life holds another such epoch of suffering as I have gone through in store for me among its dark secrets, I may be taken away before its time draws near.' The chief cause of suffering which emphasised the religious differences between Mary and Charles was Paulina's death:

I have not sufficient strength or grit of character to endure adversity. At present I can only be thankful and glad and hope if trouble does come I may face it better than I have done yet. How can I write such things to you? It is because you are my other self. My inmost thoughts and feelings and confidences, from which I should utterly shrink to share even with those others who are nearest to me, seem natural and right for you. I think the love I have for you is quite unique amongst my feelings—very strong and deep; underneath all upper currents of disagreement and want of sympathy, a strong, full stream that I am only perfectly conscious of at times.

In one of the letters Mary gave her husband a highly individual portrait of herself, sitting on the balcony in her brown cotton frock, having just come in from a bathe. She has pinned up her bun which is still damp, and her hair and the ink dry together as she pours out her thoughts to her husband: 'Oh, if I had you here and could put your chair near mine on the balcony and sit with you looking at the blue loveliness of the sea and listening to the band, while we could watch our small quartette taking their pleasure on the beach just outside. I would put my hand in yours and you should tell me all about Boston and Gloversville and New York and Mr. Kuttner, and I would tell you nothing at all but that I am very comfortable and lazy and feeling sleepy.' Mary's generosity in sharing all Charles's business worries was not matched by any interest on his part in her difficulties over the faulty drains and the smoking chimneys of Grenville Place. He seldom or never mentioned them, and left every domestic decision to Mary.

But it was not his fault that she was so often left at home. He always hoped to have her as his companion, and most women would have accompanied their husbands wherever they went, leaving children with relatives, but Mary was different. Rather pathetically she often asked him if he was homesick, but the answer was that he adored business, and travel:

Wherever I am in America I always say I like that place best—and the denizens thereof—but that is my civility. For it is New York for me— New York's the place for me. What is it about your great City—your metropolis—so different from a provincial place, however large?— a difference applying not only to the aggregate of the place but to each part of it. I have never seen one-tenth of Boston, never even one-tenth of Liverpool, and yet I dub them small! There seems to be something subtle, an essence, belonging to the great metropolitan cities, and altering everything—so that life seems more lively, busier, larger; the individual less, the community more. I like it—it does me good, but I know that it has another aspect and I am not surprised when people feel crushed by the wickedness of it, the ruthlessness, the heartlessness of its grinding mill, as you did in Paris. What place for the individual is the question?

The following year he shipped to Bordeaux in search of good quality skins. He called this excursion a holiday; the pattern was always the same. In every place he met his 'skin friend', did a great deal of work, enjoyed finding some humble lodging, made arrangements for a bath, and 'dined leguminously', as he put it. He spent a week in the Cévennes, putting up in the most primitive farms and inns. On one occasion he gave a baby its bottle while the mother cooked him a delicious meal, serving it on a rough wooden table in the single living room with the beds stacked round the walls. From Orleans he wrote: 'My holiday task has been most successful. I have had pleasure and rest and interest and all that man could wish for. I like France and we will come here together and travel comfortably. For me, I like foreign ways, as you know, and take to them as a duck to water, but not so my little wife, and when she and I travel we will do it quite differently.' In this their characters were completely divergent. Charles could write, eat, sleep and wash with the minimum of apparatus. He had absolutely no sense of class, and was as happy with his 'skin friends' as with his own family. Mary liked her own desk to write at; her day to be ordered; her bath-tub set out in her bedroom. The sights he described would have been a great pleasure to her, but his methods of seeing them were not hers.

My grandmother had a strong sense of race, of continuity, and of class in that sense. She once told me that she was sorry the old ways of addressing a duke as 'Your Grace' and a bishop as 'My Lord' were going out. She felt there was virtue in demonstrating the respect due to great titles. I was rather taken aback by this, and asked, 'But what about respect for very great people, who have no title?' 'That is entirely different,' was Mary's answer. 'But in Macaulay's case it was the same,' I continued argumentatively. 'Why should one historian be "My Lord" and not another?' 'It is a very pretty compliment,' said Mary, 'when the absence of children makes a peerage an appropriate mark of a country's recognition.' 'Do you mean that if Macaulay had had children he oughtn't to have been made a lord?' 'Yes, I do,' she said, 'the Macaulays are Highland gentry, not aristocracy.' Mary knew her place, so to speak, and was proud of it.

Charles never knew his place, because he had not got one. The nearest approach to this sort of identification comes in a letter in which he describes with acute interest and innate sympathy the house and character of Jacques Cœur at Bourges:

He was a great merchant from whom one of those precious French kings borrowed money and then paid his debt by murdering his creditor, and now his magnificent house has been renovated for an Hôtel de Ville. One may well talk of a 'Merchant Prince' for such a man as this must have been. I wonder what was the secret, and what the combination of opportunity and character that gave such wealth in some cases in those days. Honesty was one element I have no doubt, and I think a large mind another.

I have had my supper and lighted my candles and will go on 'til it is time to post my letter. My writing is very bad today, almost illegible

I fear, and I must take more pains. I hate on principle to bother a correspondent with illegible words or unintelligible sentences, hating the same myself. . . . It is delightful and like a sort of home-coming to find one's letters awaiting one's arrival. Many, many thanks.

An entry in Beatrice Potter's diary for 9 February 1882 gives a picture of the Booths' home life at this time and an impression of her own quality of prescience and sympathy:

The last six weeks spent in London, with friends and sisters. The Booths' house dark and airless, but the inmates exceedingly charming and lovable. Mary, really a remarkable woman, with an unusual power of expression and a well-trained and cultivated mind. She makes one feel, in spite of her appreciative and almost flattering attitude, 'a very ignoramus'. To me there is a slight narrowness in her literary judgements; they are too correct, too resting on authority? hardly the result of original thought? Perhaps it is this very orderliness of mind and deference to authority which makes her so attractive as a woman; for, added to this culture and polish of the intellect, there is a deep vein of emotion, of almost passionate feeling.

Charles Booth has a stronger and clearer reason, with a singular absence of bias and prejudice. It is difficult to discover the presence of any vice or even weakness in him. Conscience, reason and dutiful affection, are his great qualities; other characteristics are not observable by the ordinary friend. He interests me as a man who has his nature completely under control; who has passed through a period of terrible illness and weakness, and who has risen out of it, uncynical, vigorous and energetic in mind, and without egotism. Many delightful conversations I had with these two charming cousins, generally acting as a listening third to their discussion.

In the spring of 1882, Charles developed shingles, the children had fever and Mary suffered from severe rheumatic pains. Mr Macaulay was exasperated by such a series of misfortunes: 'Most people have some trouble or other to bear; but for the most part the troubles of peoples arise from some permanent cause—poverty, disappointed homes, unhappy domestic surroundings—but you are happy all round and yet scarcely a month passes without some serious cause of worry! Why the devil can't you both take it easy? Neither of you profit from the exhaustion of the other.' He goes on to say that 'the best English team' has been beaten by the Australians, and 'I can't hold up my head'. His cricketing commentaries have as general an appeal as Bernard Darwin's golfing articles.

Mary's brother, Charlie, spent a good deal of time with the Booths at Grenville Place, sang funny songs, strummed on the piano and made himself a great favourite with the children. He could have practised in those days as a country doctor without the university degree in medicine which he failed to obtain, but he never did: he never worked at all. Mary behaved with tact and loyalty and the relations between him and the young family in Grenville Place were very pleasant for several years. Then one day something must have been said about Charles Booth's growing reputation and jealousy crept in. Uncle Charlie came no more to sing and play with the children. He missed them more than they missed him.

Mary's sixth child arrived in October 1882, and the Old Paw welcomed 'Mary Imogen' as he did the night-gowns of swans-down calico sent him for Christmas. 'How could I have been content with common linen for seventy years?' he wrote. 'I do worship the dear holly spirit.' His letters echo the companionship that Mary and Beatrice Potter were enjoying. In February 1883, for instance, he sent his love 'to dear Beatrice. Tell her I would give a pretty penny to see her in her crimson satin and white lace dress, but tell her not to be proud of the power of her beauty. It is a grand possession but it has its dangers and should make her extra careful of her choice of mate.'

Mr Macaulay was referring to Joseph Chamberlain, MP for his home town, Birmingham, who although twice widowed and almost twice Beatrice's age, had fallen in love with the beauty and drive of this unusual girl. They were both ambitious, both genuinely humanitarian and there seemed much to be hoped for in such a marriage. Chamberlain was impressed by her work on London housing estates and Beatrice, taken aback by the solemnity of provincial life at Highbury on her first visit, was later enchanted by her host's powerful oratory at a big political meeting, and carried away by his high-handed wooing. The courtship between these two could not of course be kept quiet. In one of Mary's letters to Charles in April 1883 she said: 'I had forgotten so entirely that you were going away to Liverpool that I had arranged with Beatrice on Thursday morning for Maggie [Hobhouse] to dine with us to be out of the way of the Chamberlain Dinner Party, and for you to take her back in the evening to have a talk with the Great Cham.

to keep him off Beatrice who would have had him all dinner. When I saw Maggie yesterday I remembered all about it and had to write to Bee that you could not do it. I am sorry for I should like to help her in any way possible.'

Thus from the first amused and not over-sympathetic view of Beatrice's character, Mary's attitude had changed to intimate admiration and affection. The Booth children called their cousin Aunt Bo, and Mary used her Uncle Richard's nickname for his daughter, Bee. Beatrice was now an established and fascinating third force to the Booths' many discussions, and an integral part of their life both in London and the country. Her influence and interest were harnessed to 'political agnosticism tempered by individualist economics', as she expressed it. Charles was particularly interested in the subject of working men's apartments and the opinions of working men on political and social questions, and the fact that the poor were getting poorer as the rich became richer.

Charles himself was in the second category, as his capital now stood at £50,000. He and Mary felt justified, therefore, in looking for a country home somewhere between Liverpool and London, where the father could join his family at week-ends during the holidays. They decided to take a short lease of Haselour Hall in Staffordshire, a charming black and white timbered house, with eighteenth-century brick additions. It still stands in a particularly beautiful setting of trees and park-land, and it would have become the Booths' permanent home if Charles had had the money to buy it when their lease came to an end two years later and the owner put it up for sale.

Mr Macaulay wrote to Mary there: 'I commend you to your Hall, your coach, your fine terraced walk and your State bed.' Ill and alone, he adds, 'What a wonderful place this world of ours is! . . . It seems to me that one must be seventy years old in order to appreciate the full force of this truth. Not 'til then does one feel the same sort of amused surprise at the passionate longings of *young* men and women that adults feel for the stormy years of childhood.' On 16 October, when Mary sent him a rose for his birthday, he wrote that for seventy years he had loved her 'better than anything else on earth. Surely there must be something immortal in love when the wearied body says, "Goodnight".' In February 1884 Mr Macaulay responded to Mary's recurrent unhappiness over the death of little Paulina by questioning, ' . . . why should God gather such sweet buds as Polly and leave such full-blown cabbage roses as me on the stalk . . .?' He ended on a cheerful note: 'Do you want a good novel—read "Treasure Island" by Robert Louis Stevenson. It is the only novel I have read that is absorbingly interesting without having one word in it of love.'

In the following year Mr Macaulay's looking-glass letters reflect the prevailing preoccupation with the problem of a satisfactory settlement in Ireland. Charles believed that the choice was between separation or benevolent despotism, and as in his view despotism never proved benevolent in the long run, he drafted a letter to *The Times* in these terms. Mr Macaulay advised his son-in-law to put his arguments forward at greater length, 'as the idea of separation to most people was both startling and absurd'. Taking his point, Charles wrote and subsequently published a leaflet entitled 'England and Ireland—A Counter Proposal', which advocated eventual Dominion status. Auberon Herbert, a Liberal aristocratic friend of Beatrice Potter's, wrote a supporting letter to the *Pall Mall Gazette* favouring a modification of Charles's scheme for Ireland. Mary's attitude was sceptical: 'If only the Radicals and the Irish would agree to such a plan—or if the mass of us would determine to do it and carry it through in spite of the Irish and Radical howls—I should be for it too; but—but—I see there is dread of commotion in London from the dynamiters if the second reading of the Irish Bill is thrown out.' Meanwhile Mr Macaulay considered the only remedy for Ireland was 'the same as that for naughty wives, the stick', and in his opinion Gladstone was only interested in the problem to the extent that it brought him Irish votes in the House. His Government were already involved in another tragic muddle. 'The Times has just come in,' Mr Macaulay wrote, 'What a terrible story this is about poor Gordon. I believe it, and if it turns out to be true . . . and if the country should prefer to prolong the life of a Government so hopelessly insensible of the honour of the Nation, I shall begin to wish I was a Russian or an Italian.'

When the British troops under Wolseley finally fought their way into Khartoum they found that General Gordon had just been murdered on the steps of Government House. Mary always showed her grandchildren the two Punch cartoons of 7 and 14 February 1885, drawn by Linley Sambourne. The first, which went to press before the tragedy became known, depicts General Stuart greeting Gordon. Mr Sambourne was shopping in Bond Street when he heard a newsboy calling out, 'Gordon! Gordon!' He rushed out to buy a newspaper, discovered the truth, and went home to draw the second cartoon, entitled *Too late*. It shows Britannia weeping over Gordon's body. Mary's bitter sorrow was as vituperative in the 1920s as it must have been originally.

Without fail, on 29 April, Mr Macaulay sent greetings on 'the anniversary of my darling's wedding! A happier day for us all than the real wedding day was!'. It may be that fourteen years of trial effort and happiness made Mary want to understand the psychological changes in the girl she had been and the woman she had become. At any rate, she wrote to someone calling himself 'Graphologist', and was so impressed by the resulting character study that she kept it;[1] many people who knew her well can testify to its accuracy. Her letters from now on are far less introspective. She had accepted her limitations and was concentrating on the possible. What a pity it was she did not also persuade Beatrice Potter to consult the same oracle! Many other eyes a century later would have been deeply interested in a graphologist's exposition of their contrasting characters.

In July 1885 Beatrice confided in Mary that all thought of marriage between herself and Joseph Chamberlain was at an end. It is difficult to say which of them finally closed the door on an engrossing prospect in which each had searched for different landmarks. Neither her passionate personal attachment nor her selfless search for intellectual solutions gave him that promise of orderly support which he felt was necessary for his career. Stirred as she was by the man, and much as she wished to share his powerful political future, she could not surrender her personality to his dominance.

Mary responded with warm-hearted support: 'I can't tell you the feeling of relief your letter has given me, even in the midst of feeling sorry, very sorry . . . for all this pain and disturbance:—the worry of worries that the need to decide finally a crucial question must bring; I do rejoice to know that the decision is "No". We look forward eagerly to seeing you on the 15th. Charles sends you his best of loves. Farewell best of cousins.'

Beatrice, with much to give and no one to give it to, travelled down gratefully to stay with the Booths in the country in search of solace and understanding.

[1] See Appendix C, p. 219.

V
THE CRUCIAL YEAR
1885–1886

By the 1880s the first surge of what is now called modern technology but was then known as the Industrial Revolution had spent itself. English machinery, brilliant in its inception, was becoming out of date. Other countries were exporting manufactured goods, at competitive prices, having in some cases improved on the original industrial designs. The population of England and Wales, despite the total lack of public drainage or hospital facilities and the ubiquitous use of child labour had nearly doubled since Queen Victoria came to the throne. In order to forestall great privation in England and total famine in Ireland, where the population was almost halved by potato disease, exodus and death, the Corn Laws had been repealed in 1846. The importation of cheap food, while ameliorating the lot of the industrial worker, had caused increased unemployment among agricultural labourers, who naturally migrated to towns and cities in search of work. Boatloads of wretched Irish peasants joined the throng.

The old Poor Law dealt with poverty on a village vestry basis, paying outdoor relief, a method which was open to abuse. The reforming zeal of the great Edwin Chadwick led to a Royal Commission and the famous Poor Law Amendment Act of 1834. It attempted to solve the problems of unemployment, old age and vagrancy by grouping several villages together, calling them Unions and giving considerable powers to the Board of Guardians which managed them. Existing alms-houses continued to care for old people in some areas and the Unions built workhouses for others in need. The Board of Guardians became the Poor Law Board in 1847, and was finally merged with the Local Government Board in 1871. Whatever the name, its social application proved totally inadequate to cope with a rising population and two serious trade recessions. Upheavals in Europe led to the arrival of foreign immigrants, who, willing perforce to work for starvation wages, depressed still further the ordinary rates of pay and the number of jobs available for Britons. Thousands of willing but workless young men, old couples and defenceless children were herded into grim, unsuitable Union buildings, along with the work-shy, the subnormal and the depraved. Meant to be accommodation for migrating labourers, these workhouses rapidly became places of permanent penance where husbands were separated from wives, mothers from sons, and where the very young and very old were expected to work as hard as the able-bodied in return for their keep. If some of these institutions were run on humane lines, the majority were rightly dreaded. Fifty years later in Leicestershire, I remember the 'Union' being spoken of as the final degradation. Any privation was preferable and death itself a happy solution for the ill and old.

It seems clear now that the supreme human problem of Victorian England in the 1880s was the presence of dire poverty in a powerful and thriving country. One would have expected the House of Commons to be engaged in incessant debate on the subject. Instead it was increasingly absorbed by the Irish question. Gladstone's Government laboured in the throes of producing a palatable Home Rule Bill while the Tory Party, which had destroyed itself over the repeal of the Corn Laws, eagerly watched its opponents' equal anguish over Ireland and waited for a reversal of fortune. It was outside Parliament therefore that the problems of unemployment and poverty were wrestled with by perplexed philosophers, churchmen and humanitarians. Meetings were held and attended, novels and essays were written and read with attention, protesting processions were led and followed—all concerned with the same subject.

Early in 1881 Henry George, an American, brought out a book called *Progress and Poverty* which condemned landlordism as the root of all evil and advocated the appropriation of land tax by the State, in lieu of rent. This book had an immense impact in England, where the Government was attempting to deal with the Irish Land League. H. M. Hyndman, an Etonian Radical journalist, wrote a rejoinder called *England for All*, advocating a federation of states instead of an empire and colonies, and he gave a copy to each delegate at the conference which launched the Social Democratic League in June 1881. Both as Mayor of Birmingham and later as President of the Board of Trade, Joseph Chamberlain was always acutely aware of social conditions. He was also a convinced imperialist, and denounced both George and

Hyndman. In 1883 he brought out a Radical programme of his own, advocating free primary education, land reform and financial reform, throughout the United Kingdom, operating under one central authority. For the moment he preferred to publicise these ideas rather than to attempt to press them into legislation. Within the Cabinet he was increasingly immersed in party political struggles over Ireland, bringing pressure to bear on Gladstone through that influential triumvirate consisting of himself, the brilliant Sir William Harcourt, and John Morley,[1] editor of the *Fortnightly*. *The Bitter Cry of Outcast London*, written by the Reverend Andrew Mearns, also came out in 1883 and had such a success that it was read more as a novel than as a treatise on misery.

It was twenty years since Charles Booth had tried and failed to soften the bitter cry of Liverpool with the voice of reason. Now here in the city of his choice the same sound echoed through the meaner streets and haunted the inner thoughts of this courteous, successful merchant ship-owner. At forty-five he was an easy man to work for but he liked being the master. Indeed, since a happy apprenticeship he had never worked for anyone else and was probably incapable of so doing. He had experienced and mastered early emotional pain and subsequent mental and physical disability. Apart from his brother Tom, he had had in his youth two special friends; Tom Fletcher and Francis Prange, who both died in their early fifties. Neither had fulfilled his early promise and both had succumbed to a lingering illness. Charles did all he could for them in their suffering and for their families, but the old, close, equal companionship was at an end. So too, it seemed, was Charles's need for further friendship. Their places were never filled. All the warm affections which a man often shares with several chosen companions were in his case wrapped round his wife; all his curiosity and acumen had been concentrated for years on the business.

During the Second World War, on a crowded train, I happened to sit next to a tired old man with blue eyes and a blue duffel coat. We talked of the merchant navy, and he told me that he had been one of the captains of the Booth Line: 'The line with the best ships and the best men in the business.' As he spoke his back straightened and in answer to my questions his face kindled: 'Oh yes, I knew Mr Charles Booth very well. We all did, from captain to cabin boy. He liked meeting our

[1] Later Viscount Morley, statesman and man of letters.

families and took a personal interest in our problems. I always knew if I went down, the wife would be all right.' Just before we reached Liverpool Street I told the captain why I felt so proud to have heard all this. We shook hands warmly.

These people were the gainers from Charles Booth's way of living: his own children were the losers. He treated them as if they were nephews and nieces, enjoying their company but taking no part in their upbringing, although he knew a good deal about it by observation. His own schooldays had been so different from those of his sons that perhaps he felt unable to enter into the problems of private and public schools. His daughters' upbringing was exactly the same as that of his sisters, but the little girls were too young for intimacy, and Dodo's special position as her mother's companion in his absence made them wary of each other when together. He valued her central rôle in the family, but left it at that. In any case, when at home he concentrated on his wife, and continued vocally the pen and paper discussions so often quoted. Whenever he was away, her feelings, foibles and furies awaited him daily, on his breakfast table. He replied with even greater length and punctuality about everything that happened around and outside him, with natural humour and ease, but scarcely any mention of deeper reactions, changing beliefs or personal disappointments. His hurts, and he must have had them, were secret ones, which if shared with his wife were only once put on paper (when he had to relinquish the chairmanship of Alfred Booth and Company), and therefore leave no trace. Yet this immensely reserved man possessed deep wells of emotion and experience upon which he scarcely knew how to draw without betraying himself. Once he felt he should stay with Margaret while she had her tonsils removed, and fainted away when the operation was over.

It is symptomatic that he played a great deal of patience in his Liverpool lodgings, to calm his racing mind and enable him to digest a spare meal. It was not loneliness but a compulsion to communicate with the only human being who had penetrated his reserve that led him to write often twice a day to his wife. He got to know his landladies and their families, much enjoyed their racy conversation, walked the streets and visited the chapels and pubs round the docks, and felt admiration for the constant courage of those who have no margin of safety. 'They are so uncomplaining, so simple and so dignified about their sorrows,' he wrote. 'What a fuss we make about our losses by contrast.' He seldom saw his own kith and kin, and yet he was proud of them in his own odd way, and believed completely in nepotism. Any relation, however incompetent, was sure of a job in the business. Long ago 'Aunt Fanny', with her scorn of the Booths, had ensured that Charles would do his utmost to establish himself in the community she so much despised. Having accomplished this position, did he remember with yearning those misty passionate uplands of youth where he had been even more essential to his wife than in the peaceful fields of her later happiness?

He always preferred the simplest living conditions, which had at one time been necessary for his health and his purse, to the paraphernalia of a huge Victorian establishment, which none the less he now proudly provided for his family. He loved walking through the English countryside, but never took the slightest interest in agriculture; nor did he ever want to buy an estate and farm it properly. He wanted ships, not land; mobility rather than roots. He had enjoyed winning security for his family, but he wanted to find and give a great deal more than this in life. He joined the Statistical Society, went to various meetings of the Political and Economic Society and made new acquaintances in both intellectual and working-class circles. Some of the 'great unwashed', as Mary called them, came weekly to Grenville Place to discuss working conditions.

In 1884 two new reciprocal forces emerged which altered British history: the Labour Representation Committee, which became in due course the Labour Party, and the Fabian Society, which had immense influence among educated people. Significantly Ramsay MacDonald was active on both while Charles, who joined neither, far preferred the Labour Party. Indeed his distrust of the second deepened into dislike. In this same year Hyndman persuaded the Social Democratic League to conduct an inquiry into the condition of people in the working-class districts of London. Absolutely no evidence remains about the methods or the details of this inquiry and it may be that there was more inspired guesswork than factual reasoning in Hyndman's subsequent claim that over 25 per cent of London's workers were living in extreme poverty, but he was on the right road and unknowingly he sent Charles and Mary Booth on a 17-year-long trek.

Wedding-days and birthdays are definite in time and so is the initial meeting between two strangers; but the look across the room, the curiosity, hesitation and conviction of a courtship can never be measured. In searching for the influences that shaped Charles Booth's elusive soul I find it strange that in all his voluminous correspondence there is scarcely a reference to the two most important crises in his life, his breakdown and his breakthrough. I feel certain that they were closely linked. He possessed that inspired self-compass which according to the result can be called genius or selfishness. Incapable of doing anything against the grain he could work, when his demon drove him on, with 'an intensity all his own'. His breakdown was connected with both these forces, and his recovery came with the solution of the first and the command of the second. At this moment he might have moved in any direction. He cared for his fellow men; he could make money; he loved pictures and books; he believed in higher administration; he knew how to pick and lead a 'kindergarten'; in due course his inquiry team permeated social work just as Milner's[1] spread through political circles. Had he returned to his early love, education for all, his imagination would have opened entirely new vistas in that thicket, and could have altered the whole pattern of working-class life. But poverty was always the 'Problem of Problems' to Charles and to this immense canvas he directed the intensity of his gaze.

Far from approving of Hyndman's efforts, Charles held that his figures were 'exaggerated' if not 'totally mistaken' and that the sensational way they had been publicised was 'incendiary'. In order to refute these findings, he began to consider in depth how to conduct such an inquiry himself and wondered if it was possible to apply his own analytical business methods to the steady streams, the emotional tides and the disastrous under-tow of poverty in working-class life.

In 1884 the Lord Mayor of London[2] responded to public opinion by opening the customary Relief Fund, and then took an unusual step. Wishing to use the Fund in the best possible way he consulted the Statistical Society about how to find out which methods of assistance had proved most beneficial in the past. A new inquiry based on the 1881[3] census tables was hastily organised and rooms were set aside for the purpose in the Mansion House.

Charles offered his services at once and seconded one of his young clerks, Jesse Argyle, to work at the Mansion House, thereby discovering a cheerful, useful assistant; the relationship between the two men

[1] Viscount Milner, High Commissioner of South Africa 1897-1905.
[2] Sir R. N. Fowler, banker, MP 1868-74.
[3] Charles Booth became a member of the official committee in charge of the 1891 census.

71

grew and prospered with every year. He also discovered how misleading one-dimensional statistics can be. It was this facet of the work that was foremost in his mind when he joined his family in the country for the week-end of 15 August 1885. There he found Beatrice Potter as eager in her emotional distress as he was in the plenitude of commercial success for a new dimension of thought and action.

In her diary we catch a glimpse of Charles, that very thin, elegant, fair-skinned, questioning man, walking with the dark, vehement, untidy, passionate Beatrice under pines and Spanish chestnuts, discussing the possibilities of social diagnosis, and the Mansion House Inquiry. He told her that there were plenty of workers engaged in examining facts and figures collected by others, but that personal investigation was absolutely essential to avoid ridiculous conclusions. Charles's original intentions were entirely scientific and hers more community-conscious, but neither of them ever abandoned the principle of personal involvement. His growing vision of what needed to be done and how to do it, spurred on Beatrice's imagination at a moment when sorrow had reduced her momentum, and he found encouragement in her belief that 'the most hopeful form of social service was the craft of social investigator'. Forty years later she commented, 'It is hard to understand the naïve belief of the more original and vigorous minds of the seventies and eighties that it was by science and by science alone that all human misery would be ultimately swept away.' Meanwhile human misery was not yet absent from her own heart.

Joseph Chamberlain, unable to see that Beatrice was too hurt by the recent emotional situation to return to merely friendly terms, had attempted early in 1886 to reopen their co-operation on social questions. He had shocked her by suggesting that something *must* be done to make work for the unemployed, and concluding that 'the rich must pay to keep the poor alive'. He asked for her reactions, obviously hoping for support. In a curious reply she expresses doubts about his reason for consulting her. Was he merely looking 'for further proof of the incapacity of a woman's intellect to deal with such large matters'? She brings in a flattering reference to 'Her Majesty's ablest Minister' only to dig her pen into him the more sharply. She was obviously referring in her letter to past conversations, while he was taking a cool and dispassionate look at the future.

After this sharp exchange Beatrice turned as usual to Mary, and received an intimate and sympathetic reply:

Dearest Bee,

I wish I was a man and could relieve my feelings with respect to the conduct of the CHM a little more emphatically than decorum would allow me to do. We are both of us utterly revolted; asking, inviting your opinion, and then going into a childish pet because it is not what he expected or wanted. One thing, however, in the midst of this painful affair comes into my mind as good. You see him as he is; and, depend upon it, a man so dependent on flattery; so impatient of contradiction; so sensitive in regard to his own feeling; and so indifferent to those of others; must be at bottom a very poor and shallow creature. You are well rid of him!

Well or ill, she was rid of him, but the vacuum was only half-filled by work and friendship, and had Mary dreamt that Joseph Chamberlain's place would one day be taken by such an unlikely candidate as Sidney Webb, she might not have been so sweeping in her condemnation of the President of the Board of Trade. A few days later she told Charles that 'Chamberlain's speech shows more of the rowdy agitator that he really is', and wondered how 'poor Beatrice will like it'. Then she gave Beatrice news of Charles, who

this morning received the reports of the referees who have had in hand his paper on the 'Occupations of the People'. One man likes the paper; the other doesn't like it at all; and is very cutting in his criticism, especially of the hypothetical apportionment of 'dependents' to the different occupations. . . . I think Charlie is satisfied on the whole; he had expected objections; and knew that his criticism on the way in which the Census Department does its work must create a certain amount of soreness. He feels confident that the paper has value in it; and it is plain that the Statisticians think the same, though there may be some opposition to a youthful pretender who presumes to find fault with the experts. . . . I love you and want you always,

Your, M.C.B.

In February 1886, this hardly youthful pretender actually called on Hyndman to tell him sternly that his sensational and exaggerated claim that 25 per cent of Londoners lived on the verge of starvation had probably instigated the recent riots and could only lead to further misery. In his memoirs Hyndman recalls that he assured Charles that his statistics were accurate and that 'the more thorough any subsequent investigation might be, the more completely would his statements be verified'. At this Charles told Hyndman that he himself at his own expense intended to make an elaborate Inquiry into the condition of the workers of London, being quite certain that he could disprove Hyndman's estimate. Hyndman welcomed this public-spirited attempt to establish the truth 'in such a manner as to carry conviction to all'.

On 17 April 1886, Beatrice, having recently published her first social essay, 'A lady's view of the unemployed of the East End', which also protested against Hyndman's estimate, noted in her diary:

> Charles Booth's first meeting of the 'Board of Statistical Research' at his City Office—(it was actually the second meeting as nobody had attended the first).
>
> Present: Charles Booth, Maurice Paul.
> Benjamin Jones, Secretary to the Working Men's Co-operative Society.
> Radley, Secretary to a Trade Society, and myself.
>
> Object of the Committee: to get a fair picture of the whole of London Society, the four millions! by district and by employment; the first method to be based on Census Returns. We passed Charles Booth's elaborate and detailed plan of the work and a short abstract of it for general purposes. At present Charles Booth is the sole worker in this gigantic undertaking.

The Board of Statistical Research never materialized. Had any leaders in the social field decided to interest themselves at this point in the Inquiry the results would have been different both politically and individually. As it was, having tried and failed to obtain specialist help, Charles settled down contentedly to work on his own and thus established complete personal control of this 'gigantic undertaking'. Beatrice's constant encouragement made her his aide long before she undertook a specific task in the Inquiry. On the day following this abortive meeting she lunched with Canon Barnett, who threw cold water on the scheme which she outlined, and said it could only be accomplished by a Department of State. She must also have consulted Mr Chamberlain, in spite of the disagreements described in earlier letters, for it was he who suggested using information obtained from School Board Visitors as a means of checking the census figures. This constructive advice proved of immense value.

In the spring of 1886, when Mary was expecting her seventh child, the question of a future holiday home became urgent, and Charles decided to find one. Gracedieu Manor, built in 1820 beside the ruins of an ancient priory, on the westernmost spur of Charnwood Forest, was recommended to him. Arriving in a fly from the station with Dodo and Tom, Charles scarcely bothered to inspect the long, grey house built of forest stone, with its stylish Pugin wing, but set off with the children as soon as possible across the lawn to walk in the woods which almost encircled the Manor. He fell in love at once with the lie of the land through which Gracedieu brook flows; with the stunted fairytale oaks, and silver birch growing above the waterfall on jutting outcrops of rock, and all the bracken and bramble, which give such an untamed northern air to this Midlands forest country. Without more ado, Charles made up his mind, took the children back to the Manor, got into the fly, and wired to his wife from the station that the right place had been found.

He returned to London to present his first paper, 'The Occupations of the People of London, 1841-1881', to the Royal Statistical Society. This was the forerunner of many and stated the whole ethos of his future work:

It is the sense of helplessness that tries everyone; . . . the wage earners . . . are helpless to regulate or obtain the value of their work; the manufacturer or dealer can only work within the limits of competition; . . . the rich are helpless to relieve want without stimulating its source; the legislature is helpless because the limits of successful interference . . . are closely circumscribed. To relieve this sense of helplessness the problems of life must be better stated. . . . We need to begin with a true picture of the modern industrial organism, the interchange of service, the exercise of faculty, the demands and satisfaction of desire.

He went on to cast doubt on the value of census tables as used in the Mansion House Inquiry, the method being one recommended by many of his listeners, and suggested that statistical information should be checked against personal and other reports to achieve balance. Rather naturally, the Society's reactions were mixed.

When Mary reached Gracedieu with five children, a governess, a nursery maid, and a large staff, she found the house so poorly furnished that there was very little to sit on, and so badly roofed that buckets stood in the passages and bedrooms. It was a wet spring, and the fires smoked. As usual Mr Macaulay stated the problems of her life very clearly. He did not like to think of his own dearest

struggling in a sea of trouble, worried out of your life by bricklayers, plumbers, carpenters, charwomen, etc. Then when I know what a botheration is caused by what can be seen—dirt, dilapidated roof, twenty-nine bedrooms to keep free from bugs and spiders, I tremble to think what must be unseen. . . . I wonder whether any Sanitary Inspector would give your house a clean bill of health. . . . I try to assure myself that neither you nor Charlie could be happy unless once a month at least you plunged into a bath of water at 212 degree Fahrenheit. It is with you—and ever must be—an everlasting passage from the frying pan to the fire and from the fire back again to the frying pan. My other source of comfort is that before long you must—whether you like it or not—be confined for several days to your bed. Then at all events you must have a little rest. . . . My pencil letter is symptomatic—I am forbidden to stoop over my writing table and, in fact, it is very little writing that I can do with a pencil. You must not, however, be uneasy on my account. I am weak but I have no pain. Charles' paper is excellent. Thank him for his letter to me. God bless you all; I love the whole 'biling' of you. Old Woman sends her love.

This is a brave letter, and so are the two that followed it. Early in June, Mary commented on it to Beatrice after reporting on Charles's statistical research.

He says that the thing is alive and that he thinks the men he has got hold of by no means lose their interest in the idea; so I hope when your free time comes, you will find not probably a perfected instrument, but a usable one. By the way, he proposes himself to dine with you on Wednesday if you can have him; he has a great deal to talk to you about. I think you a little under-rate what you do at present towards helping him and the others; and I doubt much whether even during this time when your main work will have to be private study of your own, you will ever be as much shut out of the laboratory and even the wards as you think you will be.

I have a letter today from Papa. He writes in pencil and speaks of himself as suffering no pain but very weak. I don't like it and wish I could be over the birth of this baby . . . and able to be with him whenever he wants me. I can only trust no great further change will take place 'til I shall be free again. . . . I don't think I can be the only person who thinks tenderly of you, but of the people who do I certainly am. I love you and want you more and more and cling to your love.

Your, M.C.B.

On the 18 June Charles went off to New York again and Mary wrote to him: 'God bless you and bring you back safely to us! . . . the first few days are likely to be a little long no doubt . . . they always are, but . . . when we have once got our telegrams to say that you are at New York, we will begin to expect you home again. . . . As for me and the tiny one of all, we are very well to do. I wonder whether this little one will be your special pet and friend, as I have ever been my father's. . . .'

On the 22nd, Mr Macaulay wrote again in pencil:

My Darling Child,

I can't bear to think of your worries—Charlie unexpectedly torn from you and you alone in that huge Gracedieu with no-one to share the responsibilities of indoor and outdoor superintendence, to say nothing of the anxieties naturally attaching to next August. . . . Would to God that I could be of any use to my darling just now! But I am worse than useless, unable even to go upstairs but in an invalid chair, borne up sedan fashion by a couple of bearers.

Then Mr Macaulay described the death of his brother-in-law, Charles Trevelyan, and added, 'Well, after all, who can show a better record than this?—a long life of honest work, manfully done.' Mr Macaulay's only complaint was not being able to help his darling—'Oh, if I were only a few years younger, but the night cometh when no man can work.'

At the end of the month Mary begged Beatrice in a letter to expand the series of articles she was planning into something more like a book, so as to be able to express her arguments more freely. She added:

This neighbourhood would not be a bad centre in some ways for the 'personal observation' part of your scheme. We have a fearfully poverty-stricken population; left behind in the race, their special industries being partly superseded, partly better done elsewhere—a violent Irish element, disorderly.

77

The clergy seem hardly wanted . . . in consequence the churches are empty and the people mannerless to an extent that surprises one, seeing this place is such a short distance from Haselour, where our country neighbours were courtesy itself.

To Charles, Mary wrote:

The last few days have been glorious, the whole place bathed in sunshine and glorified . . . I hear from Beatrice that poor Rosie [Beatrice's sister, who had had a nervous breakdown] has come home worse than ever. Poor Uncle Richard is too far gone himself to notice the change in her, which is perhaps a happy thing so far as he is concerned but makes it all the harder for Bee who has the responsibility of both of them on her shoulders;—to say nothing of the depression of spirits that must result from the constant companionship of two people who are non compos mentis. She is now alone with them both at the Argoed where she relieves herself as well as she can by reading and planning her article on the plan to be adopted in order to make a true social diagnosis. . . . We shall soon be in the heat of the conflict [the General Election] now. I am not sanguine. Gladstone is throwing off rapidly the last restraints of tone and manner which bound him to the tradition and the company of Statesmen and men of breeding. He is hitting out right and left like the great gladiator he is at bottom, unscrupulous, rough and insolent. It is as if he knows now that he can't please God and Mammon and is resolved to cast himself entirely on the lower classes, and even the rowdier portion of them for sympathy and support. He flatters them up to the eyes and they seem to like it.

In July Charles's letters are full of what he is doing in Gloversville and New York, but he was for the first time worried about leaving his wife at such a juncture. She reassured him, 'Take the proper time to do your work thoroughly, and be at ease about me and all here . . .'. Had he known of what was happening at Gracedieu that day he might have felt less easy.

The Booths had already announced their wish to open Gracedieu wood to all comers at week-ends, and this innovation led to violent quarrels between the gamekeeper, whose job had always been to keep villagers out, and those who hoped to enter now with the owner's goodwill. Mary, eight months pregnant, walked all over the wood, quelled the rougher elements among the newcomers, and pacified Pratt, the gamekeeper. 'It is a new source of enlivenment to one's life here at any rate, and seems likely to bring me into personal relations with the poor in a way that ought to satisfy me,' she wrote. 'It certainly has amused me, and led to many philosophical reflections on the difficulties lying in the way of benevolent proprietors in the country. It is a funny world, and one in which one certainly can't do any good without having a head upon one's shoulders, as well as a heart in the right place. I hope I shan't have things in an utter mess for you to deal with when you come home to rest after Gloversville anxieties.' This was certainly not the first or the last time for Mary to have difficulty in putting Charles's ideas into practice. Action, however, never disturbed her. It was historical or emotional events which destroyed her peace of mind, and having survived the day essentially unscathed, she returned to fall a victim to Frere's *Henry III*. On the following morning she added:

I don't feel up to much this morning, having slept badly—that strange Roman Catholic Church with its grovelling, soul-destroying superstition having taken possession of my mind. I ended up my evening, after writing to you last night, with the account of the St. Bartholomew affair and the behaviour of those Valois brothers and their precious mother. . . . It did me good in the midst of this ghastly story of deceit and cruelty I was reading last night, to come upon the account of how our own Elizabeth refused for weeks even to see the French Ambassador sent over to gloss the horror down to her with excuses and explanations, and how, when at last compelled to see him on needful business, she dressed in deep mourning and stood in grim, starched silence to receive his outpourings of apology and disavowal, like the Royal thing she was with all her faults, bless her!

Charles often used odd scraps of paper to remind himself of necessary or amusing details. For instance a scribble about 'Shirts tailors thimbles' is followed by

The blood of Jesus Christ
His (God's) son
will wash away all sin
(Omnibus outside St. Francis Mission)

on the back of the letter in which Mary described election fever: 'Mr.

Goschen[1] in Edinburgh was only with difficulty able to get on with his speech. Lord Hartington had a stormy time, Mr. Bright spoke with no uncertain note in condemnation of the Gladstone—"G. fait aller son monde". It seems an instinct with him and his belief in himself and his own cause. Divine Right has curious charm—as it had in Charles Stewart's day for his followers.'

On the 7th Mary reported that 'Goschen has been beaten at Edinburgh—it is serious. Edinburgh is an odd place; turned out Uncle Tom,[2] then repented and brought him in by a great majority without even having asked him to stand and then sending to beg him to accept the Seat. Gladstone floods the country with letters, postcards and telegrams to encourage his own people. I really believe that he will never get old or die. He is more active and more malignant every month, a thriving spirit of evil.'

When the results of Gladstone's snap election came out it was discovered that the Liberals had won a victory over the Tories, but that Gladstone's Liberal opponents, now calling themselves Unionists, had defeated his Home Rule policy. Rather than give way over Home Rule, Gladstone tendered his resignation to the Queen. Lord Salisbury took office and Chamberlain made temporary arrangements to support him in the House, fully expecting Gladstone to retire from the leadership of the Liberal Party very shortly. In fact it was nine more years before the G.O.M. kissed the Queen's hand in farewell. By this time Chamberlain had joined the Tories, impelled thereto by his imperialist convictions.

In the same letter Mary gave Charles news of 'Papa's increasing weakness, but entire content; there is no pain. I wonder if I shall ever see him again. This summer is a strange one for me and often I feel as if I were in a dream and fear lest the waking should be painful. I do not feel anxious or fretted.' It is extraordinary that Mary did not get into a train and reach Southsea while she could, to make certain of seeing her father before he died. Remembering his point of view about the pain as well as the happiness of such a meeting and unwilling to break the calm

---

[1] G. J. later Viscount, Goschen became Chancellor of the Exchequer in 1887 and continued in political life until 1900. In 1903 he espoused the cause of free trade.

[2] T. B. Macaulay wrote to his brother on 17 January 1852, when urged to stand elsewhere, 'Should I leave my oil? Should I leave my wine? You remember the beautiful fable in the Book of Judges? . . .'

spell of the last month of pregnancy, she decided against the attempt. Beyond all this there is no doubt that Mary's family life and her new home filled her thoughts and fulfilled her hopes. Her father, who had fought for just this for his Polly, could now let his life ebb out quietly and thankfully.

On 28 July the last pencilled note arrived for his 'Dearest' from her father.

Your picture of the simple pleasures of the country—the milkings— the in-gatherings of currants, cherries, etc., is charming. After the experience of your Boy at Bex [where Charles had undertaken a fruit cure] he ought to be great amongst the cherries. An old friend of ours, whom you may perhaps have occasionally met at our house here, Colonel Lys, is just dead. He, his wife and daughters have been very much at home with us, running in at odd times for a game of billiards; always pleasant and always welcome. We feel very much for the poor bereaved ones. I fear that they are terribly hard up. I wish that I could be of some use to them. I must stop. God bless you dearest! You really do seem to be at peace at last. I love ou and ou Boy and all the jolly lot of you! So does the Old Woman. I put my arms right round you and give you a long, long, long clinging kiss.

Ou Old Paw.

You must read between the lines of my letter now for it seems to me that I have lost the power of writing a coherent sentence, or of telling the whole of anything I may have to tell.

Old Paw's message, whatever he may have felt about its inadequacy, comes over very clearly indeed nearly a century later. His generosity and sympathy were never more to the fore than in those last few weeks when at every turn he was hampered by acute physical weakness. There is something very sweet in the reference he made, almost at death's door, to his son-in-law, picking and eating cherres in Bex all those years before. A dawning beam of happiness reached him before his own flickering light sank under the horizon.

Mary's last child was born on 2 August. Charles took George, Meg and Imogen into the big bow-fronted spare bedroom where mother and baby lay in a canopied bed. He was in tremendous spirits, the reaction from anxiety, and he caught up Imogen and tossed her into the air so that her head was within an inch of a sharp, wooden, pointed ornament on the canopy. Mary cried out in horror, and the culprit fetched a saw and sawed it off immediately. Combining Charles Booth with family life was never easy! In the matter of religious practice Mary had always struck a balance between her husband's and her father's wishes by christening her children herself; and so with special love she named her youngest son Charles Zachary Macaulay.

Five days later the gentle-hearted old man died peacefully and painlessly. Now, as he had smilingly reminded her, the moment had come, whether she liked it or no, when she was inevitably confined to her room. Lying alone, watching the August sun striking through the bay window, she must have thought of the past with a desolate pang, and then, being Mary, turned confidently to the future. Daughterhood was at an end, with all the love, the pleasure and the duty that it entailed. As her father had been unable to visit her, and her visits to him had become increasingly irksome due to family jealousies, undoubtedly what she missed most were the light-hearted and sympathetic letters, which had followed her all the days of her married life; no one was ever a readier or more faithful scribe than Old Paw. She had no longer any need to worry about him, but she missed him direly, talked of him constantly, and loved his memory until her own death more than fifty years later.

In a long, intimate, undated reply[1] to Beatrice's letter of sympathy she agrees that although she could not 'now state in comprehensible language a single Article of religious belief, yet the need for prayer grows all the time. With Papa the body gave way when the mind was as clear and vigorous as ever. With dear Uncle Richard you are face to face with a problem [of the failing mind] before which one can only stand in awestruck depression. . . . All I can say is that one's whole soul rejects and spurns the unutterable dreariness of the conclusion that this life ends all.'

Certainly, the end of her father's life altered her own a good deal more than she realised. His literary taste, his unselfishness, his interest in the characters of the children and his devotion to Charles, gave the whole family a balance and dimension, the loss of which is noticeable in the scurrying years that followed. In addition, she was on her own now in her search for faith—a search shared by her father, but not by her husband. She suffered much over alteration and alienation of religious thought. 'You help me to be good,' she wrote to Charles, 'and of all the

[1] See Appendix D, p. 221.

innumerable reasons that I have for being grateful to you, that must stand first. You will remember it used not to be so; I used to think you made me feel wrongly.' It was not exactly that he made her feel wrongly, but that she could not find in his intellectual humanistics the inspiration she needed. When she spoke of religion in later life it was almost always with great reserve. She preferred to review different faiths in an analytical way, rather than state her own opinion, but she always clung to Church observances. Once, when we were laughing about a clergyman who had made matters worse in a sick-room, I said: 'If I were dying I would only want my family near me—never Mr Shrewsbury.' My grandmother became very grave: 'No,' she said, 'No. There is something else. I should need the Church's blessing, whoever gave it.' She had a compelling historical imagination and experienced the significance of the laying on of hands. Then with her dislike of conversation taking too serious a turn, she put her hands down in front of her and added with a comical expression, 'I am so *curious* about death.'

Charles's attitude was entirely different. He expected beneficent action from religion, but did not yearn himself for spiritual solace, inspiration and peace, as Mary did. While she read the collects, his favourite hymn was 'New every morning is the love'[1] and for him 'the trivial round, the common task' did indeed furnish all he asked of life. Humanity itself was his inspiration. In his concluding essay on *Religious Influences*, written fifteen years later, he sums up his thoughts thus:

What religion has to offer . . . is a revolution of the soul . . . which instead of ending life's activities, renders them, with the heightening of conscience, even more acute. . . . There arises contest within contest, with ourselves and our own passions, with others and with their passions. . . . Like wrestlers we strive wrist to wrist before the decisive throw, and no throw is final. Fresh adversaries spring up. . . . Our emotions and passions prove the dragon's teeth in the fable. The very idea of repose is banished to another life. In this one we do not desire it.

This August of 1886 was a watershed for both the Booths. He was getting on for fifty, and she was nearly forty. They had had seven children, and they decided that the seventh should be the last. The

---

[1] By John Keble.

Inquiry, in effect, became their eighth child. This crucial decision cost them dear. Repose was banished. Passions were wrestled with. All Charles's emotions were centred now upon his dual work, while Mary turned more and more to Dodo for daily companionship, and to the baby for the tenderness her temperament demanded. The lack of physical emotional solace no doubt contributed to her increasing migraine, but her role as A.D.C. to her husband at last gave her talents their long sought outlet. The greatest of all the Booth ships, the Inquiry, was launched.

VI
ENTENTE CORDIALE
1886–1889

For the next seventeen years Charles and Mary devoted every spare moment to the Inquiry and its results. Both of them were over taxed, often ill, but completely absorbed. She moved the children, the nurses, and the staff to and fro, holiday by holiday, and went on working at her desk in London or at Gracedieu. He flitted in and out like a blackbird in a garden, a day or two here, a night there, a month in the United States, as he worked in train or ship. He lived his whole life between one set of problems and another, and enjoyed the process of solving them as others enjoy a game of bridge. Talking or writing to each other, and taking brisk walks with a favourite dog in Gracedieu woods, were the Booths' chief relaxations. When life got on top of them, he made an occasional solitary dash across the Continent while she dug in at home. Charles enjoyed the feel of the Gracedieu ship in full sail and the presence of the children on board, but there was neither time nor wish for intimacy. The children admired him immensely and longed to know him better and find out what he was thinking about, but even when they grew up he never discussed the Inquiry with them. This was Mary's territory and hers alone. There is something curious about this, something as clear, chilling and hard as a glass wall. Beatrice was to come up against it in the years ahead when neither Charles nor Mary could respond to her changing views. At this time, however, letters and ideas flowed between all three of them and she was as much part of their home scene as of those other compelling vistas of pain and poverty.

On 27 July Charles wrote to Beatrice 'I have read with great interest your letters to Mary. I could not do a long course of reading . . . to save my life. Did you get enough done . . . to prove your point that we are not governed by general principles ? It seems evident to my hasty mind.' There followed a phrase about 'voluntary action being even more impulsive than political action', which certainly applied to his own recent efforts, and he added his belief that the statistical method was needed

> to give bearings to the results of personal observation or personal observation to give life to statistics: the figures or the facts may be correct enough in themselves—but they mislead from want of due proportion or from lack of colour . . . it is very difficult, as you say, to state this—to make it neat enough and complete enough. I don't think reading will help us—but talking may, and trying to do it over and over again is the best plan. The theory and practice must also go hand in hand, and there is no key better than a little ignorant self-confidence—humble quality compared to proud reserve and much more useful.

In September 1886 in answer to one of Beatrice's letters, he outlined his three-year project, which was now based on the suggestion which Chamberlain made to Beatrice about using School Board Visitors as the main source of information.

> Many thanks for your letter which is pregnant with ideas. I think we . . . need . . . to talk things level and I hope we may meet before I go to New York next month. Our meeting last night consisted, as I had expected, of Paul[1] and myself. . . . We have slightly enlarged and improved the tabulation of employments and brought it into such shape that each heading can easily be made the subject of a special series of trade enquiries. The two plans will thus absolutely converge, and will fit in as well as can be contrived with the census returns. The scheme thus becomes complete, and every bit done will be so much towards the whole statement of London. I don't think the whole work is beyond our reach and I think it *might* be completed in three years. The district figures will be classified according to occupations, and the trade figures, starting naturally with occupations, will be classified according to earnings, also. We shall start in earnest next week.

Mary also wrote, advising Beatrice to allow herself time for further consideration before sending her manuscript, 'The rise and growth of English Economics', to the printers:

> It is not yet as good as you can make it, but the last burst of feeling brought tears to my eyes. Is it intentional that you omit all mention of J. S. Mill? I have never been disposed to rate him high; he floundered

[1] Maurice Paul, son of Kegan Paul the publisher.

in a logical quagmire and was often inconsistent with himself. Still, to omit all mention might be thought to savour of affectation. You see I have written just what I think, sans phrases, which you don't want and which would be quite unworthy of the trust you repose in us in letting us see your manuscript. Charlie took it with him to Liverpool.

Mary reported to him there: 'The more I think of that paper the more I like it, and feel that it has an inspiring ring and force of its own; which I hope it will not lose in the revision which I recommend. Beatrice has the power which is to my mind one of the most characteristic notes of great ability, the power of investing what she takes up with charm. She has a genuine enthusiasm and can impart it.' Treasured among Beatrice's papers at the London School of Economics is a detailed, line-by-line criticism in Charles's writing, ending up with a note in Mary's writing—'M.C.B. withdraws her strictures on your remarks about Pitt!'

A few days later Mary told Charles about her visit to Rothley Temple, which her cousins the Parkers had inherited.

They were very kind, friendly, and cousinlike and the house delightful. Going there, however, upset me more than I expected. . . . It is strange to think of the bright life there that I have heard of all my life, drinking it in, and always asking for more and more stories of the sayings and doings of that large party of clever, eager cousins with their arguments and their interests and their dear warm friendship, all gone. I lay in bed in one of the oak-panelled rooms, wondering and thinking and wishing to grasp more than I can the meaning of this fleeting existence of ours.

Her father had been one of these clever, eager cousins with their arguments and warm friendships. It was his voice that she heard and missed as she lay wakeful in bed. Equally it was the clannish instinct in her Macaulay heart that made her feel welcome in the new Leicestershire environment.

Early in October 1886 Beatrice went to London for a two-day visit to the Booths, 'to talk things level'. She notes in her diary: 'Charlie absorbed in his Inquiry, working all evenings with three paid secretaries. I have promised to undertake the Docks[1] in my March holiday. Dear, sweet little Mary, with her loving ways and charming mother-

---

[1] 'Dock Life in the East End of London'.

hood! They become each year more near to me. Perhaps they are the only persons who really love me.'

But were they as close to her as she thought? She had made friends with Charles at a time when he was uncertain of his health and his future. Changing fast, he had grown larger in mind, more confident in character. Nor was she conscious of Mary's development. An unmistakable touch of condescension lies in the phrase 'Dear, sweet little Mary'. No doubt this was the sort of person Beatrice would have liked Mary to be, while she—Beatrice—monopolised and guided Charles's intellectual life. If a hair crack had already appeared in the fabric of this friendship, it arose from a weakness in the foundations—not in the superstructure. None of the three people concerned noticed it; they were all three immensely busy; two of them intensely happy; the third instinctively searching for a partnership of her own.

After this visit, on 18 October, Charles sent a succinct account of how he proposed to set about his Inquiry to a new acquaintance, Professor Alfred Marshall, the celebrated Cambridge economist, and asked for advice:

I am now engaged (with some others) on an attempt to describe analytically the industrial and social status of the population of London, that is, to state the proportions in which different classes exist, with the actual present conditions of each. It is a very difficult undertaking, and any results obtained will be much open to criticism of all kinds.

What I wish to ask for from you is criticism, in advance, on the method adopted. It is proposed to place together information from as many different sources as possible, so as to make the evidence check and complete itself, so far as possible. The frame-work will be found in the facts obtainable from the School Board Visitors, who among them provide something very like a house-to-house visitation of the condition of life, of every family where there are school children, in the lower middle class, and all below it.

As a trial I have completed a preliminary analysis, from School Board information, of a sub-registration district in the East End of London, with 20,000 inhabitants, and it is this analysis which I desire to submit to you before going further with the work, as much depends on the soundness of the system adopted.

Professor Marshall's reply must have been encouraging, as it led to a lifetime's appreciative co-operation.

In order to carry out this programme, Charles had to reorganise his working life, and therefore outlined another plan to his brother, writing from Gracedieu:

My idea is to transfer the whole of the ordinary London work to Christopher Garland, so as to make my presence when in London that of a visitor at the office. The business statistics and private business correspondence, which have always been a large part of my personal work, and which tend to increase, I shall work from home [i.e. wherever he happened to be sleeping] . . . and shall employ your Pearson as clerk for it, being myself at London or Gracedieu about three days, and at Liverpool about four days, every week. So far as I can see, this will work when it gets into shape—at any rate, I am ready to try it for eighteen months.

Charles's plan of action would have been arduous in any circumstances, but he added the extra ingredient of continual visits to the United States where, in fact, the different work, the different climate, and the delight he took in practical commerce, gave him the extra energy which was so badly needed at home.

During November 1886 Mary wrote to him in New York about Beatrice's visit as 'Miss Jones' to a working-class family in Lancashire: 'On Saturday I dined with Beatrice, and on Sunday Beatrice dined with me. Both evenings were very interesting. She is struck with the happiness and liveliness of factory life, and the pleasant intercourse with the sexes which results from their working together. She told her hosts before leaving them who she really was and, far from being annoyed, they were much pleased . . .' Mary does not mention what Beatrice must have told her, that these people were distant cousins, who bore no grudge at all that their branch of the family did not share the Heyworth prosperity. Instead Mary describes *The Princess Casamassima* as 'a wonderful book which has many touches, characteristic of our strange life, as when the hero on Sunday afternoon goes to tea with the beautiful Princess, and finds her sitting before the fire with a heavy work on Capital and Labour lying on her knees'. However, when Mary met the author, Henry James, at dinner one night she found him 'heavy and provincial'. Had he spoken with a French instead of an American accent she might have taken a more lenient view! A few days later however she advised Charles to read Walt Whitman's poems, 'for you would like the strong sense of the human bond of . . . sympathy; and I think his philosophical view would appeal to yours. By the way, the last "Edinburgh Review" in an article on politics has a very clever sentence of Lord Palmerston's, "If we give way to what is wrong for the sake of having an easy life, we shall end by having a life without a moment's peace."'

There was certainly no peace in London in the autumn and winter of 1886–7. Sir Charles Warren, the Permanent Under-Secretary at the Home Office, prohibited a procession of those in need of relief which had been arranged by the Socialists, with the result that a monster meeting was held in Trafalgar Square instead. Bernard Shaw in his play *Major Barbara* makes game of the fact that after this meeting a disorderly mob smashed windows in Pall Mall, the heart of London's clubland, with the surprising result that the Relief Fund was doubled in a week! Cardinal Manning, whom Mary cordially detested as an arch humbug, and the Bishop of London wrote to *The Times* with suggestions for alleviating the distress that was sure to prevail in the coming winter. Canon Barnett responded by exposing the mischief done by the methods employed in dispensing the Mansion House Fund in 1885, saying that inquiries as to whether families were deserving or not robbed it of all grace. He considered that five shillings all round should have been given to those whose living conditions fell below a certain standard. In the event it was Canon Barnett's intervention, based on his knowledge of day-to-day life in Whitechapel, which successfully altered the procedures by which the Mansion House Fund was distributed. Mary admired him wholeheartedly.

In 1887 she began to keep a factual diary, and kept up this habit for the rest of her life. *De La Rue's Improved Diary*, about the size of a Penguin book, with blue linen covers, contains useful dates, university terms, Quarter Sessions and a Hebrew as well as a Mohammedan calendar. After estimated populations, celestial phenomena (which certainly would have pleased Mary) and thirty pages of other information, come the birthdays of the Royal Family and the Sovereigns of Europe.[1] A dozen blank pages are sub-titled in Mary's writing, 'To call on', 'To write to', 'To bear in mind', 'To ask to dinner'; and sixty or so names have been written down, and all but half a dozen crossed through, indicating no doubt that calls had been paid, matters borne in mind, invitations sent. Then follow four pages filled with the names of books: Creighton's *History of the Papacy*, and *Memoirs of the Duc de Broglie*

[1] These would not occupy much space now!

beginning the list; *Industrial Peace* by Price, and *The Privy Council* by Dicey continuing it; Mary's taste being for the former and the necessities of Charles's Inquiry leading to the latter titles. Further down the list a different note is struck: *Little Peter* by Lucas Malet, Tolstoy's *Confession* and Dostoevski's *Crime and Punishment*; and for the children, *Dandelion Clocks and Other Tales* by Mrs Ewing.

Mary's diary for 1887 often notes, 'C.B. late with S.C. [School Board Visitor]', or 'C.B. Liverpool' or 'C.B. U.S.'. Beatrice's name occurs sometimes twice or thrice a week, in connection with a lecture or a concert, and her own diary adds to the picture. In February 1887, for instance, she dined with Charles and took the tram down the Commercial Road to visit the Secretary of the Stevedores Association. If not a celestial omnibus at least an idealistic tram-load.

In May Charles put the results of this period of work before the Statistical Society in a paper entitled 'The Inhabitants of the Tower Hamlets'. The survey itself was such a remarkable contribution that the Statistical Society, many of whose members had laughed at his pretensions hitherto, now took Charles and his methods seriously, and elected him to their Council. The Press greeted his achievement with refreshing vigour and acclaim. The *Morning Post* commented, 'It is extraordinary that a private individual should not only have dared to take in hand, but should have been able to carry out an elaborate investigation as to the occupations, earnings and social conditions of half a million people . . . yet this is what Mr. Charles Booth has done.' Only one journal, the *Pall Mall*,[1] criticised his paper severely, on the extraordinary grounds that it read like 'a complacent and comforting bourgeois statement'.

In the spring Mary gathered some village friends together and inaugurated what were called 'Mothers' Meetings'. Every Monday at Gracedieu 'her women' came to sew and knit while she read aloud Dickens or Scott, and afterwards, over cups of tea, there was companionship. Meanwhile Charles laid out a cricket pitch in the field which lay at the foot of the sloping lawn below the Manor and instigated the formation of a cricket club in the village. Tom and George invited some school friends to play the Gracedieu Park Eleven during the summer holidays, and after the match all the players had supper in the servants' hall, which was enlivened by speeches and songs. This match became a yearly fixture, but a once-only treat took place on 25 June 1887 and was

1 W. T. Stead, Editor of the *Pall Mall Gazette*, had publicised H. M. Hyndman's Inquiry.

entered in Mary's diary: 'Fireworks for Jubilee. Gracedieu and Charles' photograph in paper'. Charles at this time was living in humble lodgings in Liverpool for three or four days a week. He used to say that the only possible disguise was to be himself, and he never made the smallest alteration in his clothes or his conversation. 'The object,' he wrote in *Life and Labour*, 'which I trust was a fair one, was never suspected, my position never questioned. The people with whom I lived became and are still my friends.'

Unfortunately, reports of the illuminated grounds, the games and sports, and the finale of fireworks which completed Queen Victoria's Jubilee Celebrations at Gracedieu, were not confined to the Leicestershire Press. In Liverpool a photograph of 'Mr. and Mrs. Booth welcoming their guests to Gracedieu Manor' was a front page feature. The Mathews family with whom Charles was lodging at this time were upset by the disclosure. It made them feel uncomfortable and, though he had never pretended in any way to be anything but what he was, one can understand their initial feelings. When Charles died, they gave his daughter Meg, as a memento, the wooden chair on which he used to sit of an evening in their Liverpool kitchen, long ago. The preference for living in such humble quarters at four or five shillings a week which no immediate survey made necessary is hard to understand, unless the simplicity as well as the curiosity of his mind is taken into account. The following year, when he had moved into other lodgings, Mary wrote: 'Certainly you don't need £5,000 a year to make you happy.'

Beatrice wrote in her diary that summer: 'The visit to the Booths has recovered my spirits. The beautiful old place, filled to over-flowing with happiness and youth, checked my egotistical suffering. The Booths' home life at Gracedieu is perfect. Mary says her life is one of continual sunshine. Charlie has the three sides of his existence complete—profession, home and intellectual interest. His business, he says, is the most important of the three, but I expect he underrates the constant happiness of satisfied affection. They, and their family are the bright spot in my life, a continual source of strength and everlasting upspringing interest.' In their company she found 'relief from an agony of strong but useless feeling'.

This 'perfect' home life was not achieved in 'continual sunshine', and every now and again Mary burst out with fury and frustration over the necessity of becoming a 'houschold machine . . . turning out orders for food and carriage and making calculations as to wages with weary monotony'. The day after, she always sent a penitent letter to her 'own most dear and tender of all boys', regretting having caused him pain 'yet feeling a certain lightness of heart at having got rid of it all', and 'feeling ready for life and work again'. Once, after a particularly gruelling period, she was able to reassure Charles that

as I walked up at 5 o'clock of this lovely afternoon from Newbold's cottage there stole over my being and into my heart the first impulse of love and home attachment, that I have ever felt in this place. . . . this is decidedly hopeful, especially as Gracedieu has been most Gracedieuish;—the passages in spite of fires feel like a cold bath, the sheets on one's bed almost defy fires and hot bottles altogether; water everywhere where it should not be and nowhere it ought to be, and a pervading atmosphere of upholsterers, strokes of the hammer and plumbers bearing ladders and making a mess already of our pretty new walls. However, the servants are very good-humoured and the baby is well. Wherefore, oh Boy, make glad thine heart against the time when I shall pour out to you another Jeremiad, and don't remind me of this when I do.

While Mary was telling Charles that 'Beatrice is low about her own work, its values, etc., East End facts, feelings; in fact about nearly everything. It is disappointing not to be able to help her', Beatrice was writing about Charles in her diary: 'We are more fond of each other than ever . . . a close personal relationship between a man and a woman without sentiment (perhaps not without sentiment, but without passion or the dawning of passion). We are fellow workers, both inspired by the same intellectual desire. Only in his life it is an extra; in my life if it becomes anything, it would become the dominating aim.' To Charles, Beatrice was the 'extra'. It is certain that he would have been startled by the phrases in her diary concerning a 'close personal tie'. Only Mary was essential to him and went 'right through the outercrust', as he once wrote to her, 'and touched his heart'.

On 15 October 1887, Mary told Charles that Beatrice's article 'Personal Observation and Statistical Inquiry' had been well reviewed in the *Daily Telegraph,* and that the allusions to 'Mr. Charles Booth's Inquiry' were 'quite imposing'. She goes on to say:

. . . I have been reading 'Candide' with the result that I have promptly returned it to The London.[1] It is witty certainly, but indecent to an
_____
[1] The London Library was founded in 1841.

extent that I should hardly have thought credible if I had not read it;—worse than Sterne if anything and at any rate more obtrusive. Really the French are an extraordinary people, and there will always be to me something not quite comprehensible in their natures. I think I can understand Sterne; a man who had said goodbye to respectability, had little moral sense and the craving for animal excitement, but Voltaire—with his great purposes, his penetrating sympathy, his passionate love of truth and scorn of cruelty and tyranny; one would have thought it hardly possible that he would care to write such a thing as 'Candide'. . . .

She also read *The Story of an African Farm, Rhoda Fleming, Henriette d'Angleterre, Sa Vie et Correspondance avec Son Frère Charles II* and *A Counsel of Perfection,* for herself; *Scientific Religion* by Laurence Oliphant and *A History of Agriculture and Prices in England* for Charles; and *Practical Socialism,* by the Barnetts, with him. The Barnetts were always common ground.

In 1888 Charles moved his Inquiry work away from Alfred Booth and Company's office into one of its own in Gracechurch Street. Two able young men, both graduates, had joined his staff, Hubert Llewellyn-Smith and Ernest Aves. They were living at Toynbee Hall at this time with a group of like-minded friends, some of whom joined the Booth team later on. They were all hard at work on Charles's coloured Poverty Map which graphically illustrated the living conditions of Londoners. Black represented the lowest grade of poverty and was linked with Class A; dark blue represented the very poor of Class B; light blue represented the moderate poverty of Classes C and D; purple represented mixed poverty and all classes from B to E and F; pink represented the working-class comfort of E, F and G classes; red represented the well-to-do with one or more servants; and yellow the wealthy with three or four servants, scarcely found at all in East or South London. With the exception of this mention of servants the Poverty Map of 1900 has a great deal of relevance today. The black patches persist in isolated locations between the gas-works and the railway lines where 'streets are narrow and communications poor. The dark blue and black classes disperse only upon the demolition of their buildings.' Charles's statistics for Poverty are separated from those for Crowding and show that crowding was nearly twice as bad as poverty in Belgravia, poverty more than twice as bad as crowding in Streatham, and Kensington was worse than either in both respects, 33 per cent of its population living in poverty and in crowded conditions. He mentions in his final volume that 'the extension of the county area or some arrangement which shall ensure uniformity of standard is one of the problems awaiting London or Greater London in the near future'. Was this the first time that phrase was used?

The map was hung up at Toynbee Hall and Oxford House, another new university settlement, so that mistakes could be corrected by those who knew the neighbourhoods. Very few corrections proved necessary. When it was displayed at the French Exhibition of 1900 two years later, Charles arranged for Argyle to go over and see the map 'which may perhaps never hang again being so monstrous big'.

He was not neglecting his business commitments, on which of course the whole project depended, but entries in Mary's diary such as 'C.B. went to live in East End', followed by 'C.B. came in the evening, Oh my!', prove that he was hardly ever at home, and absorbedly busy on the few occasions when he looked in. At this time extra haste, without improving his circulation, increased his natural clumsiness so that he was constantly bruising and cutting himself. He patched up his fingers with stamp-paper—the glue must have been stronger in those days—and Charlotte saw to it that a fresh pair of socks always lay by the fender in his study so that his clammy feet could be warmed the moment he came in. Sometimes discarded socks were the only signs of his visit but usually Charlotte managed to catch her master with hot milk and boiled eggs before he left. Some people have devoted service just as others have perfect pitch. Charles moved his lodgings in the East End constantly, for they were taken to give him the flavour of a street or a district; not for him the central stability of Toynbee Hall.

In the spring of 1888 Mary moved her caravan to Gracedieu and sent Charles 'Beatrice's interesting and rather pathetic letter. Poor dear old Beatrice! She is a fine creature and very true to her friends.' This comment shows a touch of weariness along with affection, but at this moment it must be noted that Beatrice and the Booths were completely at one over women's suffrage, which all three abominated. Beatrice even signed Mrs Humphry Ward's Anti-Suffrage Manifesto. Mary and Beatrice were unconsciously defending their own right to take part in vigorous intellectual effort in a male world while denying it to other less fortunate women. Beatrice regretted her attitude in later years but Mary always derided votes for women. She used to tell us how the women of France held more power rocking their cradles than mischievous intellectuals trying to influence their menfolk. I see now that this was one way of expressing distrust of Beatrice.

When her man spoke to the Statistical Society on 'The Condition and Occupations of the People of East London and Hackney, 1887', she took Dodo to hear him. In this paper he admitted that his findings surprised him, and more than justified Mr Hyndman's dictum that 25 per cent of the population were 'living in extreme poverty'. In some districts 32 per cent could be taken as being a conservative estimate of those in dire poverty. 'To the rich the very poor are a sentimental interest,' he stated, 'to the poor they are a crushing load.' At the outset Charles had attempted to define poverty which he divided into two main categories. The 'poor' were those with meagre but steady wages of between 18 and 21 shillings a week. The 'very poor' were those who fell below this standard. His statistics excluded moral causes and grouped 'loafers, casual work, low pay, small profits' under Employment; 'drink, thriftlessness' under Habit; and 'illness, infirmity and large families' under Circumstance. He discovered that nearly 50 per cent of the very poor and nearly 70 per cent of the poor were in need because of unemployment; so proving that one skilled worker was more vulnerable to the eddies of trade, than the labourer.

Abandoning his original determination to provide facts so that others might arrive at the right solution, Charles now pleaded for drastic remedies: regular employment where at all possible and 'organised leisure' for those reduced to casual labour. He emphasised that the 'individualist community will find itself obliged for its own sake to take charge of those who . . . are incapable of independent existence'. This obligation went clean against all Charles Booth's original predilection for complete industrial responsibility and the least possible State interference with economic forces.

After the presentation of this important paper Charles immediately travelled overnight to Liverpool to take charge of a hurtful and hopeless situation caused by a member of the Booth firm who was drinking too much. In an introspective letter Mary urged him to be sympathetic to his brother, Alfred, 'over this trial. The difficulty is in his case not made less by the absence of personal liking and ease which softens it to you. Oh dear, human judgement is a difficult matter, wrong at best and yet when one appeals in one's own case to a higher tribunal, one feels crushed by an awful severity made overwhelming by its passionless calm. I always know myself to blame wherever I have unsatisfactoriness to meet. . . .' Poor Mary, she had met a great deal in her own family. A satisfactory occasion occurred a little later on at Gracedieu:

Yesterday cleared up after all, and the Baptists came and had a pleasant afternoon. They managed it all beautifully. A strong staff of helpful men and pretty young women in trim summer dresses and charming hats[came] to see their children through their tea and games and to lead the singing which was exceedingly good, ending up with the Doxology. The English are a *serious* people and I am certainly English enough to enjoy the touch of gravity that they like at the end of a day's pleasuring. . . .

One pencilled note from Charles to Mary gives a glimpse of the kind of life he led in Liverpool:

16th July, 1888.
Dear Wife,
I found myself new quarters very speedily—a room in Harford Street out of Mount Pleasant. Nice respectable people but quite poor (Class D). A blind old man with a small pension and a pleasant wife who ekes out a living by letting lodgings. I take the first floor front, partly furnished (that is, I keep what I want of her things in it) and am to pay 4/–. I like the look of the place and the people very much. . . . I shall certainly study my native town a bit. I feel content. I do like the grip of the business which attaches to the management of the Liverpool office. . . .

Mary's answer came the next day: 'I am so glad you have found a nice place wherein to lay . . . your dear wandering head, that is very easily contented with its position always. I can sympathise with the pleasure you feel in being really at the business'. In another letter, unaware of the *double entendre*, she describes how she 'enjoyed an hour and a half's rest over a good fire yesterday night with Karl Marx in our own bedroom. Marx is decidedly amusing. His style is simple and lively and he has got ideas, but is steeped in the German craze for distinctions, as Comte is in the French chart system. A Frenchman must have a chart and a German a formula, while we English—are perfection of course...!'

Mary often began her letters to Charles on a sad note, and then—as if drawing sympathy from the thought of him—ended happily:

I am most awfully low, but I fancy it can't be helped. One can't expect to have no troubles, and my life has been and is singularly free from it, considering the strange tragedy in the middle of which I have grown up. Thank Heaven my own married relation is a straightforward one, and that esteem and confidence, and a trust beyond all telling go hand in hand with my love for you. This feeling makes a kind of refrain to my life, a burden of deep repose ending every stanza, disturbed with wild agitation and anxiety and complicated indignation which shake me 'til they are stilled by that recurring sense of home peace.

By this time Mary had picked up with the circle, recently called the intellectual aristocracy, into which she was born. Her Potter cousins, Teresa Cripps and Maggie Hobhouse, whose husbands were distinguished MPs, brought a family touch to the House of Commons; Sir Frederick and Lady Pollock, very old friends, held a pre-eminent position in legal circles; and the Macaulay-Trevelyan-Knutsford connection added scholarly and humanitarian attainments to this strong web of educated non-aristocratic people. A new friend sought out Charles at this time and penetrated his smiling reserve, Norman Grosvenor of the Westminster family, a gifted musician who wished to move out of his own aristocratic groove into other worlds. His daughter married John Buchan, whose literary and administrative ability led straight back to the House of Lords! When Norman Grosvenor died Charles said he felt he had lost his only friend. They were both rather isolated men, whose outlook estranged them from their own kin.

All these people gave enormous dinner parties—enormous both in the matter of numbers and of courses and wines. Even when the Booths decided on principle to serve only three courses, the complexity of silver, glass and china involved in one meal makes staggering reading in Mary's detailed lists. In October Beatrice came to one of these huge affairs to meet the Holman Hunts. Her fame was as great as theirs because her *Pages of a Nineteenth-Century Work-girl's Diary* had become a best-seller. Mlle Souvestre, a mutual friend and famous headmistress, greeted this achievement with the words 'Mais que le public anglais est bête!' Beatrice told this story against herself and Mary always shook with laughter over it, but in the depths of her being she agreed with Mlle Souvestre, while Beatrice did not. At a return match with the Holman Hunts a few days later the Booths met Professor J. W. Mackail and his wife, whose sister had married Edward Burne-Jones. This Pre-Raphaelite circle suited them perfectly, combining as it did literature with painting. Had they known of the extraordinary emotional entanglements out of which so many of these pictures-with-a-message emerged,[1] I am certain they would have been too shocked to pursue the paths of friendship, which their children also trod so rewardingly.

In November Mary heard of Aunt Fanny's death, and wrote to Charles describing the last days of this redoubtable Macaulay: 'During the week before she died, she dined out three times, talking with all her usual brilliance and finish, and suffered no pain. She was bed-ridden for a few days only, and told her last visitor a story with the most vivid enjoyment and delight on the very evening before she died.' Neither Aunt Fanny nor Aunt Hannah had shown Mary real affection, but there was something in them both that attracted and amused her, and she would never hear a word against them.

Early in 1889 the Booths set themselves to house-hunt. The lease of Grenville Place was fast running out, and the business was doing so well that they could afford a more attractive London home. They looked at Scarsdale House with its long garden wall which bordered Kensington High Street, and reluctantly decided it was 'too far out'. When demolished it made way for huge shops along the front and many pleasant suburban streets at the back. They chose instead a spacious, dignified Georgian house in Great Cumberland Place, hard by Marble Arch. Mary found that her old friends Mr and Mrs Arthur Cohen and their children lived next door. Soon after this Winnie Cohen, then a little girl and later Mrs Bernard Butler, remembered seeing Mary and Charles walking off together towards Marble Arch, 'he the philosopher with ideas and she the engine to put them into action'.

In a detailed estimate of the expenditure entailed in moving to and doing up the new house, Mary budgeted for £2,000, including furniture, carpets and extra china. The actual cost seems to have been a little less, and even allowing for inflation this sum seems amazingly low. She lists the staff, with their appropriate wages for the year; each member received £7 at Christmas, irrespective of wages. As Charlotte had recently married, not without a Booth dowry, her name disappeared from the staff list, but remained on the list for Christmas presents. On the next page of the diary there is an estimate of the whole family budget for 1890: £4,120 in all. The cook earned £45 a year, the kitchen-

[1] See Diana Holman Hunt, *My Grandmothers and I* and *Holman Hunt: his wives and loves.*

maid £8. There were 9 maids and 2 men indoors, and the 'stables' cost £400 a year. C.B. had £50 and Mary £80 for personal expenditure; £200 went on charity, and £50 on pleasure. The word 'Statistics', listed as an item of expenditure, is followed by a question mark. When completed, the total cost of the Inquiry was supposed to be about £40,000. This figure must be wrong. The salaries alone over seventeen years would have amounted to more, without the expenses of office accommodation, cleaning and postage.

There is no mention in Mary's diary, owing more to the central character of Charles's work than to the flurry of the move, of a notable event which took place in April 1889. Volume I of the *Poverty Series* of *Life and Labour of the People in London*, sub-titled *Trades of East London*, had just been published, and was greeted on all hands 'with wondering admiration', according to the *Daily News*. Beatrice Potter's work, which consisted of 'The Docks' and 'The Tailoring Trade' (already printed in the *Nineteenth Century*), and 'The Jewish Community', was considered particularly brilliant. Charles himself was credited with 'a faculty for taking pains beyond even the fabled capacities of genius'. *The Times* called it 'the grimmest book of our time', because it substantiated the fact that over 30 per cent of Londoners lived under 'the Poverty Line', in Charles's expressive phrase. This came to be known as the Booth Line, a pun on Charles's shipping line. The *Pall Mall Gazette*'s only criticism was that 'If Mr. Booth could only get himself and his young men to write better English, we should not know where to find fault'. Charles collected his impressions with a kindly camera; there is no literary gloss to his words, but the result is refreshingly readable.

On 21 April, Beatrice—then at Gracedieu—noted in her diary: 'The book a great success. Leaders in all the principal papers and C.B. quite the head of the statistical tree.' But it was at this moment that these two pioneers found they were looking in opposite directions. Charles was determined to go forward and tackle the description of Central London now that he had completed his Inquiry into the East End. He asked Beatrice 'to undertake a more thorough study of women's work', but this she refused to do, on the grounds that she preferred to examine the Co-operative Movement, as providing a possible alternative to the capitalist system. It can be seen that while Charles felt that he must do everything in his power to lay bare the causes of failure, and discover the means to make the prevailing system more humane and more efficient, Beatrice had decided to look for another system altogether. He referred to the conflict between them in the conclusion of Volume I —'The unanimity of thought and expression in the book . . . is much more noticeable than are any divergences'. Beatrice's diary at this time contains these words: 'My friendship, or rather my companionship, with Charlie is for the time dropped. Our common work is ended. His brave vigorous life, with its varied interests and unselfconscious and disinterested pursuit of them will always be an encouraging thought. His thoughtful kindness and true affection will always be one of the comforting memories of my life.' And so it should have been. But human beings looking back on past perfection often find in it an additional source of irritation when enduring subsequent imperfection. They sweep the floor for the sixpence they have lost.

VII
THE RIFT
1889–1891

Mary gladly bore and reared Charles's children, ruled his household, read his notes and rewrote his paragraphs, but on no account, if she could possibly help it, would she go to America. Therefore, when the doctor recommended sea air for Meg, who had been ill, it was his 9-year old daughter, in the charge of a nurse-maid, who accompanied Charles to New York in 1889.

Mary wrote to tell him that Kitty Lushington, a young friend who later married Leo Maxse, editor of the *National Review*, had been to call on Sir John Simon in Kensington Square. He was the first physician and philosopher to concentrate on health rather than disease, and he succeeded in draining the city of London in the teeth of bureaucratic and civic opposition. 'This delightful, elderly gentleman whose name is pronounced French fashion, asked Kitty: "Have you seen the most wonderful and interesting book of the day?", and he produced, what do you think? "Life and Labour".' . . . He says its value is of the very big and prominent kind, and altogether said so many nice things that I feel very warm about the cockles when I think of them.'

In the following year, 1890, General William Booth's *Darkest London* came out and very naturally both the book and the author, who founded the Salvation Army, have always been confused with Charles Booth and his *Life and Labour*. Strangely enough the two men never met. Nor did their wives.[1]

Having sent the boys back to school, and settled Imogen and Tarla at Gracedieu for the summer, Mary travelled to Milan with Dodo. She reported that 'The Italian porters and officials, and even the French and Swiss ones, have not the chivalry of our beloved London and North

---

[1] Mrs Catherine Booth was also better born and better educated than her husband and worked at his side.

Western and Midland folk, who fly to the rescue of a weak woman struggling with bags and rugs too many for her, and supply information free gratis and for nothing, just to cheer one on one's way'. After this patriotic encomium she swiftly denigrated the cathedral and America in one devastating sentence: 'It is the sort of thing one would imagine the Americans might do if they ever build a cathedral, but you must keep this opinion to yourself and not read it out loud to a circle of New York friends. . . . Your wife never thinks you can do anything right without her! However, she feels still more strongly that she can do nothing right without you. All alone here, without you to guard and see to me, and with Dodo looking fragile and depressed. I feel an old woman. If you were here I should feel like a bride on her wedding tour.'

The tone of Mary's next letter, from Florence, is entirely different because she was welcomed by friends and relations at the station. Her pleasure at the sight of an English tea-table is deliciously funny:

Mr. Moncrieff's clerical figure, most home-like to behold, cheered our very hearts. . . . He drove us off through this beautiful city to Piazza de Cavalli, where we found home indeed—a lovely Italian suite of rooms all opening out on each other . . . and inhabiting this pretty foreign-looking abode dear Cousin Sophy's comfortable person. . . . In the innermost room, with closed shutters, carved chairs and fantastic drapery, rose . . . an English tea-table, silver tea things, bread and butter, just delicious to behold, and when we sat down amongst kisses and friendly, tender, welcoming ways, we began to feel different people. Oh my Boy! You will smile and say how dependent she is! So proud and unbending and unamiable; so fearful, needing all the indulgence of affection and protection. Yes, it is so. Now with the sense of being guarded and cared for, I can throw myself into Florence and its loveliness, and enjoy it all. . . .

She goes on to describe High Mass at the Certosa, which shook with bursts of song while the service was performed with marvellous grace by lazy, well-bred priests in glorious robes, who pushed curious children good-humouredly to one side. Dodo said, 'How surprised Jesus Christ would be—what would he do?' Mary whispered back, 'Accept it all and go on.' She then states her view of faith in Christianity.

Surely that great practical genius would make very light of the absurdities and contradictions, would join in the service very easily and think it waste of time to disturb these sweet motherly Italian girls when they kiss the virgin's feet and beg the protection of a favourite saint for one of their black eyed boys. It seems to me nothing prevents one from being Christian so much as the tendency to attach oneself to an accurate view of our relation to the Divinity. The disputes resulting from this must tend to be bitter; must make us exclusive and Jesus' notion was all the other way. To understand, to forgive; to take in; to shake off the yoke of old systems. Yes, but only when they impeded full exercise of our faculties and our humanity. I can't make up my mind whether I am thankful or regretful that the Crucifixion took place. On the one hand one feels the great loss; how much further one has got at forty than at thirty! With such a mind, so matchless in its immaturity, with such an extraordinary, fearless grasp, such easy power, what would not another ten years have done? Yet, if He had had them, perhaps we should not have known about Him even as much as we do, for it is the Cross which won for ever the doubting hearts of His own disciples and which wins and holds us now, touching all alike.

She finds Italian services 'as completely natural as our little Dissenting Chapels. I am sure that in the days of the Druids there must have been Dissenters in England. Perhaps the real difficulty of discovering Druid doctrine may lie in the fact that they had none and that each individual Druid was an Independent Congregationalist Minister, only uniting with his brethren in the great annual mistletoe affair, with no doubt, a distribution of coals and roast beef to the poor afterwards!' Timid as a traveller, Mary was very bold in thought.

Meanwhile 9-year-old Meg was just as miserable on arrival in New York as her mother had been in Milan. The whole month spent there would have been one long disaster except that she got to know her father. He insisted on her cleaning her teeth night and morning, and tidying her room. He read to her a great deal and spoke with tremendous pride about his book. She had no idea what was in the book but remembered that he pronounced the word as if it rhymed with 'Luke' in north country fashion.

In spite of Beatrice's feeling of detachment from Charles Booth, the cousins often wrote to each other and in one of these letters Mary described being once more alone at Gracedieu without the equal or still better the superior mind. . . . Charles . . . seems rather at a stand just now over his 'Women's Work and Wages'. . . . Otherwise the work goes on. He is really enjoying his East End life. I think it rests him more in some ways than even Gracedieu's quiet and beauty. . . . He likes . . . the people and the evening roaming and the food! which he says agrees with him in kind and time of taking better than that of our class. You must be plunged into the thick of your paper ['The Lords and the Sweating System']. I don't believe in its being dull, if it is what I suppose it must be—a record of ascertained facts, for I can't help thinking that a good many people must share one's sick distaste for the highly spiced messes we have had served up to us of late—so as to take refuge gladly in a 'plain unvarnished tale'—much as Charlie does in the oatmeal porridge and thick bread and butter of his East End landladies. . . .

On 11 August 1889, Mary comforted Beatrice about Professor Marshall's criticism of her manuscript: 'Don't let dear, good Professor Marshall depress you; the best and kindest of men, but not without his fads, especially in all that concerns the capacities of our sex. He does you the compliment, in spite of this, of talking to you as if you were a man.' Evidently his dictum that 'the woman must not develop her faculties in a way unpleasant to man. If you compete with us we won't marry you', had reminded Beatrice of the Chamberlain affair, which still troubled her heart. Mary continued:

I am sorry that the old thing still shows signs of its deep root. I don't like the idea of a lonely future of nothing but work for you, however tempered by kindliness on your part and affection from your friends. If it is so, darling, it can't be helped but I think it is a pity. . . . Charlie is very busy first and foremost with the business which needs as much thought and work as he can put into four or five days a week. The other work has had a slight check in its progress owing to the fact that the Authorities have happened to call in the Schedules of the School Board Visitors for purposes of their own just at holiday time which C. had hoped to utilize. . . .

The author of *A Liverpool Merchant House* (Arthur Henry John) mentions that after 1885 'with the immediate problems in the leather and shipping sides of the business solved . . . Charles Booth was able to turn to his great social enquiries'. The inference is that he was set free from daily responsibility for Alfred Booth and Company. Mary's letters however, which the author did not see, prove how regularly Charles worked in Liverpool, London and the United States.

'Poor Beatrice, she is as low as low can be' was one of Mary's comments to Charles in Liverpool, and was soon in much the same state herself, due to the drunkenness of the cook, who had to be sacked immediately, and the move from Grenville Place to Great Cumberland Place. However, Charlotte was 'perfection—always handy cheery sensible and nice'. They found a terrible smell of gas because 'the gasfitter has done the taps all wrong'. Gas-fitters never held that place in Mary's heart reserved for L.N.E.R. porters! It is disappointing that Charles, who must have smelt a lot of gas in other people's homes, never mentions his own wife's household problems in his letters, but on this occasion it is known that he took a hand. Some years later when Mary was impressing on Meg and Imogen the necessity of obedience on the wife's part in marriage, they began to laugh. 'When have you ever obeyed Father?' they asked. 'Of course I always do, I always have' she answered, and there was a silence while she tried to remember one single instance of obedience. Finally she raised her head triumphantly. 'It was when we moved into Great Cumberland Place', she told them. 'Your father wanted electric light and I was against it but I gave in.'

She was always generous over his affairs: 'Bless the Boy! You have all these ships! How big your affairs sound: £18,000!' (the cost of the new ship). 'I don't much like any of the proposed names. We have rather used up the good ones, haven't we? "Hilary" is a good-sounding name, but he wasn't anybody very much. "Hildebrand" was more of a personage, but not much of a saint.' Two saints and personages were as much involved as Charles at this time with the serious and justifiable unrest in the docks. Cardinal Newman supported the dockers in their demands for better conditions and wages. Mahatma Gandhi, then a London University student, called on the author of 'Lead Kindly Light' to congratulate him on his stand, and to tell him how deeply he admired the famous hymn. Mary in later life absolutely detested Gandhi but she shared his deep feeling for Newman.

The desk diary for 1890 is once again a mine of information. The household servants are noted as usual but the outside staff at Gracedieu and their wages are now listed separately. Bale, the gardener, earned £5 5s. per month; Newbold, the handyman of the place earned £4 a month; Toone, the coachman, £5 a month and Hoult the stable-boy

£3 15s. The Hoults were and are true Leicestershire yeoman farmers. They lived and their descendants still live in a farmhouse built of forest rock at the east end of Gracedieu Park.

Under the heading 'Norwegian Novelists', Mary has listed books by Björnson and plays and books by Ibsen. Taken at random from the ordinary list of books are: *Old Deccan Days* by Miss Frere; *George Washington* by Henry Cabot Lodge; *A Yankee at the Court of King Arthur* by Mark Twain; *There and Back* by George MacDonald; *The Book of the Forty-Five Mornings* by Rudyard Kipling, the title of which has been changed; and *Travels with a Donkey in the Cévennes* by Stevenson and *The Wrong Box*, another master-piece by the same author, which was particularly apposite to Charles Booth's activities. One of the chief characters, Joseph Finsbury, while neglecting his family leather business spends his time collecting extraneous and appallingly boring facts about income and expenditure in all parts of the world! Among the special list of books for Charles, such as *The Conflicts of Labour and Capital* by Howell; *History of the Science of Politics* by Frederick Pollock; *How London Lives* by Gordon; and *Free Trade in Capital* by Egmond Hake, *Socialism in England* by Sidney Webb stands out now on the page. Then, it was just another unknown book by an unknown author. Probably Beatrice, already attracted by both Socialism and Sidney, had recommended it, without realising that she and Mary, alike in their energy and their intense reactions, had been steadily growing apart in judgement. Women who have never surmounted the Matterhorns of domestic life rarely believe in the effort involved. Envious of the obvious rewards they tend to enlarge on their own hard work and interests while belittling those of the woman with family cares. Unconsciously a certain sharpness, even sarcasm, creeps into conversation between the two, and resentment rises on both sides.

Beatrice's feelings of admiration and attraction for Charles had also cooled. Her comments both on him and on Mary in later life convey passionate bitterness; and the egoism of one who demands friendship on her own terms. Had the undoubted emotional link between Beatrice and Joseph Chamberlain become permanent, her friendship with the Booths would have ceased to be such an important part of Beatrice's life. Mary and Charles, secure and happy in each other's love, did not realise how essentially lonely Beatrice was. It was in these circumstances that Beatrice met Sidney Webb, whose industry and wit would have at all times commanded her attention. The deeper intuitive sympathy that followed may have sprung from Sidney's awareness of her predicament.

Meanwhile, life flowed on as usual in the Booths' new home at Great Cumberland Place, and after Christmas 1899 Mary dutifully waded through the list of 'calls to make'. Today it seems more than absurd, almost wicked, that worthwhile women spent so much time on paying calls. Mary used to describe how she handed in her cards with the corner turned down, to indicate a personal call, and how—greatly relieved—she would hear that 'Madam was not in'. It amused her to realise that this was not always the truth.

On 14 February 1890 Beatrice invited the Booths to dine to meet Sidney Webb and when they had all gone she sat down to describe this unlikely Valentine in her diary: 'A remarkable little man, with a huge head and tiny body . . . a Jewish nose, prominent eyes and mouth, black hair somewhat unkempt, spectacles and a most bourgeois black coat shiny with wear. But I like the man.' On the following day, when Beatrice dined with the Booths, no amount of discussion about this ugly, able, amusing and labyrinthine little man could ever have reconciled their different reactions.

A fortnight later Mary wrote to her dear love:

Tomorrow morning we shall have [been] married nineteen years: partly clouded and sad but mainly very, oh very, happy. Tonight as I sit here the prospect of the twentieth year unrolls itself brightly and peacefully before me. May it be so in reality. If not—if trouble waits for us, at least the nineteen years have given us love and trust in each other and strong hearts that will try to bear whatever may come.

God bless you.

Mary always had a dread of tempting fate. She often used to say *unberufen*! when hopeful statements were made about babies arriving safely or even the prospect of a fine day. Charles evidently chided her for her fears on this occasion, for she immediately replied: 'Thank you for the dearest and sweetest of wedding-day letters. Happy we are, too happy, only that is really not so. It is a kind of weakness to feel afraid of being too happy: when one ought to feel one's heart overflowing with gratitude. I think mine does overflow. I feel so safe and guarded under your dear wing and so very happy too to know that you are so and that the six children are growing up in such conditions of peace and gladness.'

A month later she urged Charles to read *The Kreutzer Sonata*. Tolstoy's account of the difficulties of marriage always fascinated Mary. Perhaps it was her realisation that she and Charles had found unity in spite of their very different characters and needs, that drew her to speak so often of this book. She also read *What then must we do?* at this time, in which Tolstoy advocates giving away all personal possessions, and commented: 'I am sure we rich and cultured folk are attaching enormously too much importance to the effects of what we can do, or ought to do, with our wealth; and the whole wealth and poverty question is looking altogether too large. What we are and what the individual nobleness of one man may do for the rest—limitless good, are all important considerations.' This sentence indicates some of Mary's deep feeling for a different social order from that which her husband had in mind. She ends with a 'Bless you!' This was one of the phrases her father had used when he felt that his letters had become too serious.

She visited Folkestone later that summer and her 'heart swelled and the tears came at the thought of the old, happy careless days when Papa's goodness, oh his goodness! made everything in life a joy and one little thought of all the mischief abrewing in the dim future. But the evil shall die and the good shall endure, say the Positivists; and pray Heaven his goodness may have struck some responsive notes and live again and act in some faint way in his daughter and her children.'

In October Beatrice consulted Mary about the possibility of becoming Mrs Sidney Webb. Like most people who ask for advice what she really needed was encouragement. 'Dearest,' replied Mary, 'Your letter is of interest indeed. How I wish we knew more and could give advice worth having. Fortunately, it will be quite easy for us to make advances towards a closer acquaintance without any suggestion that we are considering him critically for a special purpose.' When in the following week 'Mr. Webb came to dinner', Mary liked him no better than he liked her. Criticism of a man to whom Beatrice was already drawn could only cement the new relationship and disrupt the old. Perhaps Sidney should have felt grateful to Mary after all: her absolute approval might have deterred Beatrice.

In November Mary and Charles dined with their old friends Sir Frederick and Lady Pollock to meet Miss Octavia Hill, who became a new one. This tiny, gentle-spoken woman, not only devised a new system of house-management which is still followed by countless housing associations, but also, in collaboration with Canon Rawnsley, founded the National Trust. As a girl at Hyde Park College, Mary had been taken by the remarkable Miss Harrisons to help with Octavia Hill's first venture—a playground for children. She was drawn to Charles by a common wish to X-ray the problem of poverty, but her perception of the necessity of preserving the independence of the poor led her to decide on remedies diametrically opposed to his. Because of its inquisitorial aspect, Charles and the Barnetts came to abominate the Charity Organisation Society which Octavia Hill stuck to through thick and thin. Canon Barnett wanted books and pictures just as much as hot baths and playing-fields for the poor. His book, *Practical Socialism*, published two years earlier in 1888, put forward such startlingly improbable ideas that the Establishment were amused, not frightened by them. Yet even in his own lifetime they took shape.

In February 1891 Mary told Charles that she was glad he was struck with '*The Vikings*':[1] 'How absurd it has been of us to Christianise the Northern Tribes. One sees how they mix it all up with the most undoubting conviction of the existence and power of their own old gods and sworn allegiance to the leader of a new divine enterprise, with a feeling doubtless that Heaven was wide enough for both, and it was a matter of taste whether you preferred the society of the saints in Paradise or the stalwart heroes of Valhalla. . . .'

In May Mary entertained the heroes of the Press in Charles's absence to launch the forthcoming second volume of the *Poverty Series* of his Inquiry, which completed the picture of London with a survey of Central and South London. Charles had undertaken the Classification of Schools himself as well, of course, as writing the introduction and overseeing the whole production. Miss Octavia Hill contributed a moving account of the difficulties of family life in block buildings, which struck Mary's heart more than anything else in this volume. She was also much flattered and pleased that Miss Nightingale had written to ask Charles's advice about a scheme for the alleviation of poverty in India. The comic aspect of this invitation strikes the reader immediately and perhaps it struck Charles too, for nothing further came of this Nightingale-Booth attempt to join Canute by the sea-shore, although the two met on his return from America.

In one of her letters Mary sent Charles a character sketch of herself as reported to a Gracedieu guest by his groom, who had also stayed at

[1] *The Vikings of Western Christendom*, by C. F. Keary (London, 1890).

the Manor: 'They have to do what she tells them, but if they do she is very kind to them but she won't stand no nonsense, and quite right too.' After a rather satisfied smile at herself over this statement she carries on about books.

I see Meredith in 'One of our Conquerors' makes Natalie give Victor something of my idea of the mission of the easy classes. . . . How I should like to satisfy, satiate, glut our people with luxury in all its refinements so that they might rise through experience of its unsatisfactoriness to a higher conception of happiness, but all this is a long way off. Meantime it is depressing to see how bad and embittering the absence of money and ease is for people. . . . Lord Salisbury spoke from bitter knowledge when he said, 'It takes so long to get the chill poverty out of the blood' but there is no royal road out of troubles; of that I am more and more convinced.

Mary's last letter to America described the aftermath of an influenza epidemic which had paralysed English life. It was so bad that Dodo actually 'had to drive herself alone' in the governess-cart to do the family shopping! Now that the worst was over Mary hoped they would all be together again in London soon. 'I have just said goodbye to Dodo, Imogen, Tarla, Rosie, Alice, Jane, Sarah, Fanny and Ellen who with Ray[1] . . . went off to catch the 11.36 a.m. to London. I stayed to see the Doctor and if he continues to report all well of Meg I shall go up myself by the 6.31 this evening, leaving Maria, Martha and Kate to take care of her.' The coachman took the horses up to London by rail leaving the shooting-brake and governess-cart behind. The very thought of such a household makes the heart of the modern housewife quake. Mary added: 'Oh dear! I believe I am at last learning what it is to be in love. I have never really been in love with anybody 'til now, and I feel Oh such a longing for you that I think I must be in love with you head over ears.' Charles came back from America very fit and well, spent one day at Harrow with the boys, met Beatrice at lunch the next and caught the evening train to Liverpool. He treated his home like a first-class waiting-room.

During the next fortnight Mary and 18-year-old Dodo heard Paderewski[2] play the piano, took factory girls to the Zoo, called first at

[1] The stableman.
[2] I. J. Paderewski was born in 1860, became Prime Minister of Poland in 1919, and remained a great pianist until he died in 1941.

Lambeth Palace and then at the shoemaker's, looked at Holman Hunt's picture in the Academy, dined one night at the House of Commons before listening to the debate, and gave a dance for young cousins and friends on the Friday of the Eton *v*. Harrow Match. These became annual events, and were known irreverently as 'Our Lord's Dances'. Elderly people have often described them to me in young voices. The band and the refreshments were conventionally excellent but the 15–65 age-group added the zest of unsophisticated informality. Individual polkas and waltzes were followed by a round dance of complicated concentric movements called the Lancers. A really rowdy gallop brought these Dickensian revels to an end.

In this swirl of youthful activities the old alliance with Beatrice was moving towards dissolution. 'Tea and talk with Beatrice', on 14 July, must have been the occasion on which Beatrice revealed that she was already 'privately pledged' to Sidney Webb; marriage was to follow when such a step could be taken without upsetting her father. Against all probability Beatrice still trusted that the Booths would sympathise with her in taking a step which worldly people might have considered downward, not forward, but which Mary disapproved of because she disliked Sidney, while Charles did not warm to him. The next day Mary wrote two letters; the first was to Charles:

Dearest,

I enclose Professor Marshall's most kind letter. . . .

I went to see Beatrice yesterday and read a long, very kindly criticism of her book from him.[1] He does not like either her methods or her authorities, but believes she has abilities of her own, and great ones if she will only use her own mind. I am better satisfied about her after seeing her. First she looks remarkably well, young, pretty and blooming, like her old self. Norway has set her up. She is evidently happy and believes in Mr. Sidney Webb thoroughly. The difficulty about marrying is that until Uncle Richard dies she thinks they will not have enough to live on. As she has £400 per annum now and he has enough to keep himself even if he leaves the Colonial Office, I don't see the difficulty. Beatrice talks a little comically about the extreme poverty of the marriage, her willingness to live in the humblest middle-class style and her fear of [crossed out and replaced

[1] Probably the beginnings of *The History of Trade Unionism* by B. and S. Webb, published in 1894.

by] indifference to the probable disapproval of us grand folk, ignoring the fact that she and Mr. Webb will have a much larger income than the greater number of people we know at all intimately. . . . Heroics over the self-sacrifice of living on an income of about £1,500 sound quaintly in my ears;—but all the same, I think better of the affair after seeing Beatrice.

Mary then wrote a letter to Beatrice which, unlike her usual pell-mell phrases of affection, leaves a chilly impression:

Dear Beatrice,[1]
It would be of no use to pretend that we are not sorry it is so, but your happiness and satisfaction has a reassuring effect even upon our minds and indeed, dearest friend, we will prepare ourselves to think and expect all the good we wish for you in the life that you have chosen. Is the secrecy really desirable? . . . Our best love to you. You must thank Mr. Webb please for his kind and generous expression of wish that we may not be separated from each other by your engagement. It is very good of him, as he knows (?) that we have been to a great extent his enemies. . . .

Meanwhile Charles wrote more kindly.

14, Castle Street,
Liverpool.
15th July, 1891.

. . . It will give me great pleasure to become better acquainted with Mr. Webb and I feel I shall gain much from a close and cousinly contact with the school of thought and action of which he is so brilliant a representative. Yours will now be a life of action I suppose rather than of investigation or abstract thought. Your powers would take you far I think in any of the three, perhaps they are hard to combine— I find it so myself. To action I have never pretended and any claim on abstract thought I abandon as a childish delusion—so nothing is left for me but investigation.

Your too kind appreciation of Vol. II was delightful reading to me. I have had too much praise but must try to work up to it. Just now I am all the week and every week in Liverpool only getting to London for Sunday, but still I hope we may meet.

[1] The two following letters are in the possession of the London School of Economics.

The oddest quirk of all in this situation was that Mary and Sidney—how they would have hated to admit it—shared two important characteristics; a power of work and that predilection for the back room found in the highest ranks of the Civil Service. Charles and Beatrice each possessed that gift which is rarer than any other: originality. No four halves could conceivably have fitted better into two wholes. Once joined, the Webbs gathered force and moved out of the Booths' orbit into the centre of their own still more remarkable sphere.

On 15 July 1891 Beatrice expressed in her diary the feeling that she had to tell the Booths of her engagement for two reasons; not only did she consider them her most intimate friends, but also she was connected with work for Charles's Inquiry. She hoped that they would try to appreciate and understand Sidney: 'But evidently it is supremely distasteful to them. . . .' She suggested at one interview that the Booths should ignore the engagement, and Mary 'heartily concurred. That curious little look of veiled determination came over her face, and she said "You see Charlie and I have nothing in common with Mr. Webb. Charlie would never go to him for help, and he would never go to Charlie, so that it would not be natural for them to see each other. When you are married it will be different."'

In fact when the marriage took place it deepened the rift. Beatrice was bitterly hurt and poured out her feelings in her diary—'Mary has a narrow and conventional nature; and in spite of a genuine affection for me she cannot take with loyal trust my view of my own life and accept it. But from Charlie I expected something different; he is too big a mind for that and his feeling for me was warm and strong. A shadow has crept between us and has deepened into a darkness.'

Beatrice would not accept the law of the swings and roundabouts. Since Sidney and Mary did not like each other, there was no possibility of enjoying the old intimacy as well as the new, but her tenacity fought against this conclusion. There is a theory that the friendship between these three was broken because Mary became jealous of the close working association between Charles and Beatrice. This interpretation, for all its simplicity, cannot be accepted because it was Beatrice's growing attachment to Sidney Webb, in addition to political differences, that chilled Mary's hitherto warm appreciation.

Two years later, in June 1894, Beatrice in her diary refers with bewildered surprise and sorrow to the reality of the rift, and notes that Charles writes kindly to her, but does not attempt to see her: 'Obviously he is vexed or simply indifferent, and she [Mary] still treats me as an unfortunate misled person who is to be pitied and gently repudiated for the impropriety of her conduct.' As to their close 15-year-old friendship, Beatrice comments: 'When I strained it, I should have thought slightly, it broke—or rather I found it was already broken. Even today I have not yet recovered from my amazement and wonder at this fact.' It is strange that Charles and Mary were not more aware of Beatrice's suffering, and did not make some effort to alleviate it.

Asquith once said that Beatrice was a tiresome woman married to a saint. Whether Sidney was a saint or not, he was certainly married to a seer, and all prophets have their tiresome side. Charles, who acknowledged this prophetic quality, had to choose not between two women, but between two views of life. The practical, immediate, palliative, next step on the traditional ladder was Mary's view; the leaping power of revolutionary thought belonged to Beatrice. We live now in a country shaped by her imagination. Had Charles joined forces with Beatrice and Sidney Webb, the likelihood is that social security would have emerged earlier as a practical approach to our extremes of poverty and prosperity, and that we should now be experimenting with other ideas. In choosing his own way, Charles also moved in Mary's direction but he comprehended the power of Beatrice's vision. Mary was angered and frightened by Beatrice's indefatigable attempts to convert Charles. It was this that led her, although she kept all Beatrice's letters, to speak of her with a harsher disdain than their dear early friendship deserved.

Beatrice in a final phrase wrote, 'Though friends are not changeable quantities—another friend, however true is no substitute for a lost one— the Booths have no successors.' Mary and Charles were losers too. Beatrice's dual rôle of intimate cousin and social inquirer could never be replaced, and this left Charles and Mary without an independent critic in their inner circle. Mr Macaulay's sensitive touch of gaiety might have given Mary the necessary laughter to accept the Webbs with their warts and their grandeur. Beatrice struggled in vain for years against what she described as Mary's 'impenetrable polish', and lost her battle. Mary never wished to reinvoke the spontaneous affection and intellectual excitement of their triple association. The last touch of youth, with all its limitless unexpected possibilities, was gone.

VIII
THE COMMON TASK
1891–1903

It is unnatural to divide into two streams the life that swept my grand-parents along in one great river, but I have done it in order to concentrate the facts about *Life and Labour in London*, and the resultant campaign for old age pensions. The extracts of letters quoted in this chapter are, of course, sandwiched between accounts of the children, the business, and comments on friends and books. These will be found in Chapter IX, 'The Daily Round', and form a chronicle of Victorian family life. The present chapter deals exclusively with the Booths' common task, and their uncommon working relationship.

Charles's time-table was so arduous that he could not have carried on at all but for Mary's selfless and spirited assistance. Writing to him with the humility she always showed in connection with the Inquiry she said she thought the task of compressing his notes into cogent paragraphs was within her powers, but that no one must ever know she did it. Once she expressed fear lest her rearrangements might alter the freshness of his thought. Whether this was ever so, her judgement on how to present evidence, where to abridge, and what to expand, was impeccable. In addition, she did a great deal of background reading, saw each volume through the press, and corrected the proofs. Every wife knows how satisfactory it is to be of direct help to her husband, but in Mary's case the work suited her editorial ability and completed her desire for service.

At this time Charles collected candle ends so that he could stick them along his carriage window and work in the train; the legend is that the guard thought he must be a retired grocer with a passion for economy. Mary worked at her desk in the drawing-room, concentrating for an hour or two and then jumping up to join in family talk and laughter. The thread that broke from time to time was not interest or enjoyment but health. Charles went abroad and cured himself by cutting away from everything; Mary endured headaches in a darkened room and recovered at home.

Known as 'The Chief', Charles was from first to last the only arbiter of the seventeen volumes. He drew his Inquiry secretaries from very varied backgrounds and they changed with the years. First among them came Ernest Aves. He had 'a natural gift of fair-mindedness beyond any that I have ever met,' wrote Mary, and Mrs Barnett commented ironically that he was 'so wholly lovable and generally so tiresomely right'. His qualities both as a man and as a member of Charles's team very soon won him a place in the Booth Cabinet, but he never filled Beatrice's special rôle. This appreciation of Ernest Aves's ability was shared by those who subsequently appointed him as the first Chairman of the Trade Boards. He reflected the industrial aspect of Charles's mind. Charles's statistical mantle fell in due course on Llewellyn-Smith's shoulders and as Sir Hubert he became Chairman of the Second Survey of London instigated by London University thirty years later on. Two young men from the Booths' own circle of friends also joined the team as honorary secretaries: George Duckworth[1] and Esme Howard.[2]

Mary's favourite among the inquirers, however, was always Mr Jesse Argyle, who had devilled for Charles since 1885. He was a less cultivated but a much racier companion than Sir Hubert or Mr Aves, and the entire Booth family savoured his humour and fidelity. On his first visit to Gracedieu, Mary asked Mr Argyle which pudding he would prefer, and his answer became as famous to her grandchildren as any of the great Duke of Wellington's remarks: 'Oy'll troy a little poy if you please Mrs. Bewth.' Another morning he came down to breakfast with the words, 'Sorry Oy'm lite, Mrs. Bewth. The Mide forgot to call me.' Everything in Mary responded to the pluck and zest of the Cockney Londoner, and his visits were a joy, and Charles always said he was the best literary hack in London.

Charles's first spot check, information for which came exclusively from School Board Visitors, indicated that Mr Hyndman's guess at the numbers of those in want was probably correct. Drawing on innumerable sources of information, the three subsequent *Poverty* volumes of the

---

1 Later Sir George Duckworth, secretary to Sir Austen Chamberlain; stepson of Sir Leslie Stephen. See Chapter IX.
2 The Hon. Esme Howard, later Lord Howard of Penrith, H.M. Ambassador in Madrid 1919–24; in Washington, 1924–30.

Inquiry proved that the picture was darker than any that had been imagined, and they were read with horrified fascination by a large public. Apart from the problems of old age, with which Charles became increasingly involved, it became clear that unemployment was the general cause of want, and that the highly skilled suffered more in this respect than the ordinary labourer. Convinced that the remedy for unemployment lay in better organisation of individual firms, Charles next led his secretaries to inquire into the operations of different trades and Volume IV, the last of the *Poverty Series*, was called *The Trades of East London connected with Poverty*. The second series, known as the *Industry Series*, consisted of five volumes, on every form of employment. In the third series, entitled *Religious Influences*, the effects of Church and Chapel on human welfare were weighed, and somewhat naïvely found wanting. Happiness, that real and illogical factor, was touched on with the same cool pen that noted the kitchen sink and the daily wage.

During these gruelling years a gradual reversal of Charles's main interests in life took place. The business became his recreation, and although the pension campaign was always a labour of love, the Inquiry itself became a self-imposed burden. There is no record of any hesitation on his part to complete the picture of life and labour in London according to his original scheme. Nevertheless it is sad that some government agency did not take it over and set Charles's unusual mind free to consider trade union practices, land values, town planning and the nationalisation of transport and water supplies. When he finally came to consider these in depth, the sap of his thought no longer bubbled into action and he could do no more than express unusual ideas and trust that they would germinate in other minds. Meanwhile, volume followed volume, and gradually the Inquiry became one of England's institutions, like the British Museum, much valued but seldom sampled. The general public read the reviews, not the text, spoke with increasing respect of the author, and misunderstood his intentions. They expected him in due course to produce an overall solution to the problem of poverty whereas he had always assumed that his statistics would be the foundation on which a long-term policy could be built. He looked on himself as a surveyor, not an architect.

However in 1891 the plight of the aged poor spurred him on for once to seek an honourable practical solution to the gravest sector of misery that his recent researches had laid bare. State pensions on a modest scale seemed to be the answer; large enough to give a man or woman the hope that with their own savings they might maintain a joint home in old age; small enough to discourage inevitable scroungers and critics. After many consultations in November 1891 with Mr Tom Mann who was in favour, and Miss Octavia Hill who was decidedly adverse, Charles decided a month later to put forward his detailed and revolutionary proposals for State pensions. This was his answer to Beatrice: this was his aim; human palliative measures, not radical reconstruction.

At the beginning of this period of work, on 15 December, Mary went to the Statistical Society to hear C.B. read his paper on 'Enumeration and Classification of Paupers; and State Pensions for the Aged'. 'Place crammed,' she wrote in her diary. 'Mr Loch and Mr. Marshall spoke and Leonard Courtney.' The Marshalls were paying a return visit to the Booths who had stayed with them recently in Cambridge. 'Talked about Docks, etc.,' Mary notes laconically next day, but from another source it is known that Professor Marshall thought well of Charles's proposal. Lady Darwin, the wife of Sir Horace,[1] wrote to a friend on 11 January 1892:

> I saw Mrs. (Prof.) Marshall the other day—she told me that they had been staying at the Charles Booths for a meeting of the Statistical Society at which Mr. Booth made his startling suggestion of pensioning everybody without distinction, over sixty-five. There was no time for the discussion that evening, but Mrs. M. said it was very well received and has since been discussed. Prof. Marshall's only objection, as far as I understood, was that its consideration might prevent the consideration of a more radical reform of the Poor Law. Mr. Loch[2] of the C.O.S. was dead against it.

On 22 December the discussion Mrs Marshall mentions took place at what Mary described as a 'very hostile meeting'. During the intervening week fierce retaliatory weapons had been forged and 'State Pensions for the Aged' was bitterly attacked by the very friends from whom Charles had expected sympathy, if not support. Even his superb courage faltered. Now that Old Age Pensions, National Assistance, National

---

[1] Sir Horace Darwin, one of the many sons of the great Darwin, and a scientist of note in his own right. He founded the Cambridge Instrument Factory to provide precision tools for experiments of all kinds. Letter printed by kind permission of the Darwin family.

[2] Later Sir Charles Loch; Secretary of the Charity Organisation Society.

Health and State Education have all come in with the tide of life, it is hard to imagine the horror which greeted this first little socialist eddy when it rippled on the shores of the national consciousness. Of all Charles's friends, only Joseph Chamberlain understood his concern or was actively interested in his scheme. Miss Octavia Hill and Mr Loch condemned it utterly: 'The most outrageous and absurd scheme yet promulgated' was the comment of the *Charity Organisation Society Review*. The President of the Economic Section of the British Association was less virulent in his language, but none the less considered Charles Booth's proposition to be 'so Utopian that it did not provide food for serious discussion'.

Disturbed and miserable, the Booths returned to Great Cumberland Place after the meeting, and decided to go directly to Gracedieu. There with Mary's help Charles set himself the task of expounding his point of view in a second paper, which was ultimately called 'Pauperism: a Picture. Endowment of Old Age: an Argument'. 'Paupers and Pensions' did very well as a title to begin with, and occurs often in Mary's diary for 1892, where under the heading 'Interesting matter of Old Age Pensions' she lists a variety of names and addresses in Germany from which she hoped to glean information. It is a relief to see *The Lesson of the Master* by Henry James appearing beside *The Factory and Workshops Act 1812–1891* by Redgrave!

In January Mary interviewed Mr Spender, who had written a book called *The State v. Pensions in Old Age* before becoming editor of the *Westminster Gazette*, while Charles went to see John Morley,[1] the editor of the *Fortnightly*. The Booths possessed a natural ease where the Press was concerned and the friendships that resulted from these early contacts were lasting and fruitful. 'Worked at Pauper' occurs continually in Mary's diary until 5 February, when 'C.B. and Mr. Pell spoke at the Political and Economic Society Discussion on "Are Pensions economically objectionable?" Mr. Fletcher Moulton[2] was in the Chair.' The greater the opposition the quieter was Charles's manner. A week later Macmillan and Company agreed to publish his proposals for pensions: provided he paid the costs, he was to reap the benefit of the sales. All his dealings with the firm were conducted on these lines and to everyone's surprise, twenty years later, the takings balanced the costs.

[1] Later Lord Morley, statesman and man of letters.
[2] Later, Lord Fletcher of Bank.

In March Mary saw him off to New York, corrected his proofs, saw them through the press, and with Mr Argyle's help chose a suitable sketch for the cover. This was a picture of an old couple walking along together against an effective background of pointed railings and a brick wall. Charles held that to separate a man and his wife in male and female workhouses, just because in old age they could no longer earn a living, was wicked. He argued that it would be cheaper for the country, as well as happier for them, to assist them to live with their families or on their own. Sometimes this double attitude made him disliked.

He was away as usual when 'Pauperism: a Picture. Endowment of Old Age: an Argument' was published by Macmillan as a sixpenny pamphlet. The facts and figures were taken from two of London's Poor Law Unions and one rural one, that of Ashby-de-la-Zouch, near Gracedieu.

Due to the care and imagination Charles had given to his Old Age Pensions Scheme as well as the contribution he had made with the *Poverty Series* of *Life and Labour* he was elected President of the Statistical Society in June 1892. Considering the uproar which followed his paper of only seven months before, this was indeed a compliment. At a dinner given in his honour on 25 June, he was presented with the Guy Gold Medal, struck in the memory of Dr Guy, the eighteenth-century statistician. Charles was the first holder, chosen after some years during which no award was made. My grandmother kept the medal in the drawing-room at Gracedieu, and showed it to me with great pride, deriding at the same time the other mementoes in the show-case such as a silver trowel and several scrolls. Yet she never really explained the Guy Medal, and at least one of her children did not know why it had been bestowed. The Guy Gold Medal is now awarded every two years and there are silver and bronze medals also.

On 7 January 1893, a Royal Commission was set up, which, under the chairmanship of Lord Aberdare, former Home Secretary, attempted to ascertain the plight of the aged poor under the existing Poor Law. Royal interest was indicated by the bizarre presence of the Prince of Wales on the Commission; Lords Brassey and Playfair represented the House of Lords; and Joseph Chamberlain and Joseph Arch the Commons. The second Joseph, an agricultural trade unionist, was taken up by H.R.H. with whom he probably shared a preference for the young and rich. Charles Booth's concern for the very opposite made him an obvious choice and in order to balance the situation his negative namesake, Charles Loch, was also recruited along with eleven other philanthropists. It was a hopeless team and dissension broke out at once. Lord Aberdare's portrait hangs in a room at the Home Office where I often sat during another difficult and divided Inquiry (into after-care for discharged prisoners) and I looked at it with sympathy when my own Chairman was endeavouring to produce a unanimous report on an acutely controversial topic. Sad to say Lord Aberdare's health gave way under the strain and he died soon afterwards. Lord Playfair took his place and the Prince of Wales resigned so as to avoid being involved in controversy. Charles himself fell ill and went abroad for a couple of months to recuperate. When the Commission finally reported in 1895, he told Lord Playfair that despite much personal sympathy he felt he must sign the Minority Report.[1] The whole thing, as Mary had prophesied, was a great mistake.

Despairing of any useful conclusion to the Royal Commission Charles had already published in 1894 a further pamphlet on the condition of the aged poor in England and Wales. He thought it 'very dull' and went away to the United States before it came out. Mary urged him to send his sister Emily a copy and reported that 'The reviews are delicious, especially the "Daily News". What a curious, Colossal, Impassive Sphinx they think you are.' Charles did indeed send a copy to Emily, and she replied with quiet, almost repressed congratulations. Mary kept the letter. Charles was never a prophet in his own family but his brother-in-law, Philip Holt, certainly was.

He had bought up quietly, and systematically destroyed, a mass of slum houses in the Wavertree district of Liverpool. The whole area was then landscaped and laid out as a public park and presented to the city. There seems to be no record of what happened to the people who were evicted, but it is known that the enterprise cost Philip Holt (who was childless) about £450,000. He did not allow his part in this imaginative scheme to become known until the actual day of the opening ceremony. Charles attended the great celebrations and told Meg that if he had not had six children he would have tried to do something similar. Mary always spoke of Philip's act of generosity with unstinted praise.

The rhythm of work and travel and 'Proofs Proofs Proofs', three words which fill up whole days of Mary's diary, continued unabated

[1] Draft of letter only in London University Library.

for the next three years, during which time Charles was immersed in his old age pension campaign and in the *Industry Series*. On her forty-fifth birthday Mary told Charles how much his greetings meant and posted him a proof of *The Railwaymen*: 'Who did it? It's not up to the top level of crisp clearness.'

Indeed the whole *Industry Series* was not up to the crisp clearness of the *Poverty Series* because Charles's original aim of marrying the two inquiries and producing an infant explanation of poverty had misfired. While the Inquiry team under Ernest Aves collected accurate facts about the building, printing, textile and rag trades, the 'Chief' was putting his whole heart into old age problems. Therefore the *Industry Series* became a useful account of working conditions but lacked the double-punch quality of what should have been a right and left. The *Poverty Series* hit London in the eye. The *Industry Series* missed the chin. Overcrowding, in the centre of London, proved to be an uncertain test of poverty so the attempt to link the two inquiries on this premiss failed. No relevant statistics about the aged poor were included in the *Industry Series* although from this angle the extra support needed for just one unproductive member might have proved to be enough to reduce a family to penury. Nor did Charles do more than condemn 'dead end' jobs for boys when a direct link between them and untrained casual labourers might have been discovered. In 1892 he laid down that 'labour deteriorates under casual employment more quickly than its price falls', and pressed for at least the registration of casual dock labour. This proposal was not renewed in 1897. He preferred *laissez-faire* combined with more enlightened management to any form of central control, which he felt would only lower the general standard of living. He could not find that half-way house for wage earners which he advocated for those past their earning days, although he hinted that one would be necessary in the future.

'Whatever the system . . . individualist or socialist—the final cure of poverty must lie either in increasing the serviceableness of the work done; or in securing for the less capable a sufficient share of that which is produced by the more capable members of society; or a combination of them both.' Once again he reiterated that his endeavour was 'to present a way of looking at things . . . rather than an argument. . . . I have been glad to see my book furnish weapons . . . for absolutely opposed schools and can make shift to stifle my annoyance when it is occasionally quoted in support of doctrines I abhor'.

Early in 1897 Charles went down to Gracedieu alone in order to finish the *Industry Series*. 'After a walk round the garden and a romp with the dogs I am settling down to the snugness of my room. Here I shall be able to stand a siege so soon at least as my ammunition arrives, which should have been, but was not, at Whitwick when I passed this afternoon. I am concentrating all the Inquiry notebooks here up to date, a perfect mess it will be, and have also all the Old Age Pensions material for your special delectation.'

The following day he complained: 'My packages have not yet arrived which is a bore, though I can get on without them. Why bother you with this? Only that I always pour out my vexations on you. I shall stir up the people by wire if the things don't come today. Yours, Yours, C.B.' He had amusing ways of ensuring essential routine in the office and one of his aphorisms is often quoted today in Booth International: 'There's bound to be a fool at one end of a telegram. Make sure he isn't at your end.' No doubt the packages arrived safely after his stir-up!

In the spring Charles completed the last of his 'beloved' Trade volumes,[1] made a new partnership agreement in Alfred Booth and Company with his nephew, and went off to Spain for a badly needed holiday. He began his first letter home to Mary with the charming Argyle-like phrase 'your letter smoiled at me this morning' and went on to describe Seville Cathedral with its Moorish origins and beautiful tower. About to embark on his third series, *Religious Influences*, he summarised for her his reactions to the Catholic Church:

I took my early walk Cathedral-way and tried to grasp the whole idea, which is rather difficult, but I think I got it. Oh, it is a most wonderful building to the glory of God and for the religious needs of man! How very nearly the Catholic Church did succeed! Its absolute, ultimate, and eternal failure is perhaps the most hopeless thing of all in a rather hopeless world; such a revelation of the inherent wicked-ness of man. Of course, good is no less inherent, and one hopes even more persistent, but the bad always breaks out and does for great aims. Even so, Spain remains a puzzle to me. Why such an irretriev-able collapse? Why unable even to settle Cuba?

Neither the United States nor Castro would appreciate the word 'even'!

[1] Vol. IX of the *Industry Series* consists of comparisons and conclusions.

Mary wrote back from Great Cumberland Place:

I have a sort of hazy feeling about you as if you were wandering out of our ken entirely in the strange new world of Spain—new to you and yet so old—to my imagination more full of romance than anything we have seen together. From Scipio Africanus on through Visigoths, Jews and Moors and those wonderful 15th and 16th Century Spaniards, with their chivalry and enterprise, and deep yet fantastically pictures-que religion. Well, you are in the thick of it all, thinking many a thought as you go about all alone and cut off from all the people round you, but you, I know, like the savour of that sort of situation and dig deep in it to come back refreshed to the every day humdrum, that you know so well here. I sometimes think you should have been a 16th century person yourself and have gone seeking for the El Dorado with Cortés.

There is considerable truth in this phrase.

At home again Charles sped from office to church and from church to chapel. In 1898, for instance, he wrote from London about

a not unnatural misunderstanding as to my goings and comings. I do such very odd things. As I was not to sleep here 'til Sunday night, the maid supposed I would be at Gracedieu; instead I had a wonderful day amongst the Poplar churches, seeing them at all hours. It is the only way to do it so far away as Blackwall and I ended curiously with an Old Age Pensions meeting to hear Lansbury[1] on the Social Democratic Federation view. I was wanting to meet him so went there after the churches were finished and finally did not get home 'til 11.30 and I think it was 1.30 before I was in bed. I did not say a word at the meeting, only claiming acquaintance when it was over.

Today has been resting in its way, going to Hitchin on business where I left old Crack [his dog] at the kennels, quite comfortable I think. I have not seen George yet but we shall not escape talking business tonight. I have also Vaughan Nash[2] coming for Pensions. It is quite too complicated at present.

This would not usually be considered a resting day.

[1] George Lansbury, Cabinet Minister in second Labour Government.
[2] Vaughan Nash, C.B., C.V.O., the well-known journalist who was Private Secretary to Campbell-Bannerman 1900–8, and Asquith 1908–12.

Complicated or not, when a Newnham friend of Meg's, Charlotte Wollaston,[1] came to stay at Gracedieu in August she was taken for a turn in the garden by her host. 'Smell those lupins,' he said, 'what do they remind you of? Is it Japanese boxes?' His sudden laughter at the absurdity of the suggestion made her look at him directly. She was startled by his beauty and informality and having been brought up not to speak unless spoken to, and then only to agree, remained tongue-tied and awkward. Perhaps to break through this barrier Charles burst out into detailed aspects of old age pensions, talking and walking very fast up and down the lawn. Charlotte was shocked: '*Everybody*?' she asked, 'You can't mean *everybody* to have a pension at seventy!'

The Salisbury Government set up yet another committee under Lord Rothschild's chairmanship which declared all pension schemes to be impracticable. This opinion met with relief and approval throughout the House of Commons. Paupers had no influence in Westminster but further afield their needs and Charles's views were accepted. New Zealand brought in a Pensions Act in 1898 and at home Cambridge offered him an honorary degree of science which he accepted with unfeigned delight. The Master of Trinity, Dr Montagu Butler, a friend from Harrow days, in a felicitous address linked Burke's words about Howard, the penal reformer, with Charles's patient work and effective sympathy for those who lived after years of toil below the Poverty Line. In the following year, 1899, the Royal Society elected him a Fellow, and he replied to Meg's congratulations that at his age a man would be lucky not to have A.S.S. written after his name. But in fact of all the honours that came his way he valued his F.R.S. the highest, and it completed this modest man's happiness and wonderment at being received at the round table of learning.

At the end of the same year he returned from a trip to Magdeburg taken in connection with his Inquiry, to address an Old Age Pensions Conference at Browning Hall in London, which had been arranged by Herbert Stead.[2] As a result of the success of this meeting a series of conferences were held at five great industrial centres in England and one in Glasgow, and Charles undertook to address them all. That of

[1] Charlotte Wollaston married the painter Fritz Shepherd.
[2] F. Herbert Stead, Hon. Sec. of the National Committee of Organised Labour, patiently and quietly formed pressure groups in various great cities to assist the cause of old age pensions.

18 January 1899 in Newcastle was followed by another at Leeds on 24 February, which he described as 'a very good meeting . . . but not quite such smooth sailing as before, there being a strongish contingent of Young Socialists who regarded pensions for old people as fiddling work. However, the sense of the meeting was pulled together by Stead very cleverly . . .' After describing many meetings and journeys Charles ends this letter by writing: 'I have looked carefully over the MS. [of the final Pensions Proposal] on my way up and soon grasped that it had your general approval. I took all your suggestions and have sent it to Argyle for the printers. We shall see how it looks in type. My present plan is to get it published and done with. Thine, C.B.'

A couple of months later *Old Age Pensions and the Aged Poor: a Proposal* was published. In seventy-five pages Charles had assembled data for the United Kingdom, and recommended that weekly pensions of 7 shillings should be available at the Post Office for all those over the age of 70. Taking the census of 1891 as his basis, Charles estimated that the cost would be only £16 million for the United Kingdom, as he believed that 15 per cent of those eligible would be too well-to-do to bother with collecting their dues. He himself had assured the 1893 Royal Commission on the Aged Poor that were his proposals to be implemented, he would certainly apply in person for his pension each week. I often think of him as I collect mine.

Charles concluded his 1899 Proposal with moving tributes to two men: to Mr R. P. Hookham of Islip, Oxfordshire, the author of a pamphlet published in 1879 entitled 'Outlines of a Scheme for Dealing with Pauperism' (a non-contributory scheme); and to Canon Lewery Blackley, whose article on National Insurance which came out in that same year advocated a contributory scheme. 'From each seed a great tree has grown,' wrote Charles, 'Under which tree shall we pitch our tent?' Then he quoted Mr Hookham verbatim: 'As an obscure individual thus attempting to thrust into notice a scheme of such magnitude I may incur the risk even of ridicule: I shall however have satisfied my conscience in discharging what I believe to be a duty.' Charles concluded with charming humility: 'To the writer of these words, I very humbly dedicate this book.' The same year a Select Committee under Mr Chaplin's chairmanship was set up to re-examine Charles's proposals and although it recommended that pensions for the deserving poor should be paid through the Post Office, no political action was taken.

In 1900 both New South Wales and the State of Victoria brought in old age pensions. This wide-ranging recognition gave Charles the confidence to review and reassemble the various volumes on poverty, trades and religious influences which had come out year by year. While he was away in America in the spring of 1900, Mary worked hard at preparing his Inquiry notes for a second edition. 'I have had an interesting morning over Clapham and Wandsworth and Putney,' she wrote in one letter; and in another 'I have been reading away at South London and really I don't think your account of the Bermondsey, Rotherhithe and Lambeth districts could be much improved. You paint a wonderfully vivid picture and it makes a deep impression. It is rather horrible, I think. One feels tremendously what a precious thin veneer our civilisation is. . . . Dear, you must feel far from all this now with Matthieu and his factory and his ideas, and Heaven knows what! Anything rather than the problems of poverty and religion.'

Charles wrote back from Boston, commenting on Matthieu's process of tanning which called for

very careful thought. . . . We shall find a lot to talk about in this before I can lay off and turn to the finishing of the book. Your good words of approval of the parts you have read warm me up and will make it far easier for me to fight through to a finish. It will be awfully difficult to get it really right: to say enough and not too much; to speak the truth without hurting many good people's feelings terribly and somehow or other produce the right effect, but we will do our best, you and I— and you and I are a match for anything when we are put to it!

This time all the fascinatingly diffuse evidence of religious activity proved as difficult to analyse as the subject chosen by the Ocean Row Minister—the number of victims of the Flood—which had made Charles laugh long ago; but his complete involvement, writing in the first person throughout, gave cohesion to the nine volumes. He never tired of attending churches and chapels and open-air meetings of all kinds and watching the reactions and classifying the social background of those around him. Mary could not abide skipping about from one service to another. She gave too much of herself at each one not to be exhausted, and soon stopped accompanying Charles on these excursions. Neither engaged nor unsympathetic he became in the end profoundly disappointed by his findings. 'The treats and blankets which swell the lists of mothers and children on the books' and 'the uneasy sense of internal rivalry between denominations' upset him. Even the belief which he really shared that 'everything that is beneficial may be brought under the aegis of religion' disturbed him when it was put forward by clergymen. He felt that their faith should be 'an intimate possession of the soul, perhaps not understood by the individual and very difficult of interpretation by others'. The most penetrating remark he made on the subject touches the heart: 'If the churches instead of demanding of the people "How can we help you?" were to ask even of the poorest and the worst "How can you help us?" a road might open out: and the battle would be won if it were found as perhaps it would [be], that even the poorest and the worst would claim their right to share the work on equal terms, asking for their part not how can you help me, but how can I help you.' It was Charles's deepest wish that the poorest and the worst should claim their right to offer as well as receive.

In February 1901 the Booths were together at Gracedieu, with George and their favourite young cousin, Theodore Llewelyn-Davies. 'We had a quiet day,' wrote Mary to Meg, 'your Father reading us his Paper on the "Improvement of Locomotion" for our, and principally for Theodore's criticism, he and Theodore working away at it together afterwards with excellent results. In the evening George and Theodore read us aloud taking different parts in the most amusing play, "Captain Brassbound's Conversion", quite the best of Bernard Shaw's "New Plays for Puritans".'

That spring Charles worked principally at the new edition and found 'that the North West, like the North, has to be all re-written'. Once again when the business claimed his attention he went off to New York, leaving a mass of material for Mary's digestion, including B. S. Rowntree's *Poverty: A Study of Town Life*,[1] which proved that the same proportion of people were in want in York as in London.

Early in 1902 Charles and Mary were hard at work editing *Life and Labour*. 'C.B. began reading the book in the evening' is the entry on 15 February and 'Read book' appears continually during the following weeks. Friends, relations, young and old, trooped in and out of the house for lunch, tea and dinner, and yet somehow the work went on. Sometimes they read together in the evening, but more often they worked separately. On 9 March, for instance, 'C.B. went to the Political and Economic Society' and was off to Liverpool the following morn-

[1] B. S. Rowntree based this study on Charles Booth's survey of the Tower Hamlets.

ing, back again to dinner on the third day, and away to Gracedieu for a night with Mary to see the builders about alterations. The Webbs were constant visitors all this time both at Gracedieu and in London, because of their interlocking interests. Their hostess tried to be fair to the 'curious pair, so clever and in many ways so good, but so profoundly unsatisfactory, and always with the uncomfortable note of disingenuousness'.

Charles added a new guest and a new venture to Gracedieu life by inviting Baron Bronislaw Rynkiewicz to stay. This Polish entrepreneur had acquired during his travels in South America various important concessions, among them the Manaos Harbour Concession, on the Upper Amazon. Over the years, just as the Booth Steamship Company had grown in power by assimilating the Singlehurst Line, so had the ships themselves grown in size. It was therefore becoming more and more difficult to land cargo from big ships in a river which rose and fell fifty-four feet between the high and low seasons. The Baron was convinced that piers could be driven into the subsoil of the river bank, and that a harbour could be built which would obviate all the difficulties and restrictions of landing cargo at Manaos. Charles wrote to Mary from Gracedieu:

> This Manaos Harbour Works is a big affair, and I think we must take it up. . . . I had a great day yesterday. First the Baron and his scheme for about two hours, nine 'til eleven; then a failure to communicate with Liverpool by telephone; then an hour's letter [writing] to Liverpool; then Stead and the future of Humanity from three to four-thirty; then half an hour with the proofs and secretariat, then proofs, proofs, proofs in train until bedtime: and a good Bale[1] tea at 8.40 p.m. Today I have described already—weather delicious—place lovely—Adonis [a new puppy] sweet but staggering. Take care of yourself. Enclosed is the North East map and its notes.

At the end of April Charles described

one of the days when perfection is reached by nature. It is of the bright, windy kind, with crystal air and brilliant sunshine and every green leaf rejoices. Would you were here! Oh, can't it be managed in some way? Is it not more important than anything that you should escape from London and come to Gracedieu and to me, or rather with

---

[1] Mrs Bale, the gardener's wife, cherished her Master when Gracedieu was empty.

me if it is in any way possible on Wednesday. Oh, how nice to have you! Tuesday is our wedding day. Well, I shall see you at London just to say goodnight at any rate. . . . As to book maps etc. you ought to have had Map B and I think Argyle has D ready also, with its notes, and E. and F. to follow. I sent you G. The illustration chapters are delayed. We have changed the type. I am working away on South London, and am ahead of the office now, but still a little behind my own timetable; impossible to keep steadily at it for bothering interruptions.

The interruptions included a hectic three months in the United States and a busy autumn at home dealing with the incursion of a subsidized German shipping line into the Booths' trading area. In 1903, having arranged to go to Brazil to see about the new harbour at Manaos, Charles had to complete his final volume before sailing; so he established himself comfortably at Gracedieu in February and worked away alone but for Mary's advice. 'Your letter is welcome reading,' he told her, 'and what you say about portions of the "star book" encourages me.' (From this date he wrote the sign of a star, not the word spelt out.) 'Until I have a little word from you I never rely on not having to make a fresh start! and thankful to do it, but I get those turn-backs and fresh starts often now without your aid. Such a one was yesterday when after finishing "Housing" and packing it up I began on "Expansion" and wasted the remainder of the day. I think I am on the right course today.' The Star Book was to be a synthesis of old and new thoughts, which would complete the Inquiry series.

On 19th Charles began his letter with a cheerful 'Hurrah! I got my full 3½ hours clear this morning. . . . Oh this book! I must get it finished and the days are easily wasted. I have an engagement of some kind every single day next week, including a whole day for Lincoln which I can't avoid and Liverpool really is due though I hope to shuffle out of it. I shall try to fit everything into next week in London and then get back here. I have made a big stride with "Expansion" yesterday and this morning and think it will now be all right. You will be receiving "Housing" from Miss Duncan.' Referring to the District Nurse Scheme which he and Mary were setting up in the neighbourhood, he adds, 'The young woman from York I think most likely. The other is from Bristol, more stick-in-the-mud!' In addition to everything else he was interviewing applicants for the post.

131

On the 22nd he wrote that all went well with himself and his work: 'Weather grey but the woods charming, the catkins are just shaking themselves out, one of the most beautiful sights of the whole year. I wish you could wander with me in this fairy scene. On reading over the last section of the book I found myself in complete agreement with you. I think now there is little doubt about omitting the last two pages. I wonder what Aves's criticism will be, if any ?'

Mary replied:

Your walk sounded very good. I have read all you left with me of the 'star volume' and like the Police and the Drink part very much. As for the Poor Law chapter, I have no criticism as to wording, only a certain doubt as to how far it is desirable to bring the pension question into the book. I dare say it is right but don't feel sure. Also I am not sure whether the excessive colloquialism of some of the quotations might not be modified. After all, what passed the lips of your interviewed people is not a sacred text, verbally inspired. I am having the type-written copy you left me packed and sent. One or two insignificant comments. You say the working class if interested intellectually [in religion] at all, is struck by the Unitarians. Is this so ? Not surely to more than a very trifling extent. The statement is peculiar and it might be worth while to put in a note as to the authority for it.

On 1 March Charles thanked his 'dearest' for her letter and the bits of proof:

I am sorry you had to bother with them while still so ill but everything and everybody must be sacrificed to what I have to do every time. I don't yet see my way to cutting out the whole of Section IV but I have cut it down and drawn its teeth and certainly made it less objection-able and shall have another proof to see if it will do. . . . I think I have taken all your alterations. The Lazarus piece is certainly better cut as it struck another note. The whole will read much shorter and sharper and I hope less pretentious than it did.

The next day Charles's work 'stuck fast. I made, however, so many false starts that I went to bed and laughed at my absolute incapacity to finish my own book but today has gone better. . . . Eh Gad! I hope so for the time gets short!' On the 3rd he wrote: 'As to Volume VII[1]. . . .

---

[1] *Summary of Religious Influences.*

I feel that I have reached the "as good as I could" point. As to the final volume, that point I can't hope to reach but I hope to leave it in a decent way to get it out and shut the door behind me. I don't want to write anything more for years, if at all, or at least not publish. No magazine articles for me, but I admit all you say and shall try to go as safely as I can in my notes on "Administration". I think I have made a fair start with Part IV conclusion.'

Twenty-four hours later he wrote: 'It is delightful here today, bright, fine and cold and just enough wind to make it lively for Mrs. Duggins who pursues the fugitive leaf on the lawn. [She was known as the "weeding-woman".] I have actually written the conclusion of "star volume" to the very end; Oh Gloria! and I think it is all right. We shall have it in typewritten copy from Miss Duncan on Monday I expect.'

Charles always sent advance proofs to those who had co-operated in the Inquiry. In one case the result was unfortunate and Mary wrote about 'Mr. Herbert Stead's furious epistle. He is in a rage about your description of Browning Hall. What are you going to do? This is a foretaste of the chorus of blame that we have been expecting. The accusation of listening to gossip will be made again and again I feel sure. Oh dear! But you will have to modify about the non-religious basis of Mr Stead's work. When a man says he does it all from religious motives and to a religious end, one must believe him.' On the 15th Charles answered Mr Stead's letter and sent Mary a copy of his reply: 'I needed you very badly indeed but it could not wait so it goes. It is an excellent object lesson. Few, if any, have the same personal feelings to be roused. They will simply curse me and pass on. I am very glad to be going away and hope you will be thick-skinned enough not to mind whatever is said.'

Back in London Mary sent Meg a description of the Inquiry team at work:

We had a happy day with Mr. Aves, your father and I, bringing back old times when you were small children and Mr. Aves and Mr. Llewellyn-Smith constantly pervaded the home atmosphere amid ceaseless colloquies over the condition of the pauper and the working man. We were all three sitting at our tea, deep in the rating question over cup after cup, when to us entered Mr. Mumm.[1] He was rather disappointed to find neither you nor Imogen and still more when he found us quite unequal to change our subject. On, on we went! Round

[1] Meg's publisher.

Mr. Mumm's devoted head there whirled methods of assessment, belts of open space, fringes of population, et cetera, 'til he looked more bewildered every minute. Then Mr. Aves and your father announced they must go to work again.

Working with Charles meant much more than general discussion.

During these months, filled with triviality, travelling and ill health, Charles and Mary had managed to go through the proofs of the new edition of *Life and Labour*. Mary had originally stipulated that her intensive work on Charles's volumes must be kept absolutely secret, but of course the other secretaries knew. In August 1900, for instance, Charles wrote to Mr Aves, 'My wife is at work upon Box 1 but, like the rest, is working independently—thus I shall have no less than six critical versions to help me when I pick up the threads again.' When he rejected criticism he did so bluntly: 'Dear Aves, I liked it as I had it and so it must stand.' But advice was often taken. Again, in February 1901, after apologising that his letter 'was so ambiguously expressed' he explained, 'I have oceans to do with the revision of Part 1 but my wife is "out of work". She has been over the Outer North and all South London . . . but has not yet had any of the Inner North and West.'

On 25 March 1903 the new edition of *Life and Labour* came out, bound in white vellum with gold lettering. For once Charles was at home to read reviews and receive congratulations. Beatrice Potter's name occurs on the title page immediately beneath that of Charles Booth, followed by all his other lieutenants in alphabetical order. A diagram was included to show how many volumes each assistant helped to produce and Jesse Argyle's name occurs on every single volume.

On 1 April Charles set off in the *Obidense* for Brazil, and wrote a last note to Mary: 'I shall now be quite free at last—no book, no business, a deck chair and a tale or history book in my hand and dreams in my heart. Oh my dear I wish you could sit in a chair by my side on the deck! . . . We have a very decent set on board but I play the old man generally, a rôle that suits me very well and shall be mine, I hope, for many a year to come, with my young wife to keep me up to the mark.'

Mary's daily reports did not reach Charles until 1st May. 'The reviews in the religious papers are very good—the Wesleyan papers really heaped coals of fire; they are so candid, not denying that they are cut to the quick but admitting your fairness and impartiality. Good reviews from Jewish papers and numbers of ones in secular papers.'

A Mr Millar, the owner of disgraceful tenements, had threatened to bring a libel action. Malcolm Macnaghten had engaged a solicitor and hoped to settle without a court case, but a writ had been served. When the case came before Mr Justice Bucknall he rejected Mr Millar's application for an injunction against Charles Booth's re-publication of Volume I. On 22 April Mary described the circumstances: 'Mr Llewellyn-Smith and George Duckworth spoke in such a convincing way that the Judge soon said that he had heard enough and asked the other side what they had to object to. They could argue but little and the injunction was refused.'

Out of reach of vexatious litigation, Charles described a dinner on board the *Obidense*:

just our own employees, together with Brocklehurst's men and those of the Amazon Company. The task of bringing about harmony between our people and still more the Harbour Works and the Amazon Company, is I fear beyond my powers, but I must do anything I can and hope that time will bring about improved conditions. It is curious how very difficult it is to get people to work together. We never managed it with Brocklehurst's except in Brazil and it is all we can possibly do to prevent our own Officers at Manaos getting by the ears.

In June negotiations were 'just at the greatest moment of suspense and ten days more may decide many things which are still in doubt. Success is, I think, quite certain at every point but delays there may well be, and difficulties to be met and conquered daily. Never was anything more interesting in the way of business.'

In his absence the home team prepared the Star volume for publication. Mary was not happy about the chapter on the economic position of the different classes:

It is full of illuminating and characteristic ideas, but terribly concentrated and hard to follow. I think I can make it easier and I am in communication with Mr. Aves about it. The Religious Series continues to be enormously reviewed. Most of the reviews are very good and appreciative and others simply laudatory and unintelligent. The Wesleyans do mind very much and Dr. Nichol in the 'British Weekly' has started a sort of campaign of refutation. He has written to all the Non-Conformist clergy you have described, asking them what they think of your accuracy and prints their replies. The other denominations take it very well. 'The Pilot' says that there isn't a dull page in the book.

Charles was greatly pleased by the 'marvellously kind' reviews which arrived in batches. He was glad 'to know that "star volume" gets on and hope it will be out long before I am back. All you and the others do to make it read smoother and express itself more clearly, I thankfully welcome in advance.' This was exactly what Mary's critical and constructive work was doing:

I feel the chapter on the Economics of Industry is really too involved and puzzling for people not used to your methods of thought and expression, and I am not sure about the antithesis at the beginning. All the same, I don't like altering it much for fear of losing some flavour of meaning. I feel that I simplify but coarsen it and am not sure whether you will really like the result, though I know you will make the best of it. In the Public House Chapter I think we are going to alter the paragraph about the possible downfall in the value of licences, making it more positive because there seems to be no doubt that the decline can no longer be spoken of as 'in the future'. Then with regard to your new bit about the omitted subjects, very good it is. I want to put it in not after page 90 but on page 214, just before the end and . . . Mr. Argyle seems to agree with me. The writing of the piece itself you no doubt expected us to pull about and Mr. Aves and I have been at it.

She enclosed a letter of thanks from Mr Lansbury for the gift of *Life and Labour.* 'He is a convinced Socialist, he says, but he sees only in the revivifying influence of religion the way to better things.'

Later in May Mary wrote:

I have enjoyed down to the ground all my little work at the book . . . . I hope you will approve of what we have done: I think you will. The Secretaries are all delightful people to do anything with . . . I have been surprised to find how very ready Mr. Argyle is; and how conciliatory; he has got something quite big about him and never makes a fuss about little things and he has no vanity. He doesn't care a bit whether a thing is settled in his way or no as long as he thinks it will do; and do justice to what you want to say. I fear you will be horrified at our delays but at any rate we shall be out before you return, which is the great thing. Mr. Argyle writes that he has a little girl, his wife and the baby doing well.

After a list of various items which awaited his return, she turns to the question of preferential tariffs: 'We all try hard to make up our minds about Chamberlain's new departure and we long for light and leading and for your return. Theodore [Llewelyn-Davies], very strong, of course, in opposition, has been seeing a great deal of Mr. Balfour and doesn't think much of him though he has fallen quite a victim to the personal charm. He says Mr. Balfour just loves a debate and is too much pleased with any ingenious argument against or for his own view.'

At last Mary could send a letter to Charles on dry land: 'It seems too wonderful to be writing to you in Paris and to think that on Wednesday this long time of separation will be over and we two together again, talking over all. 'Star Book' is out, thank Heaven! and looks very handsome.'

It sold out almost at once because the general public hoped to find in it the key to a new way through to better conditions for all. In this they were disappointed. I have chosen and condensed into a short résumé[1] some of the striking paragraphs describing the habits of the people, economic conditions, housing and transport for those who wish to sample Charles Booth's style of thought. His actual recommendations for unified Poor Law and old age pensions seem absurdly tame after the variety and detail of the Breughel-like pictures of London he had already painted. In his concluding essay, 'Things as they are and as they move', he reiterates that to suggest some directions in which advance could be made was no part of his original design, which was solely to observe and chronicle. 'Perhaps,' he writes, 'the qualities of mind which enable a man to make this inquiry are the least of all likely to give him that elevation of soul, sympathetic insight and sublime confidence which must go to the making of a great regenerating teacher. . . .' Only Charles would have smiled at the adjective 'sublime' even as he conjured up in all seriousness the image of the regenerative teacher who could transform the future. He had the knack of giving truth a twist of fun which makes all his notes so readable.

Mary had a more deferential and derivative style and she never lost the hope, which Charles could not share, that a higher agency would help man to make the rough places smooth; this slightly altered the emphasis. According to her children[2] she wrote the last paragraph and indeed she had earned the last word:

[1] See Appendix E, p. 223.
[2] With the exception of her youngest son.

The dry bones that lie scattered over the long valley that we have traversed together lie before my reader. May some great soul, master of a subtler and nobler alchemy than mine, disentangle the confused issues, reconcile the apparent contradictions in aim, melt and commingle the various influences for good into one divine uniformity of effort and make these dry bones live so that the streets of our Jerusalem may sing with joy.

She had set her heart on ending the seventeen volumes with an exclamation mark, as the quotation is governed by the subjunctive. She not only marked it particularly in typescript, page proof, and in a letter to the printers, but went round herself to Floral Street to see that it had been included. When the 'Star Book' arrived she opened it at once (watched by her daughter Imogen) at the last page, and saw with the keenest chagrin that her efforts had been frustrated. Nevertheless, when she turned to the dedication, as the reader may do now, her own heart must have sung with joy. Charles had written: 'My work now completed has been from first to last dedicated to my wife without whose constant sympathy, help and criticism it could never have been begun, continued or ended at all. C.B.' These words, written in pencil, on a grubby little piece of paper, much worked over and rubbed out and written in again, were the chief of all Mary's store of treasures, and delineate the root and the fruit of their marriage.

The Life and Labour of the People of London was begun in 1886 and finished in 1903.

IX
THE DAILY ROUND
1891–1903

There comes a time in every happy marriage when the original charm and unexpected turns of events fuse into a recurrent theme with a dominant rhythm. The price my grandmother paid for this masterful music—constant crippling headaches—she kept as secret as possible and endured in the darkness of her bedroom. Travel and solitude cured Charles's almost annual digestive breakdowns. Her zest for family life and his for commerce never failed, and pen and ink conversations solaced their lonely hours. Charles found stimulation in business contacts while Mary relied more than she realised on the companionship of friends. Few and precious are those in the joint confidence of any married couple, and still more was this so in the Booths' case.

Caroline Crompton, Charles's favourite first cousin, and the heroine of that unconventional excursion to Brighton which led to the Booths' marriage, was one of these rewarding friends. After working for some years as Bursar of Girton, she met and married Professor George Croom Robertson, a delightful Scotsman. They lived in Bayswater, and their presence at Gracedieu or in London was as natural as the seasons. Mary, for instance, never 'called' on 'Dear Carrie' in London because they were so intimately in touch. Early in 1891 the onset of cancer threatened this long association, and Carrie's death the following year was a bitter blow. Charles had shared the early days in Liverpool with Carrie; they had written for the *Colony*; they had walked in the Lake District; they had laughed and danced in each other's houses and they had each made a success of their lives away from Liverpool. Mary, always on her guard against family jealousy, could express her pride in him to the Robertsons without fear of misinterpretation, and relied on Carrie's independent affectionate nature. To the day of her own death she kept Carrie's photograph in her bedroom, and treasured her obituary notice in *The Times*, which speaks highly of the Bursar of Girton.

Mary, however, never believed in higher education for women. Having managed so well herself on her own, she had absolutely no conception of how difficult it might be for less dedicated people to apply themselves to serious study without guidance and stimulation. Any reference to women's higher education always brought forth from her a vein of caustic mockery, with which Charles entirely agreed, although he gave a remarkable encomium to the 'extravagance' of the School Board in the East End: 'It was worth much to carry high the flag of education. . . . We have full value for all that has been spent.' This antipathy to the rising female 'flag of education' cut them off from a ripening process which should have been part of the Inquiry, and might have given Mary another dimension in the years of single responsibility ahead.

Indeed, I think that my grandmother suffered unconsciously from emotional and even intellectual isolation. Without an effective mother or brother, and with little or no contact with the Booth family, she had also broken with Beatrice who had been almost a sister. Carrie's death deprived her of the last remaining intimate friend with whom she could discuss family problems.

My grandmother's determination never to delegate—itself a product of the tragedy of Paulina's death—led her into the opposite pitfall. As she herself was under tremendous pressure, the younger daughters grew up with insufficient discipline and companionship, feeling insecure and uncertain. Although very critical of her own mother for spoiling the baby of the family, Mary could not resist doing exactly the same. Tarla's mixture of delicacy and intelligence swept away her judgement, and drew forth the tenderest protective love. My grandfather knew better than anyone else that her sympathy was like a blood transfusion and her contumely completely crushing. He also knew that his namesake was being mishandled but took no action to redress the balance. There was absolutely no one else with sufficient standing to suggest, let alone ensure, a different approach. In the long run it was the youngest child, not the less favoured ones, who was critical of his mother, and found life disappointing.

As the years went by my grandmother reached the point when she could no longer discuss anything controversial with any semblance of equanimity. I think this was partly due to her isolated imperial position in a large household of children and servants, where decisions had to be made and discussion was not possible. The habit of command fitted her well, she wore it with grace, and found it hard to throw off even when Charles longed for her to abandon her benevolently autocratic throne for a few days' holiday. The clay had set.

Meanwhile, new friends were made. Mary had always been devoted to Charles's young cousin, Arthur Llewelyn-Davies,[1] and while assisting in his courtship of Sylvia du Maurier, she became very fond of this fascinating family from France. George du Maurier, the Punch illustrator, had had to take to writing and lecturing because his eyesight was failing. What seemed at the time a tragedy had a happy outcome. Indeed, to later generations the descriptions of Passy and Paris in his novels seem more significant than his illustrations of the lighter side of English social life, as seen by Mr Punch. Mary enjoyed every aspect of his gift for expression, and wrote to Charles about

. . . Mr. du Maurier's lecture at The Royal Institution for which Sir William Grove[2] had sent us tickets. It was delightful—the lecture I mean—Mr. du Maurier has the gift of perfect simplicity. You could hardly imagine anything more simple, even childish, than the lecture, full of witty turns and a sort of gentle mockery, keeping us attentive from first word to last; waiting now and then, looking round . . . with a rather timid, kindly smile . . . for us to finish our uncontrollable bursts of laughter before he went on again.

The Robert Holts remained staunch friends, and Charles and Mary went to Liverpool to take part in the festivities connected with their silver wedding. 'Real warm feeling for her and her husband shown on all sides,' wrote Mary in her diary; it was as Lally's bridesmaid that she had first seen Charles Booth. During this period another old friend reappeared in Mary's life: 'Charlotte joined us with her husband to take care of Great Cumberland Place.' My grandmother told many stories about Mrs Rumbold's imperturbable manner and effective action. Once, for instance, a deafening crash was heard in the middle of the night. Mary and Mrs Rumbold met on the landing, both having armed themselves with fire-irons. As they reached the stairs a second crash made them pause, and look at each other. 'Shall I scream, Ma'am?' asked Mrs Rumbold, in her quiet, deferential voice. In fact, the snow was lying so heavily on both basement skylights that each had broken in turn.

[1] See the Fletcher family tree, p. 232.
[2] Sir William Grove compiled *Grove's Dictionary of Music and Musicians*.

A chance meeting with Mr Leslie Stephen in Kensington Gardens led to a lasting friendship. As editor of the *Dictionary of National Biography*, and President of the Alpine Society, his combination of genuine scholarship with intrepidity on mountain peaks instantly appealed to Mary. Invited to tea in Hyde Park Gate the following week, she met— and immediately lost her heart to—his second wife. Leslie Stephen's first marriage in 1862 had been to Minnie Thackeray, the younger daughter of the novelist. Her sister, Anne, lived with them until Minnie died in childbirth eight years later. In 1877 Anne married Richmond Ritchie, and Leslie married the beautiful widow of Herbert Duckworth. The Duckworth children were called George, Gerald and Stella and, as has already been mentioned, George became one of Charles's honorary Inquiry secretaries. Virginia the author, Vanessa the painter, and Adrian and Thoby were children of the second marriage.

In October 1892 Mary and Charles took a holiday on their own for once. They went to St Ives and called on the Stephens. 'All of them at home,' wrote Mary, 'Dear, beautiful people. Delicious day. Went for a long walk with Mr. Stephen, Stella, her brother Adrian and C.B. to a cliff overlooking St. Michael's Mount. Had nice talks with Mr. Stephen.' The following day 'Mrs. Stephen rubbed my neck and made it better'. This astonishingly beautiful, sad-looking woman had an unexpected gift for the homely and comfortable. The Booths went on to Penzance and Porthgwarra. Day after day passed in the same way with long walks, 'heavenly weather and beauty never to be forgotten'. When they said 'goodbye to dear Porthgwarra', Mary returned alone to London. This was the Booths' first real holiday together in all the twenty-one years of their married life. It was a blissful, contented and romantic time—the honeymoon that they did not have when they were first married.

Mrs Leslie Stephen's early death was a real loss to Mary, whose letter of grief and condolence drew from the reserved and sensitive widower a terse but moving reply. He gave her a photograph of his wife, which she kept in her bedroom beside that of Carrie all her life. The friendship with Leslie grew and deepened, but they continued to call each other Mrs Booth and Mr Stephen—or Sir Leslie, as he became soon after.

At the beginning of 1893 Mary's impression of Gladstone, still leader of the Opposition, corresponded with that of his Royal Mistress:

You will be amused to hear that Alice Dugdale invited me to see Mr. and Mrs. Gladstone on Saturday. I went and was introduced at once to Mrs. Gladstone, who talked most graciously and then went across the room to bring up her husband to be introduced. I felt rather comic but sat down on a little sofa all alone with the great G.O.M., who talked away. Very soon we two were joined by Mr. Herbert Paul,[1] who began a brilliant literary conversation, wandering from Froude to Taine, Newman, the Church of England and Rome; anything but politics which the G.O.M. skilfully avoided. . . . Mr. Paul told me afterwards that he expected every moment that Mr. Gladstone was going to announce himself a Liberal Unionist[2] to please me. Well, I am flattered of course, and pleased with the notice, but I don't like him a bit better than I did before. As I sat close to him, he all huddled up with his chin in his collar, I thought he was rather like an old, grey vulture, but this is very ungrateful for he was most kind and so was she.

Back in Leicestershire, Mary did what she could for those involved in a local miners' strike:

One gets strangely mixed in one's feelings—fonder and fonder of the people as one becomes more thoroughly disillusioned from the ideal view of them. Today Mrs. Wardle, who has been receiving up to 36/– a week of strike pay, came to ask assistance. I told her good-humouredly that she was one of our rich people and whilst we had so many poor to see to, the rich must stand aside, whereat she grinned good-humouredly enough too. Her daughter came up with her baby and asked help. I told her her husband was getting work from Henson, whereat she smiled and went off. The inevitable Griffin family arrived also, telling the servants simply that they had come for their breakfasts.

When the miners' strike came to an end Mr Frank Pickering, Secretary of the Leicestershire miners, wrote to ask Charles for an interview to discuss the terms of the settlement. The phrasing is unusually touching: 'I hope this will find you well, as it leaves me not very well at present.' The two men met and remained on friendly terms thereafter.

[1] A well-known Liberal journalist who married Richmond Ritchie's sister Elinor.
[2] Liberal Unionists opposed Gladstone's Irish Home Rule policy.

The Bishop of London, Dr Creighton, also became a friend, although when he first came to dine with Charles his host was too ill to appear. Strain connected with the Royal Commission and complete overwork had eroded his health to danger point. When he was able to travel Mary took him to Palermo by easy stages for a long convalescence.

They got there in February 1893 'after an awful night; a very poor ship and a wild evening; ship tossing; C.B. trying to sleep downstairs; M.C.B. trying to enjoy the night upstairs, holding on to the seat to keep from rolling off. Strange experience. The ship sprang a leak in the night, and the men were at the pumps early in the morning. The sight of Palermo and the coast line very beautiful.' This adventurous voyage brought out all Mary's love of the sea, of the night, and her spirited reaction to physical danger. At the end of the week they moved to Agrigento—'Hot Southern feeling in the air; lemon groves innumerable and orange trees. Streets more steep, more picturesque and effective and poverty-stricken than any I have yet seen. A sort of epitome of poor, beautiful Italy.' Charles began to sketch and to 'feel more soldier-like'. Then, to complete Mary's happiness, she 'made friends with two nice English women who turned out to be friends of the de Lisles and Mrs. Herrick, and heaps of other people in England'. This sense of identity with home, was to Mary, when abroad, what a dash of salt is to a boiled egg. The travellers went on to Rome and Mary thought St Peter's 'enormous, dull, profoundly secular', but the Forum appealed to her as 'the most exciting place I have ever been in'.

Once back in London the Booth life went on along the old lines, as recorded in Mary's diary: (23 June 1803) 'Delightful talks with dear Edith and Mr. Holman Hunt; To Economic Club in the evening with C.B.—Co-operation, Production and Distribution: keen discussion between the Webbs and the Co-op men. Dodo to cricket with Mrs. Spender and to the Holman Hunts in the evening. Chicks to swim. M.C.B. and Tarla to buy fancy things for Meg and Imogen at Burnetts.' (24 June) 'The Marshalls came. In the evening Professor Foxwell, Harry and Mary Fletcher[1] dined here. Harry, Mary and Dodo to Lohengrin. M.C.B. and C.B. to uncovering of Mr. Goschen's portrait and to his Address on "The Ethicks of Economics". Met all the faithful.' Mary was loyal to the core, but it is obvious that she found 'the faithful' rather heavy going, and would so much rather have met the Holman Hunts or been to *Lohengrin* than have studied 'Co-operation,

[1] Charles's cousins (see the Fletcher family tree), p. 232.

Production and Distribution' among the statisticians. Her turn for enjoyment came in July when Charles took her to the garden party at Marlborough House, where she 'saw all the Royalties beautifully, as well as the Gladstones, Salisburys, Stanleys, Indian Princes and a great many friends'.

What did she wear? In her diary for 1893 there is a list of her dresses for the past five years. A grey cotton, a black spot, a heather skirt and jacket and another of drab stuff, make up the morning list. In the evening she wore a black crêpe, a black and white silk and even a yellow brocade. Her boots were made by Marshall and Willett and her evening shoes were black and beaded. A grey fur-lined cloak and a golf cape are listed as 'Mantles' (she never played golf). As for 'Hats', two only are tersely described: 'One grand. One common.' She enjoyed dressing for an occasion such as a dance or a wedding, but was absolutely indifferent to everyday clothes.

She was also indifferent to the properties of various medicines, keeping several old prescriptions in her medicine cupboard, all labelled 'Precipitated Chalk'. The contents were often a surprise. Writing the following year to Charles who was abroad with Meg she sent her this message: 'I am covered with shame and confusion of face in having treated her so atrociously in the matter of tooth-powder. She must have thought she had fallen in the way of an anarchist bomb.' A gunpowder plot? She adds, 'How happy I will be when our two dear folk are with us for Sunday morning. What will you have for breakfast, Miss Margaret? Eggs, bacon, sausages? Get Mr. Booth his hot milk. Oh that will be joyful!'

Charles's breakfast was hot milk. In the evening he much preferred tea or coffee, brown bread and butter, a boiled egg and an apple on a tray, at about 6 p.m., to long, set dinners. This gave him more time to work, as well as suiting his exhausted digestion better, but on the right occasion he enjoyed a good dish and a glass of wine. When he dined with his family he very often slept quietly in his chair afterwards, while they talked, and then at 9.30 or 10 would go off to work till the small hours. Remembering the arguments and laughter at Gracedieu thirty years later, I feel that my grandfather must have been exceedingly tired to sleep through it all so soundly.

On 4 November 1893 he wrote from Gracedieu to Mary in London, an unusual reversal due to the necessity of country quiet while he dealt with Inquiry notes:

Your birthday. Oh, my darling, I wish you were here with me but the children are the gainers. I have no buffday gift to offer only love, strong eternal love. I hate to be away from you. . . . I wonder if there is any chance of you coming here still for a day; that would be nice, nice. Do if you can. Your message found me in the park looking at the hounds and all the fine people of the Quorn Hunt who hunted foxes in and out of the wood all morning. It was a pretty sight. I saw a fox slink off towards the Lime Holes and after a bit the dogs followed him and all the mounted folk galloped away down the drive. They were successful in keeping to the paths, doing no damage, so it seems much better that they should be allowed the pleasure.

The Booths, who had opened the woods to the village in the summer, were now extending the same privilege to the Quorn Hunt in the winter. This liberality of attitude only added to the county's mystification. A man who called hounds dogs; who spoke with a Lancashire accent; who advocated old age pensions; who sat on a Royal Commission with the Prince of Wales, and whose appearance suggested a Beau Brummel in tweeds, was a rare neighbour.

In her answer Mary asked Charles if he had seen

the terrible news of poor Percy Macaulay's death, killed in repulsing an early morning attack on their camp by the men of the Hill Tribes on Saturday. Oh, it is dreadful! Such high hopes and this good appointment to survey for the boundary, and then all in a moment over for ever! It has been a very severe affair. . . . What pluck these boys of ours have! Percy must have heard the tumult and rushed into the thickest of the fray. He was quite alone, surrounded on all sides.

On one occasion Mary sent a pack of patience cards after Charles, who had left, 'greetingless, breakfastless and fireless' by a very early train, and he posted his thanks immediately: 'You do write the sweetest, dearest, most delightful notelets that ever was! Do I know—I don't suppose I ever shall quite know—all the love that is mine.'

Later in November Mary described how faint and ill she had been feeling:

I fancy it is all quite natural and as it should be and will help me to be ready and not mind parting with the old, worn-out machine when the time comes. I think there must have been a tremendous fighting instinct in the original ancestor who impressed himself on the Macau-

lay brood, for I often find myself wishing it could be the other way—
Percy's way, just the shock of eager conflict; and the sense of power;
and then the shot that goes home and a minute over to tell a friend to
give one's love at home; but this can't be and one must grow used to
the other. . . . You, like us, will be moved by the death of R. L.
Stevenson. It is a pity he should have gone. Sad, sad! A good man,
happy and loved, wise and kind, and with that wonderful genius
shedding such rich delight around for all of us! I shall be very curious
to hear what you think about the 'Foundations of Belief'[1], and I shall
cut out and send you Kipling's pony story[2] in the 'Pall Mall Gazette'.

In the summer of 1894 she wrote to Charles

after the excitement of the [Eton and Harrow] Match all day and our
Dance, a most successful one, 'til four this morning. Now, as play
begins early, the young ones are all gone and I am to follow in about
an hour. The interest yesterday was tremendous, almost too much for
one. We have a very inferior team, and Eton a very good one, and
with the prestige of having crumpled up Winchester in one innings
with 71 runs to spare. They went in first and made a magnificent
innings; Chinnery, a beautiful player, making 75, total 260. We went
in and Vibart was bowled almost immediately. Then a second wicket
fell and the thing looked hopeless. Then Stogdon, playing very carefully, began slowly to put runs together one at a time. For about a
quarter of an hour not a run did he make, and I thought we should
never see 50, but he gave no chances and tired the bowling. Then he
began to hit, and amidst the ever-increasing cheers of the boys, sent
ball after ball to the boundary, and did not leave off 'til he had carried
our score well over 200, and made his own share of it 124. It was a day
to live through! 'Day of fresh air in the wind and the sun.' Oh how
delightful they are, these days!

Delightful or not, Mary was completely exhausted, and the doctor
insisted on a new method of life for her. She had to stay in bed for
breakfast, and to lie down for an hour before dressing for dinner. The
lazy mornings did not last long, but the habit of resting before dinner
continued throughout her life, and not only contributed to her ease,
but to the pleasure of those who sat with her in the evening. Her bedroom fire was lit at tea-time in the winter, and she went up to a warm

[1] By Arthur Balfour.   [2] 'The Maltese Cat'.

room and read or slept as she wished. In old age she changed from one black frock to another, so there was really very little difference in her appearance, but having often gone up a weary old woman, she came down with pink cheeks and sparkling eyes and spirits.

At some point during the summer holidays of 1895 Charles and Mary decided not to renew their ten-year lease of Gracedieu Manor, which was running out. It is hard to know why. They could never have hoped to buy Gracedieu from the de Lisles, but it was conveniently placed between Liverpool and London, and Mary loved entertaining large numbers of young people there. Charles's ideas and her work in the village had taken root during their ten-year sojourn and had given the Booths a sense of identity with their neighbours. Mary could not abide Charles's many absences; equally she could not have borne to leave her hearth and home and follow him. As well as thinking it morally wrong, she would have detested such a nomadic existence. So they planned to experiment and take a furnished house near London from which Charles could travel up and down to work.

In December 1895 they decided to lease Ightham Mote for a trial year. The poetic beauty of this great Elizabethan house, floating like a galleon on the moat, the water lapping and reflecting the walls and turrets above, had gone to Mary's heart. Looking back at the frail, white-headed man with a worn face and young eyes one can see that Charles, already overburdened, was adding an unnecessary load to his back, but giving himself the pleasure of spoiling Mary—perhaps the only time he ever did.

Mary arranged a series of farewell occasions at Gracedieu. 'My women to tea' on 7 January 1896 was followed by 'Our school treat tea and magic lantern for the children; great success . . . the women gave me a beautiful tray and the gardeners gave us a beautiful cruet stand'. She was so much distressed at the time by a letter from Lord Welby in *The Times* attributing the authorship of the Exchequer and Audit Act to Sir William Anderson, when it had been drafted by her father, that the parting from Gracedieu took second place in her thoughts. She consulted Charles about writing personally to Lord Welby rather than 'making a fuss', and with his telegraphed encouragement the matter was quietly put right.

When Tom went into the Army, Charles turned to George to follow him into Alfred Booth and Company, and the boy agreed to go straight into the American side of the business after leaving school. The following summer he came back to stay at the Mote and Mary persuaded his father to let him try for Cambridge. The whole weight of responsibility for both the firm and the family thus fell back on Charles's shoulders. He would have 'to jump several more years', he wrote, before he could contemplate retirement, or death, with equanimity.

The Booths' letters at this time are full of the débâcle of the Jameson Raid in South Africa and Arthur Balfour's laziness. Mary contrasted Rhodes's masterful bearing during the subsequent inquiry in London with that of Labouchere,[1] who 'was getting so ignominiously the worst of it, cringing one minute, and the next braving it out with a hardened effrontery that is Titus Oates all over. There is no other man in history like Labouchere. I wonder if he was "good-natured and convivial too, and a quiet gentleman in private life".' This famous phrase was used to describe Titus Oates. 'We have just finished reading "The Egoist" for the second time. What a marvellous book, but still not in it with "Rhoda Fleming"[2]. . . . we have bought "Le Cid"—mortally dull, the characters have no human motives.'

The experimental year at Ightham Mote was coming to an end. Charles's overwork, the precarious business situation, George's change of direction, all contributed to a necessary decision. Mary usually cut her losses, except for that early loss of Polly, without self-pity, but this time the strain led to a fierce disagreement. Writing to Charles after he was well on his way back to Liverpool, Mary says: 'I have thought of you much and with love more than I can say. These jars are horrid; only happily they don't leave anything that is sore or unsatisfied; only regret that they have been and a sense that they must not and ought not ever to be.'

The last page of the diary for 1896 records the names of sixty-two people 'who have stayed at The Mote'. Ten months of supreme beauty, which Mary never forgot, left a gracious ambience behind. She spoke of having lived at Ightham Mote as we might speak of having heard Kathleen Ferrier sing.

The following summer Mary chaperoned Dodo and Meg and Gladys Holman Hunt during May Week at Cambridge, and scribbled off brilliant bulletins describing George's hospitable arrangements:

All well after King's Ball which we left a little before five this morning.

[1] Henry Labouchere, MP for Northampton and a controversial journalist.
[2] Novels by George Meredith.

It was a most beautiful affair, gardens lit up down to the banks, lines of lights marking the bridges, and the river dotted with the Chinese lanterns and the lamps of the canoes. My three girls looked each in her own way perfect. You never saw anything fresher or prettier than Margaret, and she danced all the time 'til God Save the Queen.

The next day Mary described the river scene as

. . . the gayest sight I ever have seen. . . . We rowed down and took up our station to see the boats go by and, after they had passed, rowed back to Cambridge among the rest of the people, the whole river as far as you could see before and behind alive with boats as thick as thick, and all gay with the dresses of the ladies and the pretty boating hats and flannel suits of the rowers and coxswains. We had a first-rate cox, but even with the best of steering there were endless collisions and occasional jams, all taken in the best of humours by these happy boys, all intent on enjoying themselves and giving their ladies a good time.

Charles's reply shows that when he had time he was as sympathetic a father to Imogen, the schoolgirl at home, as he had been to Meg on Long Island years before:

She worrits rather over her work and looks rather worn and thin. This evening I have been trying to clear up some arithmetical difficulties for her, without success, I fear, and then we took to Patience, which was better. I am not sending Miss Sewell's[1] report, as you could do no good with it tomorrow. I will leave it in your desk. It is indeed a beautiful piece of work—an admirable example of how to do such a thing. . . . There is a card from the Chamberlains, inviting us to a Grand Reception on the 30th to meet T.R.H. the Prince and Princess of Wales, which I shall also leave in your desk for you to reply to.

The Booths went but their Royal Highnesses mortified the Chamberlains by not turning up.

On 22 June 1897, the Booths took a large party of cousins and servants to see the Jubilee Procession from seats in St Paul's Churchyard. Mary always described the great scene with emotion: the flashing uniforms, the Church dignitaries in their robes, the Guards of Honour and, finally, the arrival of a dumpy little black-clad lady in her carriage;

[1] Charles's personal assistant.

and how, with her serene dignity and naturalness, she stole the whole show, and stole Mary's heart away. 'The great Queen', Mary called her, or 'The Queen'; never 'Queen Victoria'.

On hearing that the Booths were once again looking for somewhere to go for the summer holidays Mr de Lisle wrote offering them Gracedieu for three months or three years. It seemed the best solution. The returning châtelaine described it as 'all running to ruin', but said that the pleasure of 'seeing my women and walking in the dear woods' made up for 'the sad changes'. When the three years were up a fifty-year lease became essential. Gracedieu was home.

Mary's responsibility for her mother was very great at this time, but the feeling between the two had grown much easier. 'As for Mama, poor Mama, it is all the same thing over again, and she softens one, as she always succeeds in doing when she chooses. She has an inalienable charm, and though she makes a great mess of her life . . . I can feel tender to her now without feeling unhappy about her.' In a very frank and affectionate letter her mother told her about Charlie:

His music is a great source of delight to him. I cannot say that I do not wish there was less of it. There are people here who love him, children who eagerly welcome him. . . . It is curious that there are people in this world who are nice to everyone else but their own circle. I believe that if Charlie had had a resolute energetic Mother he would have done very well. I long for a good chat with no *referees*. When you write do not let it appear that I have written to you.

No wonder that Mary had grown fond of poor 'Old Woman' who now had to live with the jealous and miserly son for whom she had sacrificed the happiness of her husband and the respect of her daughter.

Another group of women got to know Mary well that autumn because of a terrible local pit accident. When the news came she took George down with her at once to the pit-head to see what help they could give. My grandmother often told me of the silent waiting women, with shawls over their heads, and the quiet way in which other miners, having heard of the disaster, climbed into the cages to join the rescue teams in the dangerous depths below. In those days there was no pension of any kind. The hat would go round for the women and children who looked in vain for the man of the family to return. On this occasion five men were saved and thirty-six lost. The widows found a friend in Mary.

Meanwhile Charles had embarked for New York in the *Umbria* and was reading Greville:

It is marvellously interesting what a picture it gives of Lord Brougham. I had no notion that he was so great and bad. I had imagined him a faddy pedagogic kind of man, very full of his own omniscience, and an insufferable bore. The way Greville dances round him is very amusing.
There is a woman on board—Mrs. Chapman or Chapin—with whom I was talking yesterday. She is fresh from Johannesburg where her husband acted as American Consul, and her house seems to have been a kind of neutral ground. She travelled with Rhodes when he came home for the Commission, she . . . talked to Chamberlain also, and as she came across Kruger she has been in touch all round. A Southern woman from Louisiana, rather full of herself, but interesting and able to see the big English view of the future of Africa. She says she spoke to Kruger at the time he held the possibility of a death sentence over the prisoners, telling him he could not do it. He said he should do what God said, and God had not yet spoken. Arrant old humbug! But she did not take it so, believes this to be perfectly genuine. It reminds one of Cromwell, and I found this lady thought Cromwell more of a humbug than I do.

Mary, who was always a partisan, never lost her sense of outrage at Kruger's behaviour, and kept in her special bundle of treasures two sheets of Great Cumberland Place notepaper, on which she had copied out Rudyard Kipling's 'Bridge Guard on Karroo' and another poem called 'The Old Issue'. This expresses so much of Mary's philosophy about life that the first four lines must be quoted:

All we have of freedom, all we use or know—
This our fathers bought for us long and long ago.
Unseen and unnoticed as the breath we draw,
Leave to live by no man's leave—underneath the law.

Her sympathy was entirely with the soldiers who had to fight over unknown terrain, in uniforms ill-suited to the conditions, for a cause which was as remote from them as it was unpopular abroad. She herself was in no doubt as to that cause, being rooted in the idea of authority, central government, and the retention of what her ancestors had won. Her views on India in the twenties followed the same lines, and she would certainly have been of the Suez Group in the fifties; but with this extremely rigid attitude to life she also valued unity enormously, and at the crunch would have sacrificed something at least for the common weal. She deplored the aftermath of revolution which divided the French nobility from their own countrymen, and commented on the futility of a whole cultured class of Frenchmen living and dying without ever taking part in politics or local government, or the great industrial concerns on which a country depends.

In his last letter from aboard ship Charles compared himself to Carlyle in that he took his wife's work too much for granted. Mary replied, 'You and I are almost exactly agreed about Carlyle except when my D.S.C. talks nonsense about being like him in his behaviour to his wife, but he is a grand creature at the end of all . . . his greatness of soul rises above his failings.'

At this epoch of Mary's life (she was fifty years old) her soul was definitely rising above her prejudices. She not only felt sympathy for her mother but grasped Meg's difficulties. Growing up in a household where her mother and Dodo divided the duties between them, the girl felt aimless and unwanted. In spite of Mary's antipathy to organised education for women, she suggested that her second daughter should try for a place at Newnham. Easier said than done as Meg had no Latin. After six months' hard work however she passed her Little-go, went to Cambridge in the autumn of 1897, and found there the right setting for her pilgrim gaiety. Of all the Booth children she was the most like her father, less certain and more artistic than the others and when encouraged, blissfully funny.

George, on the other hand, discovered after two years at Cambridge that he was not a born doctor. The very thought of such a career for him makes me apprehensive! He returned enthusiastically to business life as his father's secretary and personal assistant and became the intimate companion of a man so busy that only in working with him was it possible to get to know him.

A few months later Mary's special companion, Dodo, became engaged to Malcolm Macnaghten.[1] Great as was the friendship between mother and daughter, clashes of opinion—particularly over music— were inevitable. Both held decided views! Nor was there any separation, for the Macnaghtens always lived in London, and Dodo's independence made her even more sympathetic.

[1] The Hon Malcolm Macnaghten followed his famous father onto the Bench.

At the end of Mary's diary for 1898 there is a staggering list of letters written during the year, with the dates attached; fourteen columns of about seventy names each are noted, approximately three thousand letters—which do not include those to C.B. or the family at home, or incidental invitations and replies. No wonder Mary was once again completely prostrated by headaches. Charles wrote with great tenderness to her in the summer of 1899, '. . . longing to take such care of you as never was, oh my dear, dear wife'. Her answer was, ' . . . your letters are my joy. I see how precious, how undeservedly precious, I am to you.'

My grandmother detested invalidism, and fulminated about the way in which her time was '. . . cut up into such horribly short and snippy little pieces'.

Such thought and feeling as I had to spare has been going out in horror of the strange and monstrous iniquity of the Dreyfus sentence. It is too awful, too shocking! We all felt at first almost stunned, and really couldn't believe it on Saturday evening when Malcolm brought us back a sheaf of papers confirming all. Where does France sink to? Right down and away beyond the possibility of considering her as an equal, and yet so clever, so charming, so sensible. She is a mystery that one is further than ever from being able to solve.

Transvaal affairs seem drawing to a head and perhaps even now Tom and his men have left Umbala and may be on their way down to the coast to embark. Do come nearer home, dear! Marriage seems to me a great and growing thing and more than ever needed as one grows old. Is this trite?

Charles wrote back: 'I don't find your remarks on marriage at all trite; indeed I don't believe anyone ever said quite the same thing, but that is a way you have of finding a new cutting edge where everything seems blunt and worn out.'

Engaged once more on the problem of making the Gloversville and Philadelphia skin factories supply the Boston and New York agencies satisfactorily, he was continually travelling from place to place, but Mary always managed to send *The Times* and the *Spectator* to the right addresses, although she was gravely ill with appalling headaches. Charles sent her perceptive advice about accepting her limitations, letting devotion take a shape other than intense personal effort and finding a new balance in life: 'Not a bit more selfish essentially than the instincts that save one from falling downstairs.' But what Mary really needed was his presence. A phrase in one of Charles's transatlantic letters, written twenty years before, expresses I believe his support and her dependence: 'I kiss you and love you and rejoice with you if you are glad and comfort you if you feel low and above all I lay your head on my shoulder and tell you to be quiet and rest.' It was only with her head on his shoulder that she could accept fatigue and failure and let her guard down. Sure enough in 1900, which they spent together more quietly, health did slowly return to Mary.

On 22 January 1901, there is a historic entry in the diary: 'The Queen died at 6.30 p.m.

"Nothing is here for tears, nothing to wail
Or knock the breast, no weakness, no contempt,
Dispraise or blame, nothing but well and fair,
And what may quiet us in a death so noble."
Milton.'

Mary wrote to Meg in Cambridge on 4 February from Gracedieu, describing the funeral at second hand:

We have had a delightful 'Saturmonday' with dear Malcolm and Dodo who came down with George and Theodore [Llewelyn-Davies] after seeing the Procession in London, and told us the marvellous story of it all, so graphically, that I care no longer to read the newspaper account. It seems to have been simply overcoming, so that when the coffin came by all talk died, even amongst the commonest of the crowd, and everyone stood silent and weeping; Malcolm sobbing, but Dodo said that simply everyone cried. She described the King's face and bearing as wonderfully dignified, taking his people's [sorrow] and feeling and responding; the Kaiser too quite beyond himself. Lord Roberts, who had gone before, she described as strangely beautiful, very, very sad. It has all gone as it should; even the little hitch at Windsor, when the horses chilled by waiting, refused to move the gun carriage turned to good, for what could be fitter than that she should be drawn by the Blue Jackets to her rest. . . .

During these spring months of 1901 Gracedieu Manor was being altered and renovated while Charles worked at his book and reported progress on both counts to Mary, who was ill in London, adding 'if only you had been well and here today; the morning a perfect Spring, almost Summer, sunny time; quite hot and the woods bedecked with drops of catkin greenery hanging from otherwise bare bushes. I never saw that effect so perfect; perhaps because I have not been here to see it.'

In July 1901 Charles sat for his portrait to be painted by G. F. Watts almost every afternoon for a week. This was not a commission but a request on the part of the artist. Dodo described it as 'all vigour, energy and enthusiasm. He looks wonderfully healthy as he does when he is just home from America. . . . Mr. Watts said "This is for the Nation" and that the structure of father's face was "very beautiful".' The portrait was never finished because 'Il Signor', as his friends called the artist, died before the final sitting. Nevertheless, it possesses an insight and reaches a dimension never achieved in the finished Rothenstein portrait. It remained at Compton Place until 1960 when it took its place in the National Portrait Gallery—just as the artist had hoped.

In December 1901 Charles sent his Christmas greetings from New York and commented on reports of bitter English weather: 'Nothing like it since 1881 they say and that I suppose must have been the year of my mad rush to Liverpool when I left you to face a milk famine with a baby on your hands, to my eternal shame. I don't suppose you had a milk famine this time.' At the same time Mary was writing: 'I went to the New Gallery and stood opposite your picture and really felt as if I was having an interview with yourself, and gave thanks for the marvellous power of art. It is a great picture.' One can see the little figure with her head thrown back gazing up at the portrait while the painted eyes look right over her and far away into the distance, as they had so often all the years of her married life.

In the spring of 1902 Tom came home safely from South Africa and had a spell of leave in London. One evening Gerald du Maurier,[1] a Harrow friend, asked him to meet some friends at a supper party after the theatre. Tom sat down beside a young woman with a grave face, a very straight glance, and a lovely voice. Miss Alice Powell had left her home in Ireland to join her cousin, Miss Edith Jeffery, a distinguished London actress, in whose steps Alice hoped to follow. Tom fell in love there and then, and within three weeks had persuaded her to marry him. Very naturally, Mary and Charles were disturbed by the rapidity of the engagement, although when they met Tom's fiancée they were

[1] This famous actor was the son of George du Maurier.

156

immediately captivated by her unusual charm. Their fears were need-less—it was a sixty-year partnership.

After the wedding the old schoolroom at Great Cumberland Place was turned into a sitting-room for the younger daughters. Meg wrote a novel,[1] which was published in due course, while Imogen concentrated on the piano. Charles, an Oppidan Scholar at Eton, was about to go to Trinity, Cambridge. Dodo's son and daughter had arrived safely. Mary's cup was full.

[1] *The Brown House*, by Margaret Booth.

X
HIGH TIDE
1903-1912

Brisk, tanned and elegant Charles returned on 1 July 1903 from Brazil in a glow of relief at having added his final map and log book to assist others in charting their course through the reefs and eddies of poverty. Mary, however, in spite of all the work and effort concerned, was never happy about the composition of the Star Book. She would have preferred three orderly well-documented volumes even if this had meant another three years' work, to this attempt to fuse scientific facts into one volume with forecasts about the future. The general public was disappointed by this inconclusive finale and social reformers felt as if their steersman had abandoned ship. It is true that having gone so very far along a difficult road, Charles possessed the rarest possible chance of completing the journey. He had won for himself the financial independence to publish, and the personal prestige to ensure a good hearing for any major recommendations he cared to put forward to alleviate the unequal economic consequences of pre-1914 peace and plenty. Why did he not do so?

Lord and Lady Simey[1] detect a sense of disillusionment and defeat in Charles at the moment of choice and decision, but this is contradicted by the elation and vigour of contemporary letters. The Webbs blamed Mary for clipping his wings but again my impression is that his will was stronger than hers. He disliked even more than she did the idea of proposing some universal panacea which, if successful, could only whittle away the very individualism on which his marriage, his business and the Inquiry itself had prospered. At heart he was a trader and a traditionalist with the imagination of a town planner, not of a philosopher, and his temperament and experience ran counter to the logic of his findings. To Beatrice he had once written, 'To action I have never pretended and

---

[1] Authors of *Charles Booth: Social Scientist.*

any claim on abstract thought I abandoned as a childish delusion—so nothing is left for me but investigation.' He was wrong. Emotionally involved, he had slaved and was to triumph over the provision of old age pensions. This was the Booth lifeboat. The ocean remains untamed to this day.

Meanwhile, one of the Star Book's recommendations led to the setting up in 1903 of the Royal Commission on Locomotion and Transport in London. Charles's idea was that improved rail transport under a central authority would lead to better housing conditions for the workers of London. George Duckworth undertook the making of another map, which traced every method of transport by lines of ribbon, cord and string, and marked the stations with pins. Bus routes were not included becaue Charles considered that buses were already obsolete! He hoped that monorails travelling at forty miles an hour would soon replace them. He went on to discuss the possibility of free transport which in his opinion would encourage the speculative builder and the thrifty buyer to devise and demand better urban development. 'A slightly greater width of garden on the sunny side whether front or back may make all the difference; a single tree left standing can glorify a whole street' is one of his illuminating sentences. When the Royal Commission reported in 1905 on the lines he had suggested, no young Charles Booth emerged to storm existing entrenchments and produce results. This particular battle is still being waged today in the Greater London Council.

Mary had already warned Charles of another conflict of opinion: 'Sir Michael and the Bryces and that side are moving Heaven and earth to make up a Free Trade Party in the Conservative camp and to join hands with Rosebery and make war on Chamberlain. The Courtneys are very anxious for you and went at me tremendously at a party last week. Of course I said I could not in the very least tell what you would think.'

The Hobhouses gave a dinner-party on 5 July so that Sir Michael Hicks Beach,[1] the Bryces[2] and Mr Winston Churchill could win Charles over. The 17-year-old daughter of the house remembers Winston as very bronzed after his recent adventures in South Africa.

---

[1] Chancellor of the Exchequer, later Viscount St Aldwyn.
[2] Viscount Bryce, H.M. Ambassador in Washington 1907-10. Historian and statesman.

In spite of this friendly pressure Charles joined the Protectionist group, partly out of loyalty to Chamberlain and partly because he hoped to influence opinion towards an overall duty on imports as against protection for certain industries.

After only the briefest interlude at home to settle this and other questions he sailed for New York with his wife on board. She enjoyed the experience, and in September, when the *Ambrose* set out on her maiden voyage, she shared the fun with the Chairman, and so did a young neighbour, Robert Martin. Life had become easier for her and headaches no longer laid her low.

Charles had been cogitating for some time about doing for the men of Thringstone, on a more ambitious scale, what Mary had already done for 'her women'. This autumn he bought and adapted some temporary accommodation for this purpose, and on 19 April of the following year opened the Club himself. Sixty-eight members joined. No doubt curiosity and the allotments which were provided for those who wanted them swelled the numbers. 'The thing needs our presence very plainly, but will tend to settle down I don't doubt' was Charles's comment after smoothing over some initial misunderstandings. However, encouraged by the definite response, he bought a charming old gabled house surrounded by an orchard in the centre of Thringstone and gave Mary the use of the two front rooms for her work with women and children, reserving the rest for the men. Seven years later he engaged Harry Fletcher to build on a fine auditorium and games room at the back, and a small separate cottage for the Club Manager. During his lifetime Charles provided the necessary impetus and Mary never failed 'her women', but after the First World War there followed a long interregnum on the men's side during which no natural leadership emerged.

I remember walking through the Club with my grandmother in the twenties and thirties and seeing uncreased and neatly folded newspapers lying in rows upon tables in the reading room and hearing billiard balls clicking in the games room. Hastily hidden packs of cards —the Devil's books, as Mary always called them—provided other opportunities for gambling and so did the sleek whippets who lay at their masters' feet. Unkempt children played outside in the road and the miners' wives in black shawls sat on the stone steps of their back-to-back cottages and gossiped or quarrelled. In 1904 few of the original sixty-eight members had had any education and Thringstone House was too lavish and too alien to be a natural development, but there was a general reverence for learning. This was lost in the First World War, and never recovered until after the Second, when the Leicestershire County Council accepted Thringstone House from the Trustees and its Chairman, the same Robert Martin[1] who had cruised long ago in the *Ambrose*, installed a warden of the right calibre in the cottage. Something between a village college and a Butlin's holiday centre has emerged which provides in large measure what Charles and Mary Booth desired for their neighbours.

In 1903 both political parties were trying to gain the advantage of a forward-looking State education policy without actually committing themselves to increased expenditure. When Mary told Charles that Chamberlain had resigned from the Cabinet 'leaving Balfour a free hand in a good central position', she added: 'Not that I think, whatever they do, the Conservatives can win at the Polls. The education feeling and the Balkan affair [an insurrection in Macedonia which might have led to unpopular military involvement] and the cheap food cry ought to be enough to turn the tide in the Liberals' favour, but meanwhile the ship is lightened and Chamberlain's tongue is loosed.' He had actually re-signed over Colonial Preference with which Charles was in sympathy, but Mary obviously preferred Arthur Balfour's 'good central position'. A *Punch* cartoon of this period shows him lolling alone on the Front Bench with all his former colleagues huddled on 'the shelf' above holding out their hands to help him up. 'Plenty of room up here' is the caption.

Charles's former colleagues were also holding out their hands to their old chief at this time, and on 26 November 1903, Mary reported that they had surprised him 'with a really lovely cabinet of rosewood and ebony. . . . They all do love him.' During this month she also enjoyed 'seeing the tablet to Uncle Tom's [Lord Macaulay] memory unveiled at Holly Lodge before all the County Council and their wives: Lord Rosebery spoke so brilliantly and sympathetically and al-together charmingly that one could not help wishing he might always be able to confine himself to such literary and social occasions and leave politics alone.'

Soon after this Mary enjoyed seeing Leslie Stephen but she com-mented that his deafness was a terrible drawback: 'When general talk

---

[1] Colonel Sir Robert Martin, C.M.G.

and laughing goes on he looks sadder and sadder in his loneliness.' A few weeks later she noted in her diary, 'Dear Leslie Stephen is dying, at peace, and without pain or even discomfort.'

In December 1903, Meg wrote a description of what the family always called a 'Saturmonday' at Gracedieu which was

> very entertaining though too straining to the brain for such as me to stand the same often. The Sidney Webbs were here. They are clever; that ugly, little man with his fat cheeks and heavy eyelids, is full of wisdom and ideas. Aunt Bo looked very handsome. They are absurdly pleased with themselves, quite cocksure everything they do is right. Of course we had a great many lectures on eating little and that little seldom. 'Mastication is the keynote'! and poor Sidney has hardly any breakfast now, but I noticed that well screened by chrysanthemums from Aunt Bo's handsome eyes, he did himself very well at lunch and dinner. It is not only their methods of diet they approve so highly. Even on a holiday they work every morning, beginning the first morning. Sidney told me this glistening with pride.

Meg's light-hearted pen gives a revealing picture of the great Webbs, who were hard to emulate, easy to misjudge, and certainly never sufficiently teased by their adoring admirers. Charles and Mary worked just as hard but they detested faddiness, and liked life to run on normally around them, even when frugal meals for Charles and daily rests for Mary were essential.

A new project, stemming from the poetic and emotional side of Charles's character, which he hoped would provide a counterpoise to the analytical contribution already made to his country took shape this winter. Mary told Imogen:

> Your father and I are going to London to dine with the Holman Hunts . . . to meet Lady Loch [wife of the High Commissioner of South Africa] and talk over the best method of carrying out her and your father's plans about the [copy of the] *Light of the World* which Mr. Hunt has just finished painting. Your father wants to buy it and give it to the Nation; he is going to arrange with Lady Loch and Mr. Hunt about its going on tour in South Africa, Australia and Canada first; to be placed finally in a Gallery here; the National or the Tate or one of the others. I think Mr. H. Hunt is very much pleased . . . he will be assured that one first rate specimen of his art will belong to the

Nation and it is one which in a very special way embodies his ideas on religion and life.

The picture impressed Charles more and more. 'It is really grand,' he wrote. The Colonial Office helped with overseas arrangements, and the Fine Arts Gallery exhibited the picture to the public before it set off round the world in March 1904. Mary dealt with the Press, the Colonial Office and the Private View, although she privately thought the whole scheme very woolly and pretentious. In one scathing letter she urged Charles to cut out 'the unfortunate jargon about the sight of the picture healing animosities when it can't even make the artist forgive the Bishop of Southwark enough to shake him by the hand at the opening ceremony!' Charles paid £1,000 for the picture and spent £5,000 on the grand tour which followed. The original, which Holman Hunt sold for £5,000 when he was twenty-five years old, hangs in Keble College Chapel and is smaller, stranger and far more telling. Christina Rossetti, the poetess, and Elizabeth Siddall, who ultimately married Gabriel Rossetti, posed alternately for the head of Christ, while a suitably draped tablecloth did duty for the rest. This may account for the ambivalent weakness of the central figure which is surrounded by plants and planks of peculiar power. Few twentieth-century eyes can look at either the original or the replica without blinking. Mrs Holman Hunt of course had no hesitations and in the twenties would describe the beauties of the picture to an admiring audience in tones which filled the nave of St Paul's; even on occasions pointing out the cowering Ritchie girls as grand-daughters of the donor. When Holman Hunt's ashes were buried in the crypt Charles Booth was one of the pall-bearers. His own memorial is a near neighbour now to his old friend's in the artists' corner.

Early in January 1904 Mary wrote to Imogen from Gracedieu:

Your father and I lunched last Friday with the Curzons [who lived eight miles away]. On Wednesday your father is taking Meg and C.Z.M.B. to the Loughborough Ball!!! There's spirit for you! Two dinner parties in Liverpool and then the Holman Hunts to-night. Next week the Economic Club and Discussion in London on Tuesday, the Ball here Wednesday, London again on Thursday, and a grand dinner of all the Tariff Commissioners to meet Joe.[1] On Friday the first

1 Mr Joseph Chamberlain.

regular business meeting of the Commissioners, and down here by the late train. Then on Saturday the 16th Austen Chamberlain[1] here, Hugh Macnaghten[2] and Frank Dugdale[3] for the weekend.

It may have been on this occasion that Charles suggested to Austen Chamberlain that George Duckworth would make him an excellent secretary. When closing down the Inquiry office Charles had not relinquished his interest in the careers of his aides. Mr Llewellyn-Smith (later Sir Hubert) lived to undertake another survey of London in 1957. Mr Aves immediately became Chairman of the Trade Boards and George Duckworth (later Sir George) did become secretary to Austen Chamberlain. Mr Argyle alone remained at Charles's right hand.

Early in 1904 Mr Garland, one of Alfred Booth and Company's earliest employees, died. 'So we drop off one by one and what an old patriach I become,' wrote Charles.

One's thoughts go back to the oldest days when the little boy Garland kept the little office in India Buildings. . . . Tomorrow night is the Pearson Tariff Reform Dinner and otherwise I am free for office work. I have had a Mr. Lawrence[4] here this evening, one of the writers of *The Heart of the Empire*, who wrote asking for a talk. It has been very interesting indeed. I really do begin to hope that talk may be the solution of my old age—not only with you for that was certain, but with younger men. That is what an old fellow needs.

Thine, C.B.

Please instruct Geary [the footman] to close up the box of books in the gun room and despatch, carriage paid, by goods train to The Librarian, London School of Economics, Clare Market, London W.C., marking it 'No.1'.

This was the end of nearly twenty years' work and the old fellow must certainly have felt as if a large part of himself had been nailed up in that box, but the thought gave him a sense of relief, not of sorrow. There is a photograph of Charles sitting among his boxes looking up with a certain buoyancy. He had done his stint. From this date he travelled first class, doubled his tips and took permanent, but not in any

1 Sir Austen Chamberlain, K.G.
2 Scholar and Eton housemaster.
3 Warwickshire landowner, grandson of Sir Charles Trevelyan.
4 Later Sir Walter Lawrence, Private Secretary to Lord Curzon when Viceroy of India.

way luxurious, lodgings in Liverpool near his childhood home. He described them to Mary with felicitous touches:

This room is furnished in the 'All for Beauty' style of most lodging houses. Against one wall is a mirror in front of which is a 'how-now'[1] with various elegant ornaments and vase of flowers thereon. In one corner is an occasional table with outstretched wings, bearing on its surface an easel or book rest. The opposite corner is occupied by a piano on which stand photographs. There is a window seat and on each side a large-leaved plant in a pot. Another corner between window and fire is filled by a sofa behind which rises a group of bulrushes. There you see it all, except the centre table which is my part; a good solid, oblong table at which one can sit and write or work beneath a good hanging lamp such as your soul likes. Elsewhere in the house there is gas. Last night on arrival I went over to see Philip [Holt]. He is a very good man.

On 23 February 1904, Mary noted in her diary that C.B. 'was with the Prince and Princess of Wales nearly an hour and a half'. Unfortunately the Booths were together in London, so that the Royal clothes, carriage, conversation and décor were not recorded. Charles would have looked at them as at everyone and everything with the same kindly observant eye. The next day Mary ordered a brougham for a dinner engagement with the Chamberlains. On special occasions such as this it was necessary to hire beforehand, but in the ordinary way one whistle for a four-wheeler or 'growler' and two for a handsom cab had the desired result in inner London. The 'horses' remained permanently at Gracedieu at this time.

On 20 May Charles wrote two letters to his wife, who was nursing her daughter-in-law in London, to induce her to join him at Gracedieu:

Everything perfect here except your absence. I was early out of bed, my room all sunshine and the lawn just touched with hoar frost, then round the woods before breakfast and oh, the bluebells! Their beauty is almost unbelievable. I hope you may feel able to get here tomorrow. How glad we shall be if the telegram comes [to say so]—your letter has just come [to say no]. Perhaps I ought to tear up what I had written but it shall go. You dear person! Perhaps still—but I must not tease you.

Thine, C.B.

[1] A what-not.

Later he wrote again to catch the afternoon post: 'Do come—Oh the difference to me!'

People must reap what they have sown. 'Life is life,' Charles used to say, 'and whatever you do you have to take the consequences.' He had wanted complete freedom to come or go in the old days and had loved to dip into the family pool when it suited him. Mary had planned her life as chief of staff to the family and found it hard to leave her post even when he longed for her company. Disappointingly the diary records that she went to lunch with the Webbs on 21 May. However, on the 22nd she did go down to Gracedieu and found 'Bluebells in perfection. Out with C.B. among them a great deal.'

The words 'To have hair shampooed' written in Mary's diary always presaged an interesting event, and on 22 June 1904 it was at Oxford: 'C.B. dined at All Souls and M.C.B. joined him at the Evening Party.' The next day: 'Went to the Encaenia and saw C.B. take his degree of D.C.L. George and Imogen had come from London and were in the Theatre. Monsieur Cambon,[1] the Bishop of Worcester [Dr. Gore], The Vice-Chancellor, Mr. Wyndham,[2] The Speaker, Lord Tennyson,[3] Lord Curzon,[4] Lord Balfour of Burleigh,[5] Mr. Sargent,[6] Admiral Richards and General French,[7] were the others.' The list of Doctors of Science included two surprisingly contrasting figures, Andrew Lang[8] and Marconi.[9] 'Went to lunch at All Souls and came back to London. C.B. stayed on to dine at Christ Church.'

While they were at Oxford Arthur Balfour wrote Charles a note to tell him that he was to be made a Privy Councillor. 'Shoals of congratulations,' wrote Mary in her diary. On their return to London the Privy Councillor and his wife gave a dinner-party at the Savoy to all the knights and ladies of the Inquiry work-table. It must have been one of those happy farewell occasions tinged, as all such things are, with sadness.

[1] The French Ambassador.
[2] George Wyndham, Secretary for Ireland 1900–05. Tariff reformer.
[3] Hallam Tennyson, son of the poet, Governor-General of Australia.
[4] Viceroy of India at the time.
[5] The Home Secretary.
[6] John Singer Sargent, the American painter.
[7] Later Field-Marshal, Earl of Ypres.
[8] Poet and writer.
[9] The inventor of wireless telegraphy.

At the end of July the *Liverpool Daily News* brought out an editorial with the headlines:

'CHARLES BOOTH COMING HERE.

Famous English Statistician a Passenger on the *Campania*',

just as if he hadn't spent three days a week for thirty years in the city of his birth!

On 27 August 1904, the 'famous Statistician' described his beloved New York:

The effect at night of an electrified existence is extraordinary. The city seems really like a living thing. Last night, after dropping my guests at their respective destinations on Fifth Avenue, I rushed on for two or three miles past Vanderbilt's house and the Plaza Hotel which you wot of and circulating the park amongst towering buildings all alight and electric motors passing along back and forth in long trains all brilliantly lighted and flashing as they passed the points with no sign of the cause; no palpable explanation of the starting and stopping, the illumination and the movement, except some effort of will; just like life. Of the magnificence of these tall buildings architecturally there can now be no doubt at all. They grow bigger and there are enough. They no longer look like freaks. It is done. New York is magnificent.

In another letter he contrasts the charming homes and well-laid streets at the better end of Chicago with 'the most utter neglect conceivable in other parts, the roads a mass of mud, wet or dry, and rubbish of every description on each side of the tram lines and all across if no trams run. Apparently the roads are never cleaned and moreover freely used as a dumping ground of materials of any kind, old or new, ironwork, stones, old boilers, drain pipes, et cetera.' All this is true today of the outskirts of American cities.

Charles went on to St Louis and to Cincinnati, and was back again a week later to join Meg in a furnished house in New York. She remembers how he wrote letters at a shaky little table, seated on the only chair in the room, while she also wrote sitting on the floor. 'Don't you think we want some more furniture?' she asked. 'I don't see the necessity, dear,' was his absent-minded reply, scribbling away to catch the post. After all he had the chair!

In November Charles

. . . had rather a nice time travelling to Boston through glorious, rocky woods, quite wild; a glowing sunset and a rising moon. This afternoon we went to Harvard and called on Professor Peabody and wandered about amongst the College Buildings. I look forward to quite a different kind of time in America with you in June next year. John Morley has been here in this hotel and we had a long interesting talk last night, nearly an hour after dinner. He is straight from the House and much interested in Roosevelt.[1] He thinks that his ardent and evident patriotism, which has affected the imagination of the people, is the explanation of his enormous majority and that it may carry him through the difficulties he must encounter. Roosevelt said it had been an entire surprise. Morley was interesting on 'third terms'. He had told R. that to us it seemed a pity and unnecessary that he should cut himself off from a future in which he would still be a young man as Statesmen go; and then Morley said to me that he had been reflecting whether a third term had even been beneficial in the case of our Prime Ministers—Gladstone, Disraeli, Salisbury—and he rather thought not. He had been talking to Bryce, who had come through the South and described it as being 'industrially a wilderness'. I told of the increasing financial strength of the South, evidenced in the paying of trade debts and in the purchase of the manufactures of the North.

Oh how blessed do the quiet days of the voyage promise to be, while every hour brings me nearer home!

In November Mary wrote to 'Dearest of Megs'

You would be ever so amused at our present houseful—Baffy[2] and Edgar [Dugdale],[3] George's friend James Sandilands, Mary Spring-Rice[4] and Beatrice Webb. Mary and Baffy regard Beatrice with a sort of civil, respectful, astonished aloofness and edge out of her company whenever they can; but she is in a pleasant mood and to me extraordinarily interesting when we talk alone. She is as clever as ever

---

[1] Theodore Roosevelt had just been elected President of the United States.
[2] *Née* Blanche Balfour, a niece of Arthur Balfour.
[3] Grandson of Sir Charles Trevelyan.
[4] Hon Mary Spring-Rice, grand-daughter of the first Lord Monteagle, who as Chancellor of the Exchequer in Lord Melbourne's Government introduced the penny post.

she can be. . . . I am scribbling away now whilst Edgar and Imogen play 'Bumble Puppy'[1] on the lawn, and the rest are gone for a tramp on this heavenly November morning. Dante, whom I am now tackling, having finished Wilhelm Meister, is never weary of making his lost spirits dwell with a sort of caressing regret on the joys of the sweet air in the world above and the tender light. He pours scorn on those who, living in the midst of this sweetness, fail to enjoy it and he has made me feel that one does forget to enjoy it a great deal too much. The cares of the world choke one but here of late I think the dullest spirit must have been forced into joy and thankfulness—to whom? One does not know; but there must be someone to be thanked and I trust that if one pours one's thankfulness out into the air, leaving it to finds its own way, it does reach some beings who are the better for receiving it.

On the 18th Mary wrote to Charles:

The impatient stage is beginning to set in with me. I must not let it grow for there are still three full weeks ahead. . . . Our last party was amusing but a weight to pull along; Beatrice being a strangely incongruous element. It is wonderful, I think, at her age to have so much spare energy as really to care to try to shine and over-awe and spread propaganda among a set of young folk such as we had here; using every method; teasing, laughing and talking very loud; haranguing seriously, never leaving alone; except when I definitely engaged her and took her off and then, quite alone with me, she was most interesting and delightful.

During the four months of loneliness without Charles, Mary had at least enjoyed 'more talk with George than I have had since he was ten years old'. Margie Meinertzhagen had been to stay: 'Sweet and so nice, but terribly low spirited. We can't think what the matter is.' No doubt George solved this riddle eighteen months later when he asked her to marry him.

The Booths went to Rome in the spring of 1905 and Mary wrote home that the new Pope[2] was thought to be miserable by his friends:

He was extraordinarily happy and successful at Venice and has no gift

[1] A game with a ball on the end of elastic, attached to a pole.
[2] His Holiness Pius X.

for Vatican policy. When he came to Rome to the Sacred Conclave he took a return ticket to Venice, and when he was elected was prostrate with misery. His health suffers too from the want of activity and movement. Poor man, there is no way out of being Pope; no hope of any change but death. We feasted on your gossip about Adrian [Stephen] and the wise, wise old Dr. Butler. What a first-class Pope he would make! It is a pity the two can't change places. Well I fancy the Pope is a forcible person in his way; and how happy the Cardinals would be enjoying the suave amenities of intercourse with Dr. Butler.

On their return to Gracedieu a new sheep-dog arrived from Somerset to keep Charles company by his fireside. Mary wrote in her *Memoir* that no account of Charles's daily life would be complete without a word about Saxon, an Old English sheep-dog of great intelligence, who was 'on excellent terms with us all but if his master appeared would at once leave any of us in spite of all blandishments on our part and stalk majestically to his feet, lying down with a deep sigh of satisfaction'.

In spite of his holiday Charles remained 'very tired'. The long days and nights of labour were at last taking their toll, but by the autumn of 1905 there was a decided improvement.

'Your father and I had a glorious day, morning and afternoon, yesterday at the lily pond,' Mary wrote to Meg.

He was quite in his old form, shouting to the men; *and he is not a penny the worse today*. He must be very much better. He did enjoy it all so much and as we walked home together he said how that sort of thing takes all his thoughts and clears everything else out of his mind. If only he can get on like this through the autumn! I was just blissful and tramped round the pond and sat here and there on the grass in the state of absorbed and peaceful joy which this sort of work always induces in me. I wonder what sort of an animal I was in my last incarnation? Not civilised or tamed, I am sure.

A few days later she launches into a description of a County tea-party:

I do think that afternoon tea, as practised in high society in Leicestershire, is beginning to be an appalling function. The ceremony is now this: first you wait in the drawing room until all the party is assembled and then, after a decent interval, the servants announce tea. You then move in a body to the dining room and sit down as directed by your hostess at the table covered with cakes and sandwiches and flowers. Then the butler whispers in your ear 'Tea or coffee, Ma'am? Lemon or sugar?' and you whisper back your desires while the inferior attendants walk round with bread and butter, et cetera. At Beaumanor, after we had all glutted ourselves with cakes, the plates were solemnly changed and dessert plates, with knives and forks and spoons, placed before us and the attendants paced round again with fruit. The whole thing takes an enormous time and one might almost as well be at a dinner party, or rather almost as ill. Of course Mrs. Herrick was very kind and pleasant, but if this is really going to be the fashion, we will have to mourn the departure of the only informal function we possess.

The division of opinion on old age pensions and the anxiety of the public gave effect in 1906 to the appointment of a Poor Law Commission on which of course Charles was invited to sit. At the first meeting he was given charge of one of the sub-committees whose work was 'classification'. Among his colleagues Beatrice greeted him with affectionate enthusiasm and when she and Sidney stayed at Gracedieu or met in London the four found a new ease together. 'C.M. and M.C.B. to dine with the Webbs and talk over unemployment with them; and Mr. Beveridge[1] to talk over plan for his future work with C.B.' Beatrice had also interested Winston Churchill in William Beveridge with the result that this young man joined the staff of the Commission. The diary is as full as ever it was and a tremendous feeling of gaiety emanates from the pages. On 18 March Mary noted: 'Tom came over early to tell us that Alice has a boy,[2] Bless them all three.'

Charles spent a great deal of time at Gracedieu in the spring of 1906, arranging the financial and architectural details of the cottage he had asked Harry Fletcher to build so that the Macnaghten family could have a certain independence and yet spend their holidays nearby. This white, rough-cast capacious cottage stands on a rocky outcrop at the southern end of the wood, about half a mile from Gracedieu Manor. Few people would build on land with only a fifty-year tenure, but Charles's openhandedness meant that thirty years later his widow could retire to a delightful dower house.

His interest in 'The Road and its Difficulties'[3] led to the purchase

[1] Later Lord Beveridge.
[2] Chambré Thomas Macaulay Booth, the eldest of four sons.
[3] The title of a chapter in the final volume of *Life and Labour*.

of a Clément motor-car as French motor designers were then pre-eminent. Later there were two pampered Cléments at Gracedieu, one closed and one open, with a chauffeur apiece. When driving in the open one, the Booth ladies wore those extraordinary beehive bonnets made of violet gauze to protect the complexion from dust and glare. Both sexes donned long linen dust-coats which were necessary on unmetalled roads.

Billy Ritchie, a frequent visitor, came to stay again at Gracedieu in April, and by the time he left he had come to an understanding with Meg which Charles described as 'a solidly happy conclusion'. Meanwhile, in the Ritchie camp, Billy, returning home late on that Sunday night, knocked on his father's bedroom door to give him news of the engagement. 'Do you want me to get you out of it?' was the dry comment. A few evenings later, driving away from dinner at Great Cumberland Place, Richmond Ritchie[1] had taken another point of view. Rubbing one hand over another, he kept repeating: 'A remarkable woman, a very remarkable woman!', alluding to the mother of the bride, not to Meg herself; though in fact he had been captivated by both his future daughter-in-law and her mother.

Thus began a close friendship between a brilliant, complex and unsatisfied man and a brilliant, straightforward and totally happy woman. They shared an active love of French literature, and his Classical scholarship was matched by her historical knowledge. The power of the British Raj in India, to him a proud burden, to her a romance, was also a link; and then he made her laugh. It was her habit to sit in her drawing-room on a small upright armchair beside a table on which lay the two or three books she was reading, together with her knitting and her spectacles. A similar chair always stood on the other side of the table. In this inadequate receptacle the usually grave and enormous figure of Richmond Ritchie could often be seen, shaking with laughter as he described with very dry wit some peculiar dilemma, rubbing his hands together or smoothing them over his knees. These were gestures Mary herself used, particularly when, in later years, her cheeks flushed with pleasure as she told us about 'dear Sir Richmond'. He often lent her books, and on one occasion wrote to her, 'I was very glad to get your kind note but rather sorry to have the book back, which I hoped might

---

[1] Sir Richmond Ritchie, K.C.B., Permanent Under-Secretary of State for India.

have spent the rest of its life at Gracedieu which is what I should like for myself.'

The flavour of this friendship rises as pungently from old letters as the smell of freshly ground coffee. They were both senior civil servants, he with the vast India Office to work from and she with a desk in her drawing-room. When her 'dear Sir Richmond' died three years later Mary missed him deeply. They came from the same world. Charles and Richmond were as different in character and in looks as two members of the same race could possibly be. Charles looked on Richmond as a mine of essential information and pressed him with questions which Richmond eluded as far as possible. He slaved at his job but did not want to discuss it when enjoying lovingly chosen music, books and company in relaxed circumstances. I wonder how much, if anything, Charles's less exclusive education had to do with his social imagination and independent thought; and if Eton and Cambridge might have enabled him to embark sooner on his Inquiry, would they also have cut him off from the working-class life of England?

On a sunny day in August 1906, Billy and Meg were married at Gracedieu, and two months later George and Margie followed suit. Charles and Mary gave presents to every member of their colony of servants in the newly formed recognition of all that had been done for the two young couples. At the same time the newly formed Liverpool University decided to recognise all that Charles had done and gave him an honorary degree! Since then it has established a professorship of social science in his name.

In February 1907 Charles regretfully noted that there was no word of pensions in the King's Speech and then he set off round the country to hear Poor Law evidence. From the very beginning the Royal Commission had encountered great difficulties and a running battle ensued as its members travelled about between Birmingham, Melrose and Edinburgh. They scattered for the weekend of 14 June and Charles was not sorry to have Edinburgh to himself: 'But oh, my darling, I wish you were here! At Dundee there was the devil of a long day but the work went well. Loch was as usual in a very blocking position. Stutchbury is an irrepressible person and will fight viciously. Mrs. Bosanquet always supports Loch. Beatrice is at the other end.'

At last in August the Booths and their younger children slipped away to Austria. Charles went for long walks up steep mountain-sides, seeking renewal and refreshment in the old way, but this brought on an attack of *angina pectoris*. Although Dr Burkitt took 'a grave view of C.B.'s case', by the end of September his extraordinary recuperative powers enabled him to lead a fairly normal life again. No one realized that it was in quite a different key.

George and Margie's son was born in September and in November Charles wrote to congratulate Mary on a Ritchie grandson: 'Oh my dearie, what a lot of boys! What a time you will have with them!' He was quite right. Meg remembers trying to wake up her baby so that this grandfather could see his blue eyes. Charles seemed agitated: 'Don't disturb him,' he said. Meg looked up and suddenly realized that her father was an old man. Nevertheless he loyally accompanied Mary to Bath when she heard at the turn of the year that her brother was dying. His charm had been such that his landlady had cared for him and had paid his doctor's bills for the last few months of his life, unaware that under his bed were trunks filled with golden sovereigns. He had left his not inconsiderable money to a man he had not seen since school days; he had sold his father's books without giving Mary a chance of buying them; and yet he had kissed her hand at the end. Her diary records that she went to bed for several days overcome by the sadness of unsatisfactory relationships.

On 10 December 1907, Charles told Mary that he had replied circumspectly to an 'impracticable and even wild' letter from Beatrice, who felt that his advice to avoid arousing unnecessary hostility was a 'scolding' but did in fact pray for strength not to show her colleagues how much she despised them. Beatrice was no doubt 'wild and impracticable'—so had the young Charles been all those years ago, but now his heart attack had taken its toll. He had never been able to abide Loch and his 'blocking friends' but the swirling tides of the future gave him feelings of apprehension and misgiving derived as much from physical as mental impressions. Mary, who was still reading Commission evidence as in the old days, commented in her diary: 'Mr. Wakefield futile; Mr. Loch obstructive; not enough of Octavia Hill; Beatrice wordy and pretentious; an unseemly row between Beveridge and Clarke.'

Sidney Webb read Beatrice's Commission papers just as Mary read Charles's but Sidney used current classified evidence for his Press campaign, and this revived all the Booths' distrust. Lord George Hamilton, as Chairman, was moved to protest in a devastating letter to *The Times*. The Webbs' sense of mission, however, insulated them from all criticism. Charles's colleagues in turn became critical of him when he cross-examined a witness minutely for five hours on end as if the Inquiry was Mr Booth's and the date somewhere in the nineties. 'Charles Booth opened with an almost passionate denunciation of patching,' wrote Beatrice Webb. 'He wanted to go back to the principles of 1834 and start afresh from those principles.' 'Passionate denunciation' was so unlike anything hitherto heard or written about Charles that obviously a new factor had emerged. Early in January Charles's doctor insisted that Charles should resign from the Royal Commission.

Lord George Hamilton (the Chairman), F. H. Bentham, Sir Charles Loch, Mrs Helen Bosanquet, Miss Octavia Hill, and nine others signed the majority report on 4 February 1909. This advocated a public assistance authority supplemented by a voluntary aid council both centrally and locally, hoping by this double pressure to improve local conditions. Prebendary Wakefield, Mr F. Chandler, Mr George Lansbury and Mrs Webb wrote a minority report addressed to the evils of the mixed workhouse where the old, the young, the sick and the mad were forced to spend long years together in the closest contact; to the unevenness of outdoor relief; to the ineffectiveness of voluntary bodies; to the patchiness of medical assistance; and to the division of authority which led to neglect or misery for children. They advocated a child care service, a unified medical service, a ministry of labour as well as labour exchanges and a ten-year programme for afforestation, coast protection and land reclamation *to be carried out exclusively in the lean years of the trade cycle.* On the treatment of the mentally defective these four remarkable people were in agreement with the majority.

Charles Booth signed neither document. He thought the majority report 'poor stuff', but he could not agree with the minority's wish for central authority and ministerial responsibility. His own solution was to pin responsibility on local government as the Act of 1834 had done and insist on satisfactory results; but what safeguard except central authority could have successfully avoided the uneven resources, both financial and moral, of local Boards of Guardians? This was the question to which Charles could find no answer.

At this moment of disappointment one aspect of eighteen years' work came to fruition. A new select committee under Mr Chaplin's chairmanship was set up to look again at the proposals for old age pensions. One of the members was Mr Loch of the C.O.S. who, with others, was still doing his best to repel the idea. Eventually the committee recommended that old age pensions for the *deserving* poor should be paid through the Post Office. Charles believed that it was not worth while to apply a means test. Old age pensions were brought in by the Liberal Government in 1908, and the first payments began on 1 January 1909. This was eighteen years after Charles's first paper on the subject, which was considered by the least unkind of his critics to be so Utopian that it did not give food for serious discussion.

Neither Charles nor Mary gave any credit to the Liberal Government for bringing in the Bill. Mary explains this attitude in her *Memoir* by stating how unsatisfactory it was that old age pensions were restricted 'to those whose resources had sunk below a certain level'. I think their attitude was due not so much to the 'means test' as to irritation that the wrong political party had gained the glory, although my grandfather's ideas were entirely different from those of his fellow Conservatives. What would the Labour Party even today say to free services of gas, electricity and water? Mary left him in no doubt about her reactions to his kite-flying. He once rather sadly said that her arguments were always the same. I think that the changing possibilities which fascinated Charles frightened her into clinging more tightly to the established order. She often quoted from 'Uncle Tom' Macaulay's famous poem 'Horatius'—

. . . even the ranks of Tuscany
Could scarce forbear to cheer

but she was not always among those ranks herself! In the twenties and thirties she conveniently forgot that 'Uncle Tom' himself had been a Liberal and that support had come from that party for the anti-slavery movement of which she was so proud. Such illogicality made her a more attractive character.

However, if the Booths denigrated the current Liberal Party's efforts, the 9-year-old Labour Party did not forget Charles and in November 1909 paid him a debt of honour with heart-warming sincerity. An illuminated address[1] was presented to him in the House of Commons, commemorating his part in the passing of the Old Age Pensions Bill. 'To you more than any man,' they wrote, 'is this first instalment of justice to the aged due.'

[1] See Appendix F, for the full text of the address, p. 227.

PLATE 5 Gracedieu Manor from the cricket field

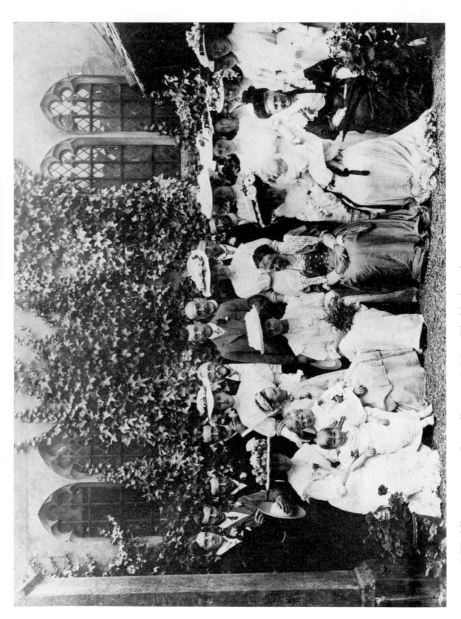

PLATE 6 Wedding group at Gracedieu 1906. Meg Ritchie in going-away clothes sits in the centre, between her mother and Lady Ritchie. Billie Ritchie

'Out in the woods with C.B.', 'To church with C.B.', are entries which occur very often in the diary this autumn and lectures and meetings were at Thringstone House, Leicester, Coalville and Birmingham, no longer at the Polecon and the Statistical Society.

Early in 1912 Charles sensed a feeling amongst his partners in Liverpool that the chairmanship of Alfred Booth and Company should pass to a younger man. He immediately suggested that his nephew, Charles, should take his place. The wrench, however, was sharp, and on reaching Gracedieu Charles told his daughter Meg that he thought he would have died Chairman of Alfred Booth and Company. Later that night he had an attack of angina and was ill for a week or two. He must have then written the little note that Mary always treasured: 'The heart knoweth its own bitterness and ought to be thoroughly ashamed of it.' Characteristically, he conquered his temporary anguish, retained a certain control over his partners, and took on other work.

In February, for instance, he presided over the fortieth anniversary of the Poor Law Conference, and his address contains the chief factors of the individual report which he would have signed had he continued to sit on the Poor Law Commission. Somewhere in this closely reasoned speech there is a reference to the Metropolitan Association for Befriending Young Servants: 'It is this spirit I welcome. Co-operation between Poor Law and Voluntary Efforts cannot be too complete. I set no limits to it. The spheres of action are different, but the same spirit of humanity should prevail in both.' It is possible that one of Charles's deepest objections to a centralised Poor Law was the feeling that voluntary effort would be frozen out. Could he but have seen how essential if not always welcome it is in the Welfare State, his anxiety about its future would have been unnecessary.

In April 1912 the new Chairman of Alfred Booth and Company decided against taking the trip to Brazil already arranged with George because of a local outbreak of fever. At a week's notice Charles sailed to Manaos, sketching with his pen, as he had done in 1903, the tropical life, the shipping considerations and the fascination of the great Amazon. He and George had a strenuous time at Manaos where the harbour had achieved all Charles's hopes. When he called at the Palace he assured the Governor that he had the prosperity of Manaos at heart. The Governor, turning to the window with a gesture, said something in Portugese. His secretary translated it for Charles: 'One has only to look around.' 'So there is my monument,' wrote Charles to his wife, with an unusual flourish. 'Manaos has great charm. I am sure I shall visit it after death, if not before. . . . Now turns the heart to England, home and all you dear ones.'

While Charles had been away, an event had taken place to which he cabled his consent with the words 'Like your news'. Imogen's engagement to Eric Gore-Browne, a young barrister who had been a pupil in Malcolm Macnaghten's chambers, met with warm approval on all sides. On 8 August the marriage took place at Gracedieu. 'Perfect day,' wrote Mary. If Manaos Harbour was Charles's monument she could certainly wave her hand with the same flourish at the Booth family plantation.

It is a curious experience to reconstruct the lives of two people from letters and reminiscences, and then at a sudden moment to find one's own identity among all the other characters. Whatever credits and debits I inherited, one possession at least is useful to the biographer—an accurate and at times overwhelming visual memory. The first time I really saw my grandmother is as fresh in colour now as it was then. In October 1912, when nearly four years old, I was the first in the family to catch whooping cough. By the time James, a year older, and Catherine, two years younger, were whooping miserably in bed, I had graduated to the nursery. One afternoon a voice called my name softly from the stairs. I ran to the door, opened it, and there on the half-height below was a sight that struck me as very beautiful, almost magical: a white bonnet, a white shawl draped over a dark slender figure, and dancing brown eyes level with mine. I knew who it was already, but the moment of comprehending the person we called 'Baba', (as did all her grandchildren following the fashion set by the first of them) occurred on that nursery landing. Our other grandmother, Anne Thackeray Ritchie—known as Grandmama—was a novelist and a fascinating friend to a large literary circle. Tall and dignified, recently widowed and always dressed in black, she was a melancholy and alarming figure to James and me. We knew her well, as she lived across Burton Court from our Chelsea home; we were proud of her but not at ease with her. She expected us to behave like her friends Henry James and Rhoda Broughton. This new, small, gleaming visitor, rapid and gay in her talk and her movements, did not seem at all like a grandmother, or even like a grown-up. She was Baba, an entity all on her own, a fixture in our lives. My Booth grandfather was not yet in this category although we admired him immensely and called him Papa.

In June 1913 my youngest sister Maisie was born, and when later on our parents went to stay with friends in Norway we four children spent August at Freshwater Bay under Grandmama's wing. She adored our nurse, Mary, who was very Irish, very pretty and very much in love. Her gentleman friend, as he was called, often joined our nursery walks. Arm in arm with Mary he teased James and me while we, utterly disapproving without in the least knowing why, pushed the pram. Perhaps to forestall our comments, Mary told terrible tales of our wickedness to Grandmama, who believed them and lectured us severely. She never knew how we were smacked and locked in our bedrooms without food or clothes for hours. We never thought of telling her and it would have done no good. In September we moved on to Gracedieu Cottage and here, after tea one afternoon when I was rocking a fractious Maisie in my arms, in came Baba. She seemed much older than before; a soft-voiced, brown-eyed little lady in black. She sat down beside the baby's bath and asked me where Mary was. When told she said, 'And is she often out?' I nodded. Trust is such a quick thing. When Mary returned Baba continued to talk in her soft voice, charming Nurse, never giving me away, and yet controlling the situation. All the smacking and shutting-up stopped, and a few weeks of unusual spoiling set in, before my mother came home and got rid of the tyrant. James was sorry. 'You never know who we'll get now,' he said. We got a winner.

In the autumn my Ritchie grandmother wrote: 'Beloved Baba. We have just come back from lunching off pheasant with James and Belinda. We looked at your pictures.[1] I said I liked yours the best, which was not saying so very much. They liked Papa. When Belinda objected, "But Papa does not keep his hat on the table beside him", James said, "He was a much younger man then remember, Belinda."' This still seems a *non sequitur* to me.

On Monday, 23 February 1914, Baba noted in her diary: 'M.C.B. to Benson & Phillips [Shoemakers] and took James, Belinda and Catherine[2] a drive. C.B. and M.C.B. dined at Lambeth to meet the King and Queen. Lord[3] and Lady Lansdowne, Lord[4] and Lady Loreburn, Lord Balfour of Burleigh,[5] The Dean of Westminster and Mrs. Ryle, The Bishop of

[1] The Rothenstein portraits.
[2] My brother, myself and my sister, aged 6, 5 and 3.
[3] Leader of the Conservative Opposition.
[4] Lord Chancellor in Campbell Bannerman's Government.
[5] Secretary of State for Scotland in the previous Government.

Yukon and wife, Sidney Colvin,[1] Mrs. Benson.[2] We saw the Crypt after dinner and Library treasures.' Baba often described how the Queen took a cigarette case out of her bag after dinner and smoked considerably; and how later, while they were looking at the manuscripts in the Library, she said that it was a terrible thing to have so many opportunities of seeing interesting and beautiful things when often one was too fatigued to enjoy them at the time, or to remember them afterwards.

In the spring of 1914, my grandfather's thoughts were diverted from trade unions and industrial affairs to the urgent question of Irish Home Rule; of Ulster's emotional and political bonds with England; and the ghastly quandary of Ulster-born officers, serving in Ireland. Civil war was very near. 'I want to prepare for further talks with Trades Unions but just now politics sweep everything else out,' wrote Charles. A few days later I went to stay with him in London, as there was a plague of influenza in the Ritchie home; I am intrigued by his description in a letter to Baba of 'a large and long breakfast party; first Belinda and me with lots of engaging conversation, and then one by one all the others; the intervals filled up with Government revelations about The Curragh;[3] A.J.B. quite perfect in the Debate. I miss talking with you very much.'

Enticed by this quiet appeal, Baba came up to London and her diary records endless engagements, such as 'Mr. Argyle came . . . Mr. Osborne of the Trades Union Non-Political Group for a long talk'; there were the usual luncheon and dinner parties, and 'a visit to Motherless Children's Committee'. Yet I very well remember how she read me *The Talisman* during this visit and how she preferred the exotic courage and courtesy of Saladin while I could never resist the rough chivalry of Richard Coeur de Lion. The scene when Richard with his sword and strength is unable to cut the gauze scarf which Saladin's scimitar easily divides was certainly enjoyed as much by reader as by listener, while we sat knee to knee riding the crest of Walter Scott's imagination. Thus began the reading of the whole gamut of the Waverley novels, many several times over, ending with *Anne of Geierstein* when I was sixteen. To be a listener was not to be lazy. Baba always read from a small green leather edition which was light enough to be held up, laid

[1] Sir Sidney Colvin, keeper of the prints and drawings, British Museum.
[2] Mrs Benson, wife of the Archbishop of Canterbury.
[3] The Curragh Incident of March 1914.

down, used as a lance, caressed as a baby. Behind the lenses of her pince-nez her swimming eyes looked enormous and, like those of a horse, hardly focused. She often cried but never lost control of her voice. When she came to conversation she suited her voice to the particular character and essayed the Scots accent with absolute confidence if not complete success. In my case, I can never imagine Meg Merrilies speaking in any other way. During the description of forest and field, torrent and lake, a dreamy look came over her face and she did not catch the listener's eye as she did during dramatic moments; partly because she was skilfully trimming and cutting the sentences. Only at a much later date did I guess what was happening. At the end of a chapter we would sit silent and relaxed for a moment, thinking of the wild night ride, the cry on the moor, the knock on the door. Then would come a little murmur, a soft hand on my knee; the book would be shut up, the spectacles put away and the curtain rung down.

In May 1914 Charles Booth read a paper on 'Labour Unrest' in Birmingham, visited London and Derby on successive days, and embarked in the *Aquitania* for America. On 29 June he wrote about the dreadful assassination at Sarajevo: 'What will come of it all? The European news is most dangerous. The Ulster news is put in the shade—that may be no harm.' The letter comments on Walter Lippman,[1] Mr Roosevelt and Felix Frankfurter,[2] new American friends, and on the death of an old one, Joe Chamberlain. 'He has been, and is, a very great figure and may stand out as one . . . if the notes he struck prevail; I think they will.'

From 31 July his letters foreshadow the grim events ahead: 'The news becomes more terrible. As far as I can see, England must be involved. It looks as though Germany thought she had a good chance of success, and—if so—we others have to do all we know all together. The fact that German boats are being held in port all ready is the worst feature as it seems to imply a sure expectation of war with England.'

Having taken the opportunity while in America of discussing trades union policy with many of his business and political friends, Charles was well equipped to accept Theodore Roosevelt's invitation to expound his views to a few chosen people at Oyster Bay on 4 August 1914. Charles's appearance and personality struck Felix Frankfurter so for-

[1] The distinguished political commentator.
[2] Felix Frankfurter became a famous judge of the American Supreme Court.

cibly that in his reminiscences, published forty years later, he included this account of a man seen once and never forgotten:

> We were to go out, spend the day and have a talk with The Colonel[1] on August 4th 1914. It happened to be that fatal day in the world's history. Needless to say, we did not talk about the American Labor Movement, or American industrial problems, we talked about the war.
>
> There was another guest there who had been asked to talk about industrial matters. He was one of the men most competent to talk about them, Charles Booth, author of the 'Poor in London', the first comprehensive, detailed and what may be fairly called, scientific attempt to study quantitatively the condition of the poor in London. But Booth was also, and this is a phenomenon one finds or did find more frequently in England than in this country, Chairman of the Cunard Shipping Line.[2] He was a man of wealth and a man of social sensitiveness. He was an exquisite looking creature, delicate with a beautiful Van Dyke beard. He had the quality of an Arab steed, that delicacy. I remember well the difference between so boisterous a creature as T.R. was, a man with so much animal zest, so much horse-power, and the refined reticence and hesitation of thought of Booth. The contrast between them in physical appearance was enormous, but also in attitude, because here was T.R. in the comfort of Sagamore Hill in Oyster Bay, shaking his fist at Mr. Booth saying 'You've got to go in! You've got to go in!!' Here was Mr. Booth, head of the Cunard Line, with God knows how many ships on the water, just sitting quietly. It was awfully easy for T.R. to say, 'You've got to go in!!' We were not going in. I'll never forget this beautiful creature, Booth. There was T.R. doing a Tomahawk dance round Mr. Booth, and this exquisite gentleman, who was seventy-four at the time, with Roosevelt shaking his fist at him and saying. 'You've got to go in!' shook his head like one of those Chinese Mandarins, saying slowly, 'I suppose we've got to go in.' While we were talking, the English Cabinet were sitting.

Charles, commenting on this meeting with his usual wry humour, told George that he hadn't been able to get a word in edgeways!

---

[1] Theodore Roosevelt.
[2] In fact Charles's nephew, Sir Alfred Alan Booth, Bt., was Chairman of the Cunard Line.

Meanwhile at Gracedieu Mary noted for 5 August 1914: 'Sir Edward Grey's statement in the House of Commons on Monday afternoon and evening announced that we supported France and will not stand violation of Belgian neutrality. War declared at 12 a.m. on the 5th. Belgians make splendid resistance at Liege.'

We Ritchies spent the summer of 1914 at Gracedieu Cottage, and I remember very well that feeling of everything coming apart, which so horribly returned in 1939. Uncle Tom was, of course, a regular soldier; my father held a commission in the Leicestershire Yeomanry, Uncle Eric a commission in the Post Office Rifles, and Uncle Charles left Gracedieu in order to join up. Some time during these first few weeks of war, Baba came and sat very still in our nursery. She was dressed in black and looked very grave.

When Lloyd George invited George to direct the infant Ministry of Munitions,[1] Papa put on harness again and returned to Alfred Booth and Company; ships were essential to the war effort. 'I believe I am doing useful work,' he wrote early in 1915. The faithful Jesse Argyle now left his master for the very first time to take a position in the Ministry of Munitions. 'No noice little words loike "Please" and "Thank yew" in this plice,' he reported to George after a few hectic days. In reply to Mary's letter of farewell he wrote:

> Oh, how good to me you and Mr. Booth have always been! The day which brought me to Mr. Booth was quite the best of my life, giving me over thirty years of happy work and comradeship; leaving me at the end with two such wonderful friends. . . . You speak of not having taken an active part in what was accomplished, but I know of what inestimable value has been your ready sympathy and wise counsel to your husband in all his undertakings. He has several times spoken of it to me, or in my hearing. Nothing in the whole work gave me truer pleasure than the Dedication—so nice, so just and appropriate.

On 21 July, Charles described the plight of his young partner Clement Jones,[2] who was back from the Dardanelles with dysentery. His wife had travelled to London from Cheshire with her new-born baby on hearing that Clement's life was despaired of, and on arrival at

[1] See *A Man of Push and Go*, Duncan Crow's biography of George Macaulay Booth.
[2] Sir Clement Jones, C.B.

her lodgings she found Charles Booth waiting there to reassure her. A few days later he visited the patient, who 'talked away vigorously. His account of the Dardanelles situation is terrible. I don't see what hope there is for it, except in the possible stoppage of munitions for the Turks . . . Lloyd George and his munitions are rather upside down. The war outlook is far from good.' In another letter on 18 August Charles wrote: 'There are stories of Zeppelins in the air. We have to take everything as in the day's work. George has seen Geoffrey Robinson,[1] Editor of 'The Times', who said that if the Dardanelles effort failed he thought it would sweep Asquith out whatever might follow. I think we are now without any unity of purpose or lead at all, and—if so—who will emerge? Balfour most likely.' On 16 September Charles thought that 'Kitchener's speech—solid and carefree as usual, points to Compulsory Service', while Mary noted in her diary: 'Account in the paper of the 4th Leicestershires and Bob Martin's splendid and valorous behaviour in the trenches for twenty-one hours after he was wounded, directing his men, having his wounded sent back and writing Orders.'

On 14 February 1916 Mary sent her usual letter to her 'dearest Valentine':

Such a strange day! Flurry after flurry of wildly driven hail and snow, the sky so dark that I had to leave the piano as I could not see to play; then clearing, out came the sun and patches of heavenly blue showed themselves among the clouds. I had made up my mind to a fireside afternoon, changed it and went out into the woods where on the top of Bilberry Hill above the rushing streams, overflowing on to the path, the sun made all the russet ground gloriously golden and I thanked God for my beautiful home and this peaceful, delicious life. No story to tell, but a happy and lazy day, good to live.

Your Wife.

A day or two at Gracedieu always replenished Mary's wells of happiness, and while enjoying them she shut out all other thoughts—even those of war.

Early in April they 'sat in the primrose valley together' at Gracedieu, but typically on the anniversary of their wedding they were apart. Charles wrote to Mary: 'Yes, we made no mistake forty-five years ago, whatever other mistakes, and how I do hope for five years more of this

[1] Geoffrey Robinson became Geoffrey Dawson and was again editor of *The Times* during the Second World War.

wonderful fruition, but am thankful for every day of it we may secure.'
He knew how precarious and precious was their time together, as he
had just had some kind of seizure.

In May, Mary noted in her diary:

Heard on Saturday morning, the 6th May, from Tom of the success
which his Highland Brigade had on the 25th April. The Germans
attacked with nine mortars and a very hot bombardment. Tom's men
went forward without a moment's hesitation and drove the enemy
back with heavy losses. They have got the thanks of the Corps Com-
mander, five M.C's, many D.C.M's and M.M's for the men. They lost
seventy killed and wounded.

Long afterwards, on being asked about the war, Tom said that the
secret of fighting was to persuade young soldiers that 'their lives did not
matter'. This could only have been done by a man who thought very
little about himself.

On 1 June 1916 Mary recorded:

Naval disaster off coast of Jutland. This turns out not to be a disaster
at all though we had heavy losses. Ships under Admiral Beatty came
in contact with the whole German Fleet coming North. They engaged
and the 'Queen Mary' was struck and blew up at once, going down
in two minutes. After the action Jellicoe swept the seas and found no
German craft of any kind left and five hours afterwards the Fleet
reported itself again ready for action.

On the 3rd Mary wrote: 'Heard that Tom has the D.S.O., and on the
5th she described the sinking of H.M.S. *Hampshire* with Lord Kitchener
on board.

The following month my grandmother noted: 'C.B. has not been so
well since we returned here and gets up for fewer hours in the day', but
the news received a week or two later must have revived them both:
'Letter from Tom received on the 28th. He had taken command of the
7th Gordons on the 21st and was very busy getting everything in order.
Had not taken off his clothes for three nights when he wrote . . . his
servant wounded at his side, his helmet hit and dinged [a good Scots
adjective] but he uninjured.'

My own recollections of my grandfather come from this summer of
1916. He and Baba would sit on the lawn or walk up and down the old
cedar and ilex avenue which they preferred to the newer part of the

garden where they had planted an avenue of sycamores. Saxon, the Old English sheepdog, was their constant companion. He was grey and white, a very handsome fellow. His son, who was black and brown and snappish, had in some mysterious fashion become part of the Ritchie household and lived with us at the Cottage. James and I often ran down the path through the wood, along the edge of the cricket pitch, past the huge oak tree by the clap-gate and up the slight rise of the great mown lawn to greet our grandparents who, watching our progress, would wave from afar. On one occasion we were absolutely appalled by a noisy, bloody, dangerous fight between Saxon and his unattractive son. They were separated with great difficulty and both were severely bitten by the time the fray was over. I found myself holding hands with my grandfather who was still sitting calmly in his chair with a light rug over his knees. He leant down to tell me that both dogs would recover completely. I looked into his bright blue eyes which were on a level with mine, and at his flushed cheeks and shining white hair and beard. Accustomed to the idea that young women were beautiful, young men handsome and old people not in the running, I was astonished to realize how exquisite Papa looked. I was also much worried about family violence. 'Didn't Saxon know he was his son?' I asked. 'Of course he isn't a very nice dog, but why did Saxon bite him? Fathers shouldn't fight their sons.' Papa took me for a little walk up the new avenue and told me what a complicated thing love and hate can be. I was seven and he was seventy-six; that was the only real conversation we ever had together.

In August 1916 Mary wrote: 'Charlie has been a very little better', and underneath this copied out James Russell Lowell's[1] lament for his wife:

How was I worthy so divine a loss?
Deepening my midnight, kindling all my morns.
Why waste such precious wood to make my cross?
Such far-sought roses for my crown of thorns?
And when she came, how earned I such a gift?
Why spent on me, a poor, earth-delving mole,
The fireside sweetnesses, the heavenly lift,
The hourly mercy of a woman's soul?

She was facing in her way thoughts of the loss of her Valentine, of

[1] The American essayist and poet.

rousing argument, of shared interest, of fireside sweetness; but the diary goes on in its usual factual, detailed way. At the end of the month Tom was severely gassed. He was eventually moved, 'still very weak', to the same hospital as Bob Martin, who was at last convalescent. Mary wrote: 'Delightful letter from his Divisional General, Douglas Campbell, full of praise of him.'

In September, 'M.C.B. had perfect walk with C.B. over High Cademan', and the next day Mary was 'out with C.B. in Calvary and Temple Woods'. These woods are a considerable distance from Gracedieu and it is a happy thing to imagine Charles and Mary stepping among the fallen golden leaves together. The following week she noted down: 'Tom is appointed to command the 1/6th Battalion of The Black Watch.' Immediately under this proud announcement is another: 'Man from Knight's came to see to heating apparatus. Put it right and left instructions.' On Saturday, 4 November, Mary noted her sixty-ninth birthday— 'All well, thank Heaven!' On the 9th Charles went 'to see dangerous ash trees near Newton's and Wilmot's cottage', but the next day he was ill and she wrote of him, unusually, as 'Charlie'.

My grandfather had a stroke on 16 November 1916, as he sat at his desk working on a paper about the industrial reconstruction which would be necessary after the war. 'The pen fell from his hand and thereafter he could neither write nor speak', but he conveyed his pleasure in Mary's company and that of his daughters by his eyes: 'He has known everyone and welcomes them eagerly one after another.'

Only Tom, summoned from France by telegram, was still travelling homeward when the end came on 23 November:

Dodo, Meg, Imogen and I were round him and he looked at us all in turn with the fullest recognition and affection. After that I did not leave him at all and he sank. For some time he returned the pressure of my hand, but that ceased and about mid-day he passed away quite quietly. Dear Tom arrived too late, having travelled just as he was straight from the trenches on receiving the telegram. He had to leave again the next day and go straight back, but he was comforted by his father's wonderful expression, as we all have been. Tom's General had told him he might tell his father that he had been recommended for immediate distinction for his conduct of his men on the 13th when his leadership carried them victoriously to the furthest limit of their objective. [Tom was awarded a bar to his D.S.O.]

On Sunday, 26 November: 'Charlie was buried in Thringstone Churchyard.' Mary's writing is touchingly uneven.

Charlie and Grace Booth and Enfield Fletcher came from Liverpool, Clement Jones and Mr. Argyle came from London, also Edith Holman Hunt; the Martins, the Beaumonts, the de Lisles and Frank Dugdale were amongst the Leicestershire friends. Mr. Shrewsbury took the entire service. The Citizens Corps lined the way to the Church. Charlie was carried by our own men. We all sang, 'O God our help in ages past' by the grave. I think there was nothing that Charlie could not have liked and no-one there who did not care for him.

On the way to the funeral service Mary, with her extraordinary lack of self-pity, told Meg of Mr Shrewsbury's difficulties in running the parish since his wife had died. Two of her answers to letters of sympathy remain to show the extent of her perception of other people's troubles at a moment when hers were so poignant. The first was to Grandmama Ritchie:

Dearest Friend,
    I have been grieved to hear of all that you have had to face—the passing away of your and Hester's loved old friend, Lord Tennyson, and then this strange tragedy of Mr. Reginald Smith.[1] Was it the war that over-strained and disturbed his brain? . . . And you are giving up The Porch! That will be a wrench. I wonder if you will fix on Ramsgate, of brown sails and beautiful sunsets, beloved of Stanfield and of Pugin.
    Dear! Thank you *ever so much* for your dear, kind understanding words. I feel a log with no zest for anything. It was all for him and with him and nothing seems to have any meaning. It is not grief for I am abundantly satisfied and secure in the certainty that all is well with him; only that I am selfish, and too much used to happiness to know how to do without it.
                                        Your loving,
                                        Mary Booth.

The second letter was to Beatrice Webb whose pen must have touched that deep-running stream of emotion shared with Charles and Mary all those years before:

1 A member of the publishing family and a close friend of the Ritchies.

Beatrice dear,

Thank you for your dear letter. It takes me straight back in thought to our old intimate days; before life, and that strange, difficult factor, divergence of opinion, led us apart, though it could not, and never will, sever the old tie. I've felt this always. And now, thank you for your sweet words. You knew him as few did, and all his single-minded, whole-hearted nature.

My love to you and Sidney,

Your ever affectionate,
Mary Booth.

This letter is touching and truthful and must have done something to fill the gap in Beatrice's faithful heart. When she came to write *My Apprenticeship*, the knowledge she had of her old friend's nature enabled her to produce a sense of astonishing completeness when making her assessment of his achievement. 'If I had to sum up in a sentence the net effects of Charles Booth's work I should say it was to give an entirely fresh impetus to the general adoption by the British people of . . . the policy of securing to every individual . . . a prescribed national minimum of the requisites for efficient parenthood and citizenship.'[1]

At the end of 1916 Mary made a record in her diary of family birthdays and festivals and, bracketed together in a special place on the page and in her heart, two anniversaries: 'Paulina Mary Booth died 18th March, 1876. Charles Booth died 23rd November, 1916. Goodbye my dear. Absens Adsis.'

When Charles lay dying, unable to speak, he gazed at Dodo for a long time with a particularly intent, appealing look; she knew that he was leaving his dear wife in her special charge. Her light touch and gay humour gave support without restraint and mother and daughter kept in constant touch. Mary, who like her father was convinced that she would die young, insisted upon Dodo accompanying her whenever she bought a new skirt or pair of shoes so that Dodo should approve of her future property! For twenty years, with just the right dash of fun and without a hint of the irritation she must certainly have felt at times, Dodo went with her mother on these extraordinary shopping expeditions.

Meanwhile the war was being fought out yard by yard and man by man and Mary copied into her diary 'The narrative of the operations

[1] Vol. II, Chap. V.

from zero on "Z" Day to the time the Battalion was relieved by Tom, Lt. Colonel commanding 1/6th Black Watch. Signed 17th November 1916'. There follow six closely written pages, written in paragraphs, marked '5.45 a.m.' or '7.15 a.m.' throughout the day. The officers' names, the number of men involved and the tactics employed are clearly defined. Casualties were 7 officers killed, 7 wounded; 70 other ranks killed, 140 wounded. Through the official language Tom's humanity shines out.

From February to May 1918 Baba was up in London and we Ritchies went to live with her. There was scarcely anything to eat and her diaries are full of the kind of recipes which may make much out of little but leave everyone unsatisfied. On 16 February 'a bomb fell on Chelsea Hospital at about 10.30 p.m. The keeper, his wife and child at the Lodge were killed. Lady Ritchie's house, 9 St. Leonard's Terrace, opposite the Hospital, had all the windows broken in. Lady Ritchie was in the drawing-room when it fell. The room was filled with dust and smoke and the smell of gunpowder.' When my governess took me there the next morning, Grandmama was lying on a sofa in the dark, because the curtains were drawn in an unsuccessful attempt to keep out the cold; the wind blew them backwards and forwards. Queues of old ladies came in with flowers and condolences which she accepted, looking rather vague and bored and perfectly at her ease. Her courage was satirical and static. Mary's was active and practical; her reaction to this event is written into her diary: 'Goethe says, "The Prussian was born a brute and civilisation will make him ferocious."'

It may well have been on the occasion of this air raid that, hearing the maroons going off at what seemed to me midnight, I came downstairs in my dressing-gown to the drawing-room where I found Baba sitting under the lamp, arguing about Ireland with Uncle Malcolm; sparkling with anger; rising to her feet; advancing upon him; bristling with contempt; quoting this and confuting that; and enjoying every minute of the waiting hours, as I did!

Early in 1918 Mary with a quiet mind set to work on her *Memoir* of Charles Booth. Others were doing what they could to commemorate his work. At the annual general meeting of the Thringstone Club and Library, the Reverend C. Shrewsbury, representing the trustees, took the chair, and a large number of members were present. The vote of sympathy with Mrs Booth and her family included the phrase: 'While Mr. Booth was ever welcomed in the highest circles of our land, let it be remembered that he was responsive to the approach of the poorest in the village of Thringstone. His was one of those characters which are unspoiled by greatness.' The motion was carried in silence, and all the members rose to their feet. Mary often quoted these words with a comical expression. How touched and amused Charles would have been.

In April 1918, during the last great lunge of the German Armies, Mary copied into her diary Queen Mary's message to the fighting forces, which always moved her very much. It begins: 'I send this message to tell every man how much we, the women of the British Empire at home, watch and pray for you during the long hours of these days of stress and endurance.'

By the spring of 1918 Booth family cares were diminishing rapidly. Tom, on his recovery from the effects of gas, had been seconded from the front line to a post in Holland with the Commission dealing with the exchange of prisoners, and her son-in-law Eric, having been awarded the D.S.O., was now safe at G.H.Q.; and in October Charles came home on leave. Mary wrote in her diary on 1 November, 'the Allies take 50,000 prisoners. Austria sues for peace. Turkey surrenders unconditionally.' On Sunday, 10 November, the entry is: 'M.C.B. to church. News of abdication of the Kaiser and the Crown Prince.' On Monday, the 11th: 'Imogen and the children left. We heard just before they started that the Armistice is signed. Mothers' Meeting and went to see Pattie.' On the following Sunday she noted: 'God Save the King in church and special prayers and thanksgiving.' Immediately underneath this is written a recipe for 'Cup Pudding: One cupful of breadcrumbs, flour, suet, jam, sugar, milk; half teaspoonful carbonate of soda; boil three hours in moderate oven.' If this juxtaposition had been pointed out to her, she would have thrown back her head and laughed outright, but basically the two items—the emotional world event and the addition to domestic lore—were not divided in her mind. A woman's life was always a combination of the two in her view.

On 23 November 1918 Mary wrote in her diary, 'Two years ago Charlie left us'; a month later, 'Tired. In all day. The "Memoir" came out'; and on the next day, 'In the woods, a dream of beauty'. As usual the woods and the conclusion of the task she had set herself brought her recovery and peace.

The *Memoir* is a short and telling story, divided into the different aspects of Charles's life and giving almost no hint of Mary's part in all

PLATE 7 Mary Booth with her grand-daughter, Belinda Norman-Butler, at Gracedieu Cottage 1936

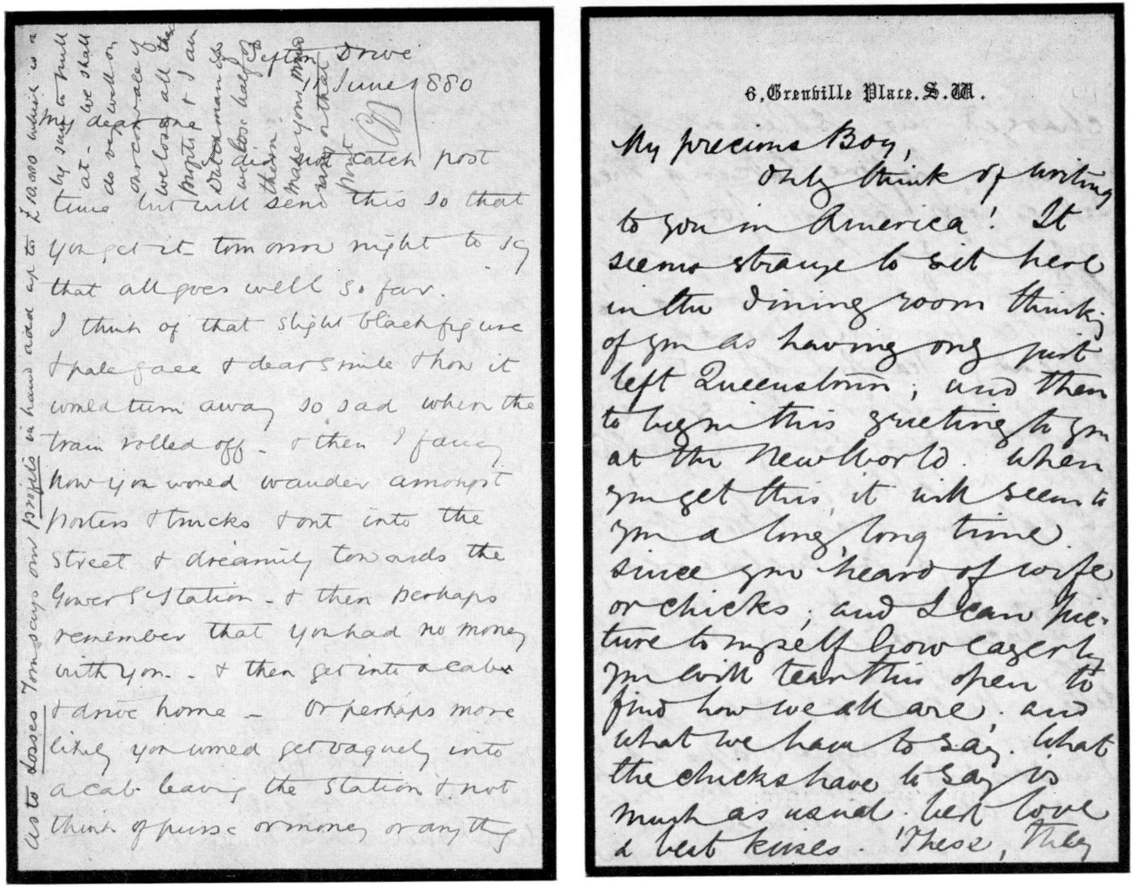

he undertook. All the reviews have been preserved. The *Positivist* begins with the lively phrase, 'It has been said with pardonable exaggeration that every goat skin in the world finds its way to Charles Booth sooner or later'. *Great Thoughts* concentrates on another angle:

The last of Charles Booth's published works is a pamphlet on 'Industrial Unrest and Trade Union Policy', issued in 1913 and this subject engaged his thoughts until his pen dropped from his hand in the autumn of 1916. His views are of extraordinary interest at the present moment, when our industrial system, like so many other things, is in the melting pot. The blame for industrial unrest, says he, lies upon us all. Masters and men must share it and onlookers with their hasty and violent judgements do not escape, but however the responsibility may be apportioned, the fact of economic loss to both parties and to the whole community remains.

The *Charity Organisation Review* generously devoted three pages to the men who were their strongest critics: 'Two names stand out pre-eminent among the popular philanthropists of London in the latter half of the 19th Century—Charles Booth and Samuel Augustus Barnett . . . The "Memoir" of Charles Booth is so slight as to be hardly more than a sketch, yet it will probably leave on the minds of most readers a clearer impression of its subject than will be gathered from the two massive volumes written [by Mrs Barnett] with admirable vigour of her husband's life, work and friends.' Still on the subject of Canon Barnett, the review finishes with these words: 'As with Mr. Booth, it was mainly the question of Old Age Pensions which attracted him away from his former allegiance to the C.O.S. and in both cases the loss was one to be deplored "for these were men of mercy".' It was right to link the two together, even though Canon Barnett was a convinced Churchman while Charles Booth always described himself as a reverent agnostic.

Gradually during 1919 the Booth family shook themselves back into peacetime life, and to Mary's great joy C.Z.M.B. became engaged to Mollie Spring-Rice and married her in July. The Booth children inherited extraordinarily diverse qualities and failings from their ancestors, but one gift they all shared—the ability to turn a love affair into a lifetime of devotion. Each of them possessed it to the full

Baba did not know that she was to live the same length of time, twenty-three years, as a widow, that she had lived as a girl at home; for twice that time, forty-six years, she had been a wife. Margie said of her mother-in-law that she was perfect at each stage of life. I feel that the constraints of the Macaulay ménage, the stresses, anxieties and sheer hard labour of her married life, were dearly paid for in heart strain and headaches, although these were as nothing compared to the fascinating companionship she had shared with her father and her husband. In old age, however, as a grandmother, she was perfectly and simply herself, and health came to her in abundance. Like many another medalled old age pensioner, she relished and enjoyed every moment of these holiday years squandering on her twenty-four grandchildren the treasure of mind and heart which fifty years before Charles had won for himself alone.

On 15 December 1920, Charles Booth's Memorial, designed by Sir Charles Nicholson, was unveiled in St Paul's Cathedral.[1] It stands in the south transept of the crypt not far from Wren's stone with its splendid Latin inscription. The English words describing Charles Booth's work are framed in twisted cables, hinting at those voyages of discovery which he had enjoyed throughout his life. Austen Chamberlain's 'perfect address' included these words: 'Something of the beauty of his life was traceable in his face: that face so shrewd and so kind; but above all in those eyes where humour and pity seemed to meet and express his soul.' As the social scientists Charles Booth had led and parted from and the church dignitaries he had criticised and appreciated walked away from the ceremony, they would have passed a picture which epitomised his passionate belief that informed goodwill is the Light of the World.

[1] In 1922 the Charles Booth Chair of Social Science was founded by the University of Liverpool and endowed by Alfred Booth & Co. Sir Alexander Carr-Saunders was the first holder and Professor, now Lord Simey, the second.

XII
GRACEDIEU
1920–1939

A year after my grandfather's death this quotation from Ruskin appears in Baba's diary:

There is a sanctity in a good man's house which cannot be renewed in every tenement that rises on its ruins and I believe that good men ... having spent their lives happily and honourably, would be grieved at the close of them to think that the place of their earthly abode, . . . was to be swept away . . . that no respect was to be shown to it, no affection felt for it, no good to be drawn from it by their children; that though there was a monument in the church there was no warm monument in the hearth and house to them. . . .

Undoubtedly Baba felt that she must keep Gracedieu going as a 'warm monument' to her husband, and George told her that her income from Alfred Booth and Company made this possible.

The reader may remember the character of M.C.B. as reported by Mr Sedgwick's groom in 1889 from the point of view of the servants' hall: 'They have to do what she tells them but if they do she is very kind to them but she won't stand no nonsense and quite right too!' Baba ran all her life at Gracedieu, or nearly all, from her desk, and the personal allegiance given to her by her staff was intense. Arthur Wilmot, the butler, Charles Wilmot who cared for the vegetable garden, Newton who ran the flower garden, Domany the coachman, and Mrs Howell, the head housemaid, all came to see her in the drawing-room, some every day, others when necessary. The only member of the staff she went to visit was the housekeeper, and curiously enough there were considerable difficulties and changes in that office, and almost none in any other.

Both Wilmot brothers were handsome, humorous and tall, but Arthur had a special grace of manner and command of phrase. It was he who, finding a flustered grandchild waiting in the dark outside the drawing-room door, wondering how to suggest an alteration or extension of plans, would give the grave advice, 'Use diplomacy, Miss' (or 'Sir', as befitted the occasion). He was only once at a loss and that of all things was a loss of temper. Maria, the parlourmaid, complained that he had sworn at her. Baba heard what Maria had to say and then summoned Wilmot. He admitted that the regrettable incident had taken place. On being pressed for an explanation he said, 'Well you see, Ma'am, Maria is always right.' Baba accepted this as understandable, and in a year or two it was Maria who left, right as ever.

Newton was a sensitive withdrawn man who looked, in contrast to his sturdy cuttings, the picture of ill-health. I held him in no respect and casually took some seedlings, without asking, for a clearing I was making in the wood. Baba scolded me and then came to smile at my 'Savile Garden'. She said that 'dear Newton was an artist', that his wife was 'no manager' and that in working class life this was a situation for which there was no redress. She gave them her entire sympathy in every difficulty. Remembering the brilliant herbaceous borders, the mown lawns and cut edges, I recognise that Newton with his seed catalogues and his eye for colour and shape was a remarkable gardener. The Arthur Wilmots, the Domanys and the Newtons lived at the top of the drive in the charming cottages which my grandparents had built for them. Wilmot's cottage and garden were exquisitely neat and pretty. In Domany's home there were prams in the passage, tricycles on the path and cups of tea always hospitably at hand in the kitchen. The third cottage was pathetically unkempt outside and in, and yet there again kindness and interest were never lacking.

Domany, the coachman, was our beloved friend, and by the nature of his occupation we had more to do with him even than with Wilmot. We talked to him endlessly and helped occasionally as he polished the saddles and bridles, cleaned the cars, and rubbed down the horses, hissing slightly through sparse, yellow teeth. We loved filling the buckets at the water pump, and putting them in the stalls, or sloshing them over the cobbles. Various people came and worked for him in the yard, but his youngest son, George, was the best mate he ever had. Domany's face was round as a melon and as red as a guardsman's jacket. He had very pale blue eyes and straw-like hair. He was very round in the middle; very active and alert, and much more intelligent than he looked. He was a great Conservative. 'Vote for the party never for the man,' he used to say, and then would launch into a full-blooded attack on the Labour candidate. He could cast a long line of invention when necessary. On one occasion he kept his master waiting and produced a brilliant explanation as to why he was late. 'That's a very good story, and I don't believe a word of it,' said my grandfather, amused.

Baba took tremendous interest in the stables, and urged on by Domany, who adored buying and selling horses, she entered into complicated negotiations and made the ultimate decisions. The first pony I remember was Johnny, who trotted round with bumping children on his back or took us bowling along in the governess-cart. He was soon joined by a roan cob for Domany's use. Then came the hunters, two of which must be mentioned by name—Jack the Australian Army horse, and Bridget, a bright chestnut mare. Baba's eyes gleamed as she asked about Bridget's prowess at the end of the day. She liked to know just where hounds had drawn, just where they had checked, and what the jumps were like. She used to watch the riders going off and would often be seen watching their return across the park from the drawing-room window. Our fun was her fun.

Mrs Howell was Baba's faithful ally. She managed the young housemaids perfectly and did a great deal in the linen department, though she was no particular friend of the children. We called her Mrs Wow. Perhaps she was rather lonely high up in her sewing-room above the nurseries. I once went to see her there and found her welcoming and pleasant, rather a different character from the one we usually met as we charged round the house. No doubt she came into her own in the quiet weeks of term time. Every evening she lit the fire in Baba's bedroom, laid out her evening clothes and ran her bath before dinner. Later she returned to clear up and put the night-gown to warm on the chair by the fire. Everyone over eighteen had a hip bath laid out daily on a numnah rug, and two jugs—one of boiling and one of cold water—placed beside it in the bedroom. Those under eighteen shared the one small attic bathroom with the maids. The tin bath was painted now and then and the surface was cracked and rough and very uncomfortable to sit on.

'Mrs Ladybird', as Uncle Tom called the housekeeper, held sway for a long while in the housekeeper's room, a sharp, difficult woman. She had an aged gentleman friend in whom we were much interested, and a horrible old spaniel which we detested. He lived under the sofa in the housekeeper's room which stood beneath the Manor's one and only telephone. Warned by all his nieces and nephews, Uncle Tom went on one occasion to make a call from this peculiar instrument. It was the kind—long obsolete even then—which had an adjustable mouthpiece. Every time he pulled the mouthpiece towards him, the spaniel growled from under the sofa. Finally Uncle Tom bent down to pat and reassure the dog, and was sharply bitten for his pains. For some reason his heartless nieces and nephews still rock with laughter when they remember this scene.

The hard tennis court, hidden behind the herbaceous borders, was used continuously in the summer holidays from ten in the morning until six or seven o'clock at night. The doyen and good fairy of all these matches was Uncle Tom. Dressed in exquisite white flannel trousers, tweed coat and Homburg,[1] he balanced little boys with big girls; good players with bad; he fetched balls; adjudicated awkward points and, like his Macaulay grandfather, invented little jingles and jokes to keep us all happy. 'Hard cheese!' has become 'Tough Cheddar!' to dozens of children because of his unusual way of expressing sympathy. Very often Baba sat with those who were waiting their turn, and watched each ball and enjoyed each rally more than the players. On wet days everyone read *Punch* in the library. Baba had the whole set bound in stiff, purple covers, and we revelled in jokes of the eighties and nineties and the First World War. In many ways our lives had enough likeness to du Maurier's pictures to make us laugh in tune with him. We were neo-Victorians.

The same group, sitting on the lawn under the ilex trees, would watch the recurrent cricket matches. These were more formal occasions. Down below on the cricket field we would see the Domany family, the Newtons and Wilmots and many village friends. I met old Mr Vestey from the Home Farm, coming down to watch a match one day, and addressed him by name. 'You 'ave the advantage of me, Miss', he said in a stately way, tipping his hat. I had not considered the necessity of being introduced before this happened. We knew everybody roundabout and everybody knew us; Gracedieu was a haven, for us and the whole neighbourhood.

Nevertheless, it was a haven in which sudden and violent squalls could unexpectedly swamp the unwary. One day at lunch I had the temerity to criticise Lloyd George's Government for blockading the civilian population of Germany in order to force the Provisional Government to accept the Allied terms. Without considering or measuring the

[1] A felt hat with a bound brim.

consequences, I said that it would have been better to have gone on fighting to achieve submission rather than to starve the children. I had no comprehension then of Baba's long anxiety in the war and her bitter fury with the nation which had instigated the conflict; nor had I the smallest knowledge of Keynes's recent book, *The Economic Consequences of the Peace*, and its political undertones. With relentless contumely Baba demolished my feeble remarks. At that time children simply did not leave the table for any other reason than extreme illness. I sat on, swallowing the tears which poured into my mouth, shaking with sobs, refusing the dishes that Wilmot and Maria handed to me as part of the traditional dining-room dance, until the meal came to an end. I spent the afternoon wandering about in the wood and, returning towards tea time along the avenue between the ilexes and the cedars, I saw Baba's tiny figure in the distance, dressed as usual in what we called 'the druid garment'. This was a cloak made of very light tweed which always hung on a peg in the lobby by the garden door, and outlasted its mistress after thirty years' wear. Baba saw me, and putting her hands together and her head down came rapidly towards me with her short, swinging steps. For an instant I thought of flight, but with thumping heart I braced myself and walked towards her. As we came nearer I saw that she was smiling. 'You spoke from the heart,' she said, 'and I may have misjudged your point of view. At the same time I think you should realise . . .'. Having begun in the most dulcet tones her voice began to rise rhythmically and furiously and suddenly I did the only thing that was possible: I began to laugh, and so did Baba, at the ridiculous way in which the whole affair might so easily have begun all over again. We walked about arm-in-arm for a while, and then went in to tea, but we never discussed this particular topic again.

Another clash of arms led to an insight into Baba's life without which this memoir would have been even harder to write. Nevertheless, it left its scars. In 1926 Beatrice Webb's *My Apprenticeship* came out. Always foraging for books, I found it put with the other autobiographies in the bookcase on the landing outside the guest bedrooms. Any new book is intriguing. Not knowing anything about the author or her particular connection with the Booths, I was immediately enthralled by the description of Papa already quoted in Chapter III. Having spent most of the morning sitting on the top step of Harry Fletcher's staircase, which came up to that landing only and was therefore a good place for quiet reading, I set off to find Baba. She was at her desk in the drawing-room as usual with the sun shining round her; one of the most satisfactory things about Baba was that she could always be found. The little scene is still in retrospect, as it was then, deeply disappointing. 'What a fascinating picture of Papa!' I said, holding out the book, and instantly it seemed that the sunshine waned. 'A pack of half truths, if not downright lies,' was one of Baba's remarks, and then a great deal about the vanities and absurdities of Beatrice Webb's flirtation with Russia. Trying to leave the political situation of that day out of it, I reiterated that it was the first account of Papa I had ever read.

Then Baba took me up to her bedroom and put her own *Memoir* of Charles Booth into my hand. We looked at the photographs in the book, and then at all the photographs on the walls. When we came to Mrs Leslie Stephen's picture, Baba said that such beauty was so great that even a cold in the nose did not affect it. I noticed for the first time that there was no picture of Papa in Baba's bedroom, and I asked to see others than those in the *Memoir*. Baba brought out a box which we carried back to the drawing-room; photographs of all kinds fell out, and I went steadily through them, asking 'Who is this?' and 'Where was that?' Then I came to the picture of a painfully thin young man with darkish, untidy hair, an eager look, a small straggling moustache and no chin. 'Who is this?' I asked, thinking that it was probably a picture of Baba's brother, Charles. 'Don't you know?' said Baba. '*It's Charlie.* That was taken when he was so ill that we had to go to Switzerland.' As a result of my reading Beatrice Webb's book Baba told me a great deal about those early years, but we never discussed the author of *My Apprenticeship* again. In her mind political divisions were a real barrier to friendship; things were right or wrong. There were no half measures because Baba minded too much. She would not have sympathized with the bipartisan spirit with which most people discuss the questions of today. She stuck to the cut and thrust of the House of Commons at all times, and deplored every action of the Liberal and Labour parties. Only once did she talk in a different vein to me, and that was when Asquith died. She sat down, looking at the announcement in *The Times*, and then she looked up with tears in her eyes. 'Something has gone from the House,' she said. 'His scholarly mind and power of—oh, what is the word?' 'Rhetoric,' I suggested, remembering her dislike. 'Nonsense,' she replied. 'There's a nobler word—oratory. That power of oratory will never be heard again. The House has lost its Master.'

Her own side did not escape without scathing comment. She was horrified that Arthur Balfour, whom she trusted, had not resigned in protest during the Peace Conference, which certainly turned out as ill as she foretold it would. She thought that Woodrow Wilson's wish to set the world to rights was completely fatuous but only to be expected from an American, and that the European politicians who followed his lead ought to have known better. She could never understand why Stanley Baldwin wished to give women the vote, but stood entirely behind him on the question of protection. Old age pensions and a limited form of protection were the two principles advocated by her husband of which Baba entirely approved. Other ideas which had passed through his mind, some of them, such as free public transport, emerging in print, were entirely rejected by her. This made things rather confusing for the grandchildren who, having got as far as realising that their grandparents were pioneer philanthropists, discovered unexpected pitfalls in the paths of conversation.

One morning I found a very seedy-looking man saying goodbye to Baba in the drawing-room after an interview. She told me that he was a Whitwick collier who had a 'grumbling' appendix and was often laid off work as a result. He had come to ask for help. I said I thought it would pay the country to enable such a man to have his operation, and what a pity it was he had to wait until the attack became actually dangerous before the hospital could help him. 'Pity!' said Baba with scathing emphasis, 'and who is to pay for all this? How can we protect our fishing rights, our lines of communication, without a fleet? How can we patrol the North West Frontier, police India, administer the Colonies, honour our treaties, without an army? Taxation is heavy enough already to hinder industry; further taxation would cripple it. Pity! Pity!' she reiterated. But later on she called me back from the garden and asked me to help her in looking up addresses of people who subscribed to the Surgical Aid Society, and she wrote to a dozen or more of those she knew, or had some link with, to ask them for their help in providing the Whitwick collier with sufficient funds to have his operation. Her sympathy was always there for the individual, as Papa's had been, but he looked further and deeper into the background to form a complete picture, and wondered why and how environment influenced man. It is only now that I realise that these snatches of argument, which made such a deep impression on me at the time, were really one-sided echoes of their grand marriage-long arguments. Without his answering voice, her positive approach was too absolute.

Papa's very large donations to charity came to an end with his death, but Baba's own list was generous by any standards, and included every year one rather startling bequest: 'Cruelty, two guineas' (N.S.P.C.C.). She collected some data on her own contribution to the well-being of invalid children, and on various pages of her diary she wrote down 'the history of St. Andrew's Home', which she was able to run with her Macaulay income, noting above the title: 'Opened at the Cross Lanes cottage in May 1910 with room for three children, those threatened with phthisis but not actually infected to be preferred. Mrs Turner was the first Matron. Sally Watton and Eva Rossell the first names. Parted with Mrs Turner in July. Miss Howard started on the 24th and left for Australia in the summer of 1911, and Miss Whiffin succeeded her and is there still.' Many girls' names follow. In 1914, 'we moved to the new Home capable of holding seven girls'. Then follows a list of twenty-five girls, almost all of whom 'improved in health very greatly' and most of whom went into service, some at the Manor; one or two became dressmakers and some went to munition work. One, Lizzie, 'was disappointed and left very soon at her own desire'. 'Edith Rossell who has been with us a long time is much better but still suffers from asthma.' This faithful friend means a great deal to all Gracedieu grandchildren.

Breakfast was a long meal at Gracedieu. Baba drank a cup of coffee with the early risers, and then made herself a cup of tea which lasted until the nine o'clockers were well into the marmalade. After that the post arrived and sitting on the window-seat with a waste paper basket and several grandchildren beside her, she would open all her letters and read them aloud, beginning with Aunt Dodo's delightful, pithy pages, which were as much a part of Baba's life as the woods and fields of Leicestershire. Next she enjoyed looking through all the circulars, bills and advertisements, discussing the latest fashions, and asking those about her whether that particularly splendid hat would be suitable for church, or debating how quickly this magnificent new motor-driven mowing machine would cut the grass. Mowing at Gracedieu, with a pony pulling the machine, took three days every fortnight, and the sound and smell of it to Gracedieu children seemed as constant as the sea breaking on the shores of Britain.

When this was all over, at about a quarter to ten, a general exodus took place, but usually one grandchild remained to walk with Baba into the drawing-room, and there on the side table, neatly folded, lay the

Morning Post and *The Times*. When being offered my choice on first graduating to newspaper level, I took the *Morning Post*, for I felt *The Times* looked more imposing and therefore more suitable for Baba. She gave me the *Morning Post* with very good grace, but I saw that her face had fallen, so I asked for *The Times* instead. She held it out eagerly. Baba loved the *Morning Post* because it was a partisan paper. She liked the cut and thrust of the editorials, and the handling of the news, but having read it not very seriously, standing upright by the fire, she would switch to *The Times*, reading the debates of both Houses with the greatest attention. Budget Day, year after year, was a great excitement to her. Of course, there was no wireless to spread the news the night before, so that sixpence on or off the income tax only became known when Baba opened the pages by the fire after breakfast.

The papers read, Baba would call on the housekeeper, visit the stables and return to work at her desk, which was always in apple-pie order. Then would come a little walk, for which preparations were minimal—the 'druid garment' thrown across the shoulders in almost all weathers, a straw hat with an elastic band behind her 'bun' in the summer, a little black velour pudding for the winter; goloshes when it was wet and sometimes a basket in which lay a kneeling-mat and an object not unlike 'Uncle Matthew's' entrenching tool of which Nancy Mitford writes. With this implement Baba used to dig up plaintains from the lawn and as the years went by and her strength declined there were fewer and fewer plantains to be dealt with, so the equation was a satisfactory one.

The drawing-room must be described next. 'I asked Charlie for £100,' explained Baba when asked about it, 'and I lined the walls with oak and stained them dark and I filled in the Gothic arches to the windows to cut out the intolerable glare, and give a feeling of quiet and seclusion.' A pale mushroom carpet covered the floor. Baba's knee-hole desk stood in the south window, and bookshelves lined the wall behind and before her. Her own little upright armchair and its pair stood beside a serviceable square table. The first lamp to be brought in when it grew dark was put on this table. When Aladdin lamps were invented, Baba found their extra light extremely convenient, and had one to read by. Large sofas and chairs stood round in different corners, all of them covered in a marvellous chintz, the dye of which Baba bought when she chose the material in 1900. Every now and again another bolt of chintz would be printed for her. The background was shining white on which gorgeous red roses and bold green foliage grew luxuriantly. The curtains were woven in shades of dark green, one of William Morris's designs, and he designed the hanging brass lamps which were made in his workshops.

In the east window a jigsaw puzzle was almost always set out, and when it was finished Baba would pack it up personally, add a note if a piece was missing, and then dispatch it to the Puzzle Club. The arrival of a new jigsaw was always a delightful moment; we enjoyed looking at the title, putting the pieces the right way up and deciding which was the sky and which the outside. Under my brother's clumsy-looking hands the most complicated background would melt into order. Baba was bad at seeing shapes, but she liked the companionship and ease, and the scraps of talk and the teasing that went on round the puzzle table. Sometimes she would sing in a quavery voice some snatch of song, 'Daisy, Daisy, give me your answer, do', or 'Knocked 'em in the Old Kent Road'. She played backgammon with a single companion, keenly rattling the dice, and took to Patience when alone.

Tea time was another of Baba's moments. Wilmot and Maria would arrive with the kind of round table that shuts up across its diameter and a white linen cloth, a tray of green and white Rockingham cups, a silver kettle, spoons, knives, cut bread and butter and Tiptree's strawberry jam. As we got older, Baba would sometimes turn to one of us and say with shining eyes, 'Will my darling make tea?', but when we were young she always made it herself with great precision, heating the pot, keeping the kettle going, and seeing that everyone had something to eat. If we had been out hunting there was always an egg for our tea, in addition to the other good things. If there were small children staying in the house, their time came after tea. They played all sorts of games with innumerable silk handerchiefs and bricks and a little wooden bucket known as 'Gibadink', which restored wounded soldiers, fed dolls and the long-suffering grown-ups continuously. Sometimes Baba would play the piano for Musical Bumps, and the tunes she played were usually Schumann's *Kinderscenen*.

It was her habit to stand upright beside the fire after dinner for at least half an hour, and while her children and grandchildren wilted around her she would tell them about the long, dreary hours spent at Miss Marshall's school, wearing her backboard. All her life astronomy had a calming, pleasurable influence on Mary, and through her eastern window she loved to watch the night sky. The stars were personal friends, and she spoke of them as people—'What can Sirius be about?'

Often after dark she would step out of the drawing-room into the garden, wrapped in a white shawl, even in the depths of winter, to show her grandchildren a particular planet.

Baba was not specially interested in the origins and history of Gracedieu, preferring to tell us of Haselour Hall or Ightham Mote, but of course we went on asking questions about the ruins down by the stream, and the locked chapel into which she did not know we could climb by a broken window. For years we wandered about inside, looking at the dusty painted statues, calmed by the quiet atmosphere, and certainly doing no harm. Unfortunately, it was chosen as a top secret meeting place by some younger cousins, and this incident led to the window being barred, after a painful interview!

The chapel and St Bernard's Monastery, four miles away, also built during the nineteenth-century Roman Catholic revival in England, seemed as mysterious and romantic to us as the mock ruins in the wood. Gracedieu Priory was founded in the thirteenth century, and was dissolved by Henry VIII in 1534, the twelve nuns being equipped for the world with red flannel petticoats and precious little else. John Beaumont of Thringstone, one of Henry VIII's ecclesiastical surveyors, was in a good position for procuring the property. After putting in Elizabethan windows and fireplaces, he lived in the Priory for some years; he was the father of the famous playwright. In the eighteenth century Sir George Beaumont, patron of poets and artists, decided to revive his mouldering Leicestershire estate and built a fine Georgian house nearby at Cole Orton. When he died he left his collection of pictures to the nation, which resulted in the establishment of the National Gallery. The Priory had already become a ruin, and was sold to Sir Ambrose Phillips of the Middle Temple, who had acquired a great deal of land in Leicestershire, after the Jacobite invasion of 1745. Prince Charlie's army reached Derby before it melted away. Many ruined Cavaliers of the district were glad to sell their land at bargain prices. Sir Ambrose Phillips's son married a Miss Lisle, and added a 'de' to the name in deference to the romantic movement of the time, but not to the liking of the de Lisle and Dudley family. The nineteenth-century heir to this extensive property, Ambrose March Phillips de Lisle, a convert to Roman Catholicism, built Gracedieu Manor in 1830 half a mile from the ruins, on higher ground, with a mind to turn it into a priory. Later, he engaged Pugin to add a chapel on the west and a wing on the east of the original square block. This wing, in which small bedrooms face north while the wide passage faces south, possibly designed as a solarium, was our nursery passage. It ended in a stone spiral staircase which led to the servants' quarters below.

In the holidays Gracedieu was always alive with children, not only the twenty cousins, but other children who lived nearby as well. For week after week Baba's spirit and enjoyment never flagged, but as James and I grew older, and both of us as students had longer holidays, the last week in September and the first in October became doubly precious to us, because we shared with our grandmother a certain sense of release from the job of organising many people. Many things having been well done, Baba could sink back into the pause which is autumn, and concentrate on the beauty of the wood. Newton and the under-gardeners, freed for a while from the slavery of flower-beds and growing grass, used to take billhooks and saws and, under Baba's direction, trim the rhododendron walks, cut down dead trees and root out brambles. James and I turned our attention to bonfires, and Baba in her 'druid garment' would come and stand beside us, watching the scene, enjoying the shouts, the crackle of the flames and the touch of chill in the air as evening drew on. Then we would walk home together across the cricket pitch, not speaking very much, half bemused by the ancient ways of man and the touch of worship which flaming boughs bring out in all human beings. Back again round the tea-table beside the coal fire, with the lamps lit,[1] conversation would run on again as if it had never ceased. Soon after six o'clock Baba would go upstairs for her rest, and following her, an hour or so later, to change for dinner, we often heard a little cooing song, the rustle of skirts, and a step or two as we paused on the steep stairs outside her door; she was dancing a little minuet of happiness.

Her bedroom was thirty feet square, with an oblong-shaped bow window thrown out to the east. The furniture was dark mahogany, the doors were stained black, and the effect was of a comfortable monastery cell. Beside the window stood an elegant sofa-table, topped by an oval eighteenth-century looking-glass. On the table lay ivory brushes, a small hand mirror and a bottle of bay rum. Baba used to say to us, 'Do what you can with your appearance and then leave it alone.' She certainly left hers alone! In the darkest corner, beyond the fireplace, a

---

[1] Gracedieu Manor was lit entirely by lamps and candles until 1932 when Baba moved into the Cottage.

door led through to Papa's old room. This was equally big, but in contrast to Baba's room, blindingly light: spare rugs on a floor of bare boards, armchairs covered with horse hair, and an enormous desk, furnished the gaunt room. On the wall by the door into his wife's room hung Papa's proudest possession: the framed certificate given him when he was elected a Fellow of the Royal Society. To balance this on the right-hand side of the window hung an ordinary photograph of Liverpool Docks.

As we grew older I became aware that Baba lived her life in compartments. To her Leicestershire friends, she was a darling old lady with extraordinary sweetness and sympathy, and though this impression was deeply true, it was not the whole of her. Her love for Leicestershire meant that she spent less and less time in London. The rough-and-tumble of the holidays over, another compartment, the quiet of the term time, suited her to perfection. Left alone, she would reread the whole of *The Prelude* ('a great deal of it very dull') or *The Faerye Queen* ('What an extraordinary idea of life, pricking over the sward like that'). This serious reading was combined with knitting, playing the piano, laughing over a George Birmingham novel or doing a crossword puzzle.

She had a tremendous respect for Byron as a poet and gave me *Don Juan*, saying that it was so amusing and also so revealing about Byron himself, and the strange destiny he shared to some extent with his hero: never able to concentrate on one person, always fated to continue the chase. She spoke quite openly about Byron's escapades at Newstead, his love affair with Caro Lamb, and even his relationship with his half-sister. The contrast of the nobility of his death and the vulgarity of Trelawney's eager curiosity about the origin of Byron's lameness always evoked her sympathy and indignation—'Low!' she would exclaim, '*Low!*' She couldn't stand Keats's poetry: 'Too cloying'; nor did his love for Fanny Brawne, or his early death, touch her heart. But Shelley was another of her wild eagles; he attracted her not only as a poet, but also as a man. His treatment of his first wife was entirely counterbalanced by his imagination and pluck.

I remember vividly how, after dinner one evening in the twenties, Baba asked me if I knew Thackeray's tribute to Macaulay which is now bound up in *The Roundabout Papers*. When I shook my head she went to the bookcase on the right of her desk, picked out the volume she wanted, without hesitation found the place and standing in the middle of the room read out the rolling phrases with emotion. She then closed the book and came right up to me, her brown eyes enormous with unshed tears, and said it was a remarkable example of sympathy between two geniuses of such different backgrounds and attainments.

She never sat in the book-lined library, but when she went to look for Taine or Maeterlinck she knew exactly where to find them. She had a little bookcase in the drawing-room for library books, and a lovely mahogany sewing table for her silks and wools. Nothing ever ran out at Gracedieu, neither books nor stamps nor knitting needles. She had complete and tranquil control of the ship.

She was by nature a very reticent woman, for all her vivacity and truthfulness, and found it difficult to change her compartments quickly. Those who had known her in past days, who came looking for that old age pension enthusiast, or dear Cousin Mary, were sometimes surprised and hurt by the Leicestershire lady who met them. Mrs Marshall, the wife of the professor, and dear friend of long ago, arrived to stay wearing long, black robes, sandals and knitted woollen socks. It is hard to say whether Baba was bored by the economics and statistics of the past or whether she wanted to emphasise another side of life; whichever it was, she inundated Mrs Marshall with county gossip. When at last conversation came round to more familiar ground the two widows, very pink in the face, rebutted each other's statements with phrases beginning 'Charlie always said', and 'Alfred much disliked'. The visit was not a success. I felt sorry for Mrs Marshall and her lost expression. No doubt she was relieved to get back to her tricycle in Cambridge. A visit from the Rothensteins went well on the whole, but I was surprised to find Baba rubbing her hands after they had driven off, and humming a little tune as she stepped back into the drawing-room. She had no need of friends from the past; her life was full enough, more than full, as it was; even Edith Hunt only came once.

Of all the imperious old ladies we knew, festooned in black lace and gold chains, whose bearded husbands had been photographed by Mrs Cameron, Mrs Holman Hunt was easily my favourite. The bonfires, boy scouts and dressing-up boxes of her extraordinary domain provided hilarious entertainment. Tea-parties with Lady Tennyson, Lady Pollock and Mrs Reginald Smith, trying not to drop crumbs, were pure torture. We never spilt anything in Melbury Road because a good deal had been spilt already and nobody minded. Mrs Holman Hunt once gave me some beads which 'Holman had picked up in Palestine'. I imagined him scooping them out of the desert and hanging them round the neck of a goat. This is an unexpected chance to say thank you to his endearingly eccentric widow.

Cousins, distinguished or not, who brought their children to stay, were in a different category altogether from visitors. They had a right to Gracedieu's hospitality somehow and these visits were delightful. The George Macaulay Trevelyan family used to come and so did the Tom Macaulays. After G.M.T. brought out his *History of England* in 1926 I remember Baba dampening my enthusiasm by saying that considering the sympathetic assistance given to 'Uncle Tom' by Lord Holland and Lord Lansdowne it was ridiculous that George's prosperous father should not have spared him the necessity of writing pot-boilers. In the long run, however, *English Social History* (published in 1944) gained by the fact that due to early cares G.M.T. remained a poor man at heart even when riches came his way. He certainly possessed a particularly affectionate and poetic insight into other people's lives. When the second survey of London was published G.M.T. talked to me about Papa and said, in his grinding voice, 'It was magnificent work done in the teeth of opposition with two ulcers gnawing away inside.'

Looking round at the cousinhood Baba felt sad that 'the Booth strain seemed to have gone in', and that the children of all six marriages had taken after the in-laws. As Papa was totally unlike his family, I do not know what strain she meant, but it was certainly regrettable that none of the Macaulay brains reappeared to take the scholarships she would have won so easily. Just once, and only once, she gave me an inkling of her pride in long past school prowess. She had been reading me Macaulay's great speech in the House of Commons advocating the Bill which finally freed Jews from all political and educational limitations in this country. I made some remark about their remarkable level of intelligence. Baba drew herself up: 'Yes,' she said, 'they are very fine thinkers, and they mature early. However, they were never first in my class at Monsieur Roche's.' I looked at her and said, 'You were first', and she blushed with shyness, and smiled and hung her head. On another occasion I owned up to the habit of pretending to be D'Artagnan or Lady Hester Stanhope or Jim Hawkins, according to the book I was reading. It was tea-time, and she was busy lighting the kettle, and she said naturally and without thinking at all of the implications: 'But *nobody* can resist that', and I suddenly realised that perhaps even as a grandmother she could not resist it either. It was this touch of fantasy that went to our hearts and made the minutes count in her presence.

Throughout the county, Baba was much in demand for opening new schools and giving away prizes. These events usually took place in term time, but on one occasion a loan exhibition of dolls and embroidery was held at Lord and Lady Ferrers' home, Staunton Harold, in August, so Baba took me with her for the opening ceremony. Domany drove us over, and laid the fine tweed rug over our knees and handed me out at the door, as well as his mistress, with just the right touch of deference. This made me feel rather grand, and rather amused, for he and I had been arguing on very even terms that morning about a new saddle. Baba looked perfectly lovely in a tiny white lace bonnet and her black corded silk 'Manteau', of which she was very proud. Made by 'Madame Rose' in 1906 or so, it reappeared for weddings or special occasions. She always wore the same sort of shoes with five little straps across the instep and her evening pair were ornamented with little jet beads. White gloves completed the outfit. When she stepped onto the plat-form I noticed to my astonishment—and it has touched me to the heart ever since—that she was exceedingly nervous. I had never seen her anything but confidence itself. She made a halting little speech, using the most ordinary of the well-known phrases, and then, having declared the loan exhibition open, she said she trusted that no one would go away empty-handed. This, of course, brought a shout of laughter from everyone, particularly those who had lent the most valuable things, and the little mistake endeared her all the more to her audience. How-ever, she was upset and spoke anxiously about it on the way home.

Of the deepest hurt she ever endured she never spoke at all. In the late twenties we could see around us the pathetic poverty of hard-working farming families and we became aware that neither the Booth ships nor the leather factories were doing any better. Business disagree-ments which are softened by success increase in hard times and flare into bitterness when family loyalties are involved. Charles left the business and Baba leant perilously far towards his point of view, but not far enough to satisfy him. Although his home was nearby he cut himself off from Gracedieu altogether for several years. Baba lived silently through this cruel time, only showing her yearning for her youngest son by being much too stiff with George, who, as Chairman of the business, behaved with great generosity. Gradually the breach was healed and a special friendship grew up between Baba and Mollie, her daughter-in-law, which was their reward for loyalty in distress. Of the three uncles, all such disparate characters, Tom the gallant soldier and George the imaginative merchant relished and relied on each other's company in old age; only Charles, who never found the best way of employing his brains, remained aloof.

On Monday, 21 September 1931, an event occurred which seems now like a storm in a tea-cup, but then seemed to mean a great deal. Britain went off the gold standard, and it looked as if other standards would have to go too. When the end of Baba's fifty-year lease of Gracedieu came into view, the future of Alfred Booth and Company seemed far from certain. Totally tranquil, she made her plans to move from the place which will always be more hers than anyone else's, to Gracedieu Cottage. Papa's idea of a nursery in the woods for his eldest daughter now became a haven for his widow. An upstairs bedroom was lined with shelves, and Baba chose her favourite books and measured the space available with effective enjoyment, assisted by my father, who shared her love of reading. Gracedieu Manor was taken over as a preparatory school by Radcliffe College, a Roman Catholic public school. It could not have had a happier or more appropriate fate. Arthur Wilmot and Domany moved their families to live nearby and went on working for Baba. Charles Wilmot gardened for the school, and Edith Rossell came to be housemaid to the founder of St Andrew's Home.

In August 1932, Agnes Howell retired. 'We have lived together for sixty-six years,' wrote Baba in her diary, and the next day she walked down the gentle slope of the lawn to the railings by the great oak tree and up the path, passing the cricket field, and through the wood to her new home. There were no regrets, or if there were they were never for herself. This ability she had of living on the day, in the hour, to the minute, brought her instant happiness. Some of us went to stay for the first time at the Cottage with sore hearts, but going into the drawing-room and seeing her in the bay window with the sun all round her and the oaks stepping down the rocky slope outside, we felt that nothing had changed, except perhaps ourselves.

But there was a change in Baba, which had nothing to do with the move from the Manor to the Cottage. She had used happiness as some folk use medicine, and had dosed us with it to her heart's content. Maintaining a great reserve about the stiles and ditches of adult life, she succeeded in giving us children a most uncomplicated sense of security and enjoyment. As we grew up, we asked and received much more, and during the last span of her life she allowed us glimpses of the strange, deepening thoughts of very old age, and the moral grandeur of those who ask nothing at all for themselves. Her own integrity, learning and sweetness had grown with every faithful year. She no longer wished for our happiness; she hoped for development. For herself, gradually stepping still further back, she was sought out more than ever by her family and her country friends. She came seldom and for still shorter intervals to stay with her Dodo, but never failed to attend all our weddings, except that of Tom Booth, who married in America. Away from home she seemed less confident, less herself; back in her own Leicestershire kingdom, she was pre-eminent.

On 17 January 1938 Baba wrote to her daughter Meg: 'Life here flows on very quietly and your old mother is very well though feeling steadily older and more tottery. We have had two amusing Sherry Parties in the neighbourhood, all of us meeting and chatting and everyone apparently in good case.' To be 'steadily older' at the age of ninety-one means different things to different people! 'I forget if I told you that Mr. de Lisle has absolutely turned down my request to buy the Wood [for the benefit of the people of Leicestershire]. 'I am very very disappointed.' Referring to her life and work with her husband she used the word 'wonderful'. 'It is strange,' she went on, 'how long ago it seems, so that I sometimes feel as I look back on the lives of two people together as if they were both there.'

In the spring of 1939 I took my 5-year-old son to stay with Baba and as she watched his hands at work among the bricks, the animals and the coloured handkerchiefs, she talked of her early days and said: 'Of course, a woman's deepest thoughts are for her children—not always the happiest,' she added, 'but the deepest.' I was surprised, because I imagined that her deepest thoughts would have been for her husband. On reflection I think she was remembering the family responsibility which had been hers, not his. One night we discussed the difficult question of religious education. 'What does Edward[1] think?' she asked. 'He leaves it to me'. 'So did Charlie,' she said, very far away in the past. 'But you knew what to do,' I burst out, 'and I don't.' 'Oh no,' she said, 'I was just the same: in a mist.' Watching her I was suddenly terrified that she was frightened of the denser mist ahead. She knew without words what had come over me, and told me comforting and yet chilling things about old age. 'All my contemporaries are gone,' she

---

[1] My husband, Edward Norman-Butler.

said, 'You dear ones give me so much that I enjoy my life, but I couldn't begin again with another generation. There is an instinct for death, as there is for life. Sir Frederick Treves told me so. It has been obscured by the fear of Hell, largely inculcated by the Roman Catholics, but it is a real thing—a natural thing—I have no fear of death; I fear incapacity.'

She spoke of the beauty of the English prayer-book—particularly of the Collects—and what a boon it was to share the setting if not all the dogma of the Anglican Church: 'How ridiculous and arrogant it is to begin to attempt a new interpretation of the Infinite.' She reminded me of Talleyrand's remark to the revolutionary Deputy who wished to set up a new religion in France: 'All you have to do is to die and rise again on the third day.' 'I love the Church of England,' she said. So many Sundays in ugly St Andrew's Church I had watched her little black back at the end of the pew by the wall, the cotton gloves laid beside the fat prayer-book, and noticed her demure expression as Cousin Albert Babington, who couldn't say his 'r's, preached about the 'Towwid zones of the south', or Colonel Bob Martin described the financial structure of the Diocesan Board of Finance, from the pulpit; and remembered how she would go home and read Fénelon's spiritual advice to court ladies.

It must have been after this visit that Baba wrote words that can only be quoted because the young woman she praised is as distant in time as she is: 'I can't tell you what a joy Belinda's time here was to me. I have always loved her dearly, but now she seems more entirely to-be-devoted-to than ever. . . . What a blessing one's own private life is! One is every day thankful to be able to throw off the terrible anxiety that comes with the reading of the daily papers with all the warnings of evil that are shadowing our country, to say nothing of other countries with their great anxieties: Oh, Hitler, Goering and Goebbels!!' She had a right to explode because she had read *Mein Kampf* in German when it came out. 'Hitler is very frank,' she said. 'You can't say he dissembles at all. It's all here—the whole plan of attack. Why don't our politicians read his book instead of exchanging delegations?' And he did attack, just as her long, peaceful dominance came to an end.

Up to the end of July 1939, Baba went walking as usual alone in her beloved woods. Sometimes she fell only to return and write in her diary; 'I took no hurt.' In the end she fell in her bedroom. When I went to the Cottage a fortnight later, Aunt Dodo's smiling face and easy command of the situation made the first moments not only bearable but even enjoyable. It seemed, in spite of anxiety, like another heavenly Gracedieu visit until the nurse, crackling in her uniform, took me upstairs.

The prisoner lay, small and crumpled and chained, in an unrecognisably light, impersonal room. She held my hand and asked eagerly for news, as I had met her friend, Dr Bell, in the hall. 'He won't tell me, did he tell you, how long I must stay in bed?' The first and only time she needed help from me I had neither the courage to tell the truth nor the grace to lie properly. 'Six weeks,' I said, halving Dr Bell's three months. Baba looked absolutely stricken and then was magnificently angry: 'It is too long. Impossible! I must be out and about. I have a great deal to do,' she said. 'You will be in the Wood again by the autumn,' I suggested, 'and we will have a bonfire and come home to Tiptree's strawberry jam . . .'—but the sentence broke. Suddenly acutely aware of her precarious hold on life, I was absolutely unable to reach beyond my own panic; even too shy to look at her. And then Baba leant over and kissed my hand and laid it to her cheek. I had told her something after all, and she was telling me the greater truth. There was no shyness left. I looked at her for a long while. We never said goodbye.

APPENDIX A
CHARLES BOOTH
'What I appear to myself—October 1878'

(see Chapter III, page 51)

I should doubt the advantage of 'seeing ourselves as others see us' if we must *change* our own point of view for theirs. It is, however, well to know what others think of us and few minds are so hardy as to be uninfluenced by this knowledge. What I imagine others to think of me, then, shall be stated first.

Firstly that I am a fool—they think it in various degrees—with kindness and with unkindness—and modified more or less by other considerations—but at bottom that is what most people think of me. . . . None of my friends would be surprised at an act of folly from me and such wisdom as I possess is apt to be disregarded and unnoticed. Of those who love me most, and think most highly of me, none would say of me 'he has wisdom'—nor do I claim it for myself. Yet I am not so great a fool as I appear nor do I fail to reap some of the rewards of wisdom.

Secondly that I am clever but shallow. I believe I pass for clever with nearly all, and with all the limit to my cleverness would come with such qualification as 'perhaps not deep', 'wanting in depth'—all down the gamut till 'very shallow', 'fanciful' and 'silly' are reached by those who judge me most hardly.

Third that I am not to be relied upon—changeable—infirm of purpose and weak, and here difference of opinion steps in—not as to a question of degree but in essence, for those who love me best would deny all of these things—but too many see these things in me for me to disregard their opinions and I question myself why such different views should be held and which one is the truer one.

Fourth, I have been thought at times and by many different people—cold—heartless—dishonest—grasping and self-seeking—but opinions of this sort are usually short lived and being only held by such as are injured or so think themselves till the injury is forgotten. . . .

215

What I think of myself is this: I am no fool—I think clearly and act from reason. My thoughts are more clear and my acts are more reasonable than those of the majority of men. . . . What is particularly true of me is that just as I have little engrained wisdom so also I have little knowledge—less that is than other men with my advantages would have—for I have no memory.

These two wants have forced forward such powers as I have of thought and given them a certain readiness and penetration unusual to a man of my common-place calibre and yet sure soon to be detected as unsupported by the real depth and acuteness of which they seem to be the sign. I however build well with other people's bricks. The clearness with which I see—as far as I do see—and the ease with which I handle all the arguments that come before me—are even increased by my mental meagreness and want of knowledge. I am unembarrassed by the mass of materials under which many men much my superior in brains, as well as attainments, are crushed. I become effective, and might be useful; but am likely to spoil it by conceit. I become full of myself and my ideas and being unable to check them by myself and for myself I can only reach firm ground by some sharp fall which in so far as it is in public is something of a disgrace and a very reasonable cause for the poor opinion entertained about me by so many.

The difference of opinion as to the third point I think I can explain. My purposes are strong and change little but the ways by which I hope to attain to them I change with a facility very disturbing to those whose purposes are vague and whose minds find rest rather in the road than the goal—and my want of thorough knowledge of what I am about often makes me confidently take a wrong road. . . . But the purpose in my mind being always clear and always the same my false steps [are] retraced and the object often attained in spite of the over confidence which is natural to a mind clear as to the goal and blind as to the intervening difficulties. . . . Of my moral failings of heartlessness dishonesty and self-seeking, I do not know what to say. . . . I know I am sufficient to myself—self-centred and though needing support, able to get it from my surroundings whatever they may be—this is the shape in which I see my heartlessness, and I think it is characteristic of a cold and rather poor nature. I know also that I am wanting in fine perceptions of honour and unscrupulous in the attainment of my ends, but I do not think my ends involve any very low form of self-seeking; and to set against this I have a genuine desire to do right and enough self government to do it when I know what it is—I am also open-minded and willing to accept humbly rebuke whether in words or from the logic of facts and I am thus continually set right.

Thus mentally and morally it is the same thing with me—I am continually deserving of rebuke and only deserving of praise in so far as these rebukes are not without effect; and though my faults may be unchanged I am able by that persistency (which is my only strong quality) to avoid many of their evil consequences, but not that of being at the mercy of hostile criticism.

C.B.

APPENDIX B

Charles Booth to Mary Booth, August 1880

(see Chapter IV, page 51)

'. . . Ocean Row is a wonderful development of Methodism, a religious watering place owned by the body and peopled by the souls of the Methodist Church and those congenial thereto. It is an effort to bring us to the aid of godliness like the lively music to Revival hymns. The place is on the New Jersey shore about two hours from New York. . . . About the centre of it is the Auditorium and under its huge roof the Services are held. . . . I never saw so large a congregation, five, six or seven thousand. The Service was of the simplest; a hymn or two, a prayer—some Bible reading and a discussion from Brother Keppler, an eminent visitor. I did not think much of the discourse which turned on the very bad shape they would be in if there were no future life.

The young people's class was engaged on a discussion on the flood; the subject at another was the number of the submerged population and it is not a subject which lends itself well to statistics. Oh dear! It is a queer world that we live in and God's work in it not the least curious thing. I don't know what is God's work if this sort of effort is not. It is strenuous effort after a certain ideal of life, sustained by prayer and glorified by praise and yet what a very poor thing it is in some ways, small and narrowing, tending to self-satisfaction; hardly touching at all the more difficult problems of Self, needing a basis of ignorance just as much as they say it is needed for the Masses in the Catholic Church, but with a difference between the ignorants who acknowledge their ignorance and therefore turn to the Priest and the ignorants who acknowledge no ignorance and who accept anything as true if it comes to them in the right form. That sentence was almost too much for me! . . .'

APPENDIX C

Correspondence between Mary Booth and Graphologist

(see Chapter IV, page 65)

'6, Grenville Place, S.W.
2nd July, 1885.

Mrs. Booth begs Graphologist kindly to send her her character from the specimen on the opposite sheet. She encloses eighteen stamps.' On the opposite page Mary has quoted from Lorenzo's well-known speech in *The Merchant of Venice*, beginning with the lines:

> '. . . look, how the floor of heaven
> Is thick inlaid with patines of bright gold. . . .'

The reply was as follows:

'Madame,
You are decidedly free from affectation, naturally pleasant, benevolent and clever, yet your cleverness is more of the deductive and reasoning order than of innate creative power. Your intellect is virile but your feelings are womanly and somewhat changeable and your intellect lives, as it were, in perpetual struggle with your feelings. You are, strange to say, more able to keep the whip hand over others than over yourself, although you are honest and have as much conscientiousness as versatility. You appreciate art to a great extent . . . but a sense of poetical beauty ought to sway you rather in the direction of literary or oratorical effort than any other, though you are a woman whose practical genius ensures comfort and elegance and sociability in her surroundings, with the occasional variation of an outburst of excitability which would be but a passing storm leaving the atmosphere more wholesome than before without a trace of bitterness or malice. You are not what would be styled a very fastidious or sensitive, proud being, but you are essentially a lady in mind, as you would be gentlemanly if you were of the stronger sex, and some of your benevolence is derived from your sense of enjoyment in life. You can stand alone or

219

enjoy society equally well and, though in the full vigour of intellect and energy—and even of ambition—you are a woman of experience and—for a being of such mobile feeling and active thought—of considerable tact. When you choose to give advice, especially with regard to matters that have no personal concern with yourself, it is often valuable advice. When you obligingly choose a dress or ribbon for a friend, we can vouch for its being in perfect taste. But you are no haggler in bargains and have a truly masculine sense of proper economy in domestic matters. On the whole you are entitled to affection and even admiration and have great capacity for happiness in this world and in the prospectively still happier world.

[*Signed*] Graphologist.

Louisa Cottage,
Exmouth,
Devon.'

APPENDIX D

Mary Booth to Beatrice Potter

(see Chapter V, page 82)

'My dear, dear Beatrice,

I feel guilty over having left your welcome letter so long without a word. I do wish I could have you in one of the armchairs by the fire to talk out sundry perplexities, instead of putting them on paper. Yes, immortality is a difficulty. I do not think belief one way or the other . . . has any effect upon one's morality . . . but without it life is so meaningless. After Papa died the conviction that he was living elsewhere bore down upon me and took possession of me in a way that surprised myself. After they had told me of the coming of the telegram and the first shock of the news was over, and the nurse left me for the night, I lay thinking. It was so long since I had seen him; and I wondered whether there could have been anything that he would have wanted to tell me or anything he would have wanted me to do, but I came to the conclusion that I knew all his mind and that he knew it was so, and would not have longed for me in any painful way. Still, it seemed hard we could not have met once more:—and then there swooped down on me all at once, with a sense of elation, such a strong conviction that after a time amounted to a certainty, that he was making his way to other work, free and rejoicing; his voice seemed to fill my ears, not talking to me, but far away, so that I could not distinguish the words, but only joyfully recognise his old, full tones of long ago. I felt that all was right with him, and I could bear to be left without him. Sometimes now I feel feeble and long after him dreadfully. Still the peace has not left me utterly. Papa never seemed to be quite suited to this world; he was so tender and shrinking in his feelings, and he had a loftiness of mind that was pained and harassed with much that he could not help seeing. I think he shut his eyes to a good deal. I do so cherish a hope that all was not over when he ceased to breathe, that he has found another life. The certainty of that night has left behind a root of hope. I was very much interested by what you said about prayer. I couldn't now state in comprehensible language a single Article of religious belief, and yet the need for prayer grows all the time. With Papa, the body gave way when the mind was as clear and vigorous as ever. With dear Uncle Richard you are face to face with a problem [of the failing mind] before which one can only stand in awe-struck depression. One needs all the help one can lay hold of in this strange confused existence. All I can say is that one's whole soul rejects and spurns the unutterable dreariness of the conclusion that this life ends all.'

APPENDIX E

The Star Book

(see Chapter VIII, page 137)

In Part I of the Star Book, Charles Booth began by reminding his readers: 'In the introductory chapter of the industrial series of this work a social classification of the population is given, to which I would again refer . . . being based as regards those without servants, upon their house accommodation, and for the rest upon the number of their domestic servants.' These servants themselves formed 4.9 per cent of the total population of London and there were over a million domestic servants in the country as a whole. A comparison with 1971 would show startling changes in this respect, but the 'habits of the people' do not seem to have altered in other ways, particularly as to gambling.

Charles quoted someone as saying, 'You must change the people a bit before you will stop betting. Police orders won't do it.' He did not feel that betting was a cause of poverty—'The more money, the more betting'—nor did he think it possible to isolate drink as a cause of poverty. 'It plays a part and a great part, but it is only as the accompaniment of idleness, extravagance, incompetence or ill-health that it is fatal.'

In the section 'Sundays, Holidays and Amusements' Charles wrote: 'The taste for music, and for good music, in all classes is undoubted. Good music would seem to be amongst the things which can with safety be supplied collectively and in this manner, as in others, the London County Council are showing the way.' The Royal Festival Hall comes to mind here.

After some general remarks on economic conditions, Charles noted that 'The poor may scoff at luxury, but they are more self-indulgent than the rich; and the rich may sigh for simplicity but even when they really wish for it, find it unattainable; and even if it were attainable would probably not like it. . . .'

In the section on housing Charles expressed his admiration for Miss Octavia Hill and finished with a remarkable appeal: 'I wish I could rouse in the minds of speculative builders a sense of the money value that lies in individuality with its power of attracting the eye, rooting the affections and rousing pride in house and home; then they would seek to use, in place of sedulously destroying, every natural feature of beauty and take thought to add others. A slightly greater width of garden on the sunny side, whether front or back, may make all the difference; a single tree left standing can glorify a whole street.' We are only just beginning to pay attention to these points. Another sentence could also have been written with truth today: 'Of the insufficiency, badness and dearness of the housing accommodation available in many parts of London I need not say anything more. It would be difficult to exaggerate the facts.' He went on to discuss difficulties in the way of improving means of communication and advocated 'bolder engineering expedients on the periphery of London, such as Tube railways, sub-surface tramways or special monorail passenger lines overhead capable of covering forty miles in twenty minutes. Without doubt the arrangement and use of the streets will tend to be further specialised. Street traffic may be regulated or new avenues made for the sake of serving motor cars.' In 1903 this was an accurate forecast for the present day. '. . . in recent years the increase of the outside population has disguised the facts of growth but it will not be long before a "Greater London" will have to be reckoned with for administration purposes.'

Charles Booth pinned his hopes for the future on 'the advancement of the individual . . . a new Middle Class is forming which will perhaps hold the future in its grasp. Its advent seems to me the great social fact of today. Those who constitute this Class are the especial product of the push of industry; within their circle religion and education find the greatest response; amongst them all popular movements take their rise and from time to time draw their leaders. To them in proportion as they have ideas, political power will pass.' This was an accurate prophecy until a few years ago when the power of protest sprang up. The recommendations when they come seem tame in comparison with these imaginative comments.

Charles Booth called for the unification of Poor Law administration, 'not only in London but throughout the country—but it is only as regards London that I now speak. Where great aggregations of population are brought together there is a tendency to uniformity of class in each section. Poor districts become more uniformly poor because the better off leave and betake themselves to the parts they prefer. If therefore under these conditions the cost of the poor under the Poor Law is to be borne locally it necessarily presses unjustly. On the other hand, if the community as a whole bears the cost it must control the management; and yet the administration in order that it may have any real life must be local.'

In addition to organised relief and private charity, he himself had advocated as a third element 'the introduction of Old Age Pensions contributed directly from the National purse, not so much in aid of poverty as of thrift. As my plan bears equally on the administration both of the Poor Law and of private charity, I will venture to recapitulate it.' Mary had suggested that it was a mistake to include a further reference to the scheme, but Charles evidently felt loath to let any opportunity go by without tackling this question. Another four years was to pass before Asquith brought in old age pension legislation.

The title of his concluding essay is 'Things as they are and as they move': 'Seventeen years and an equal number of volumes have been occupied with this Inquiry. In as many pages I must now try to sum up the results: seventeen words would doubtless suffice did I know how to choose them aright but the subjects covered offer a wide range, being no less than life and industry as they exist in London at the end of the Nineteenth Century under the influences of education, religion and administration. We see life cursed by drink, brutality and vice and loaded down with ignorance and poverty while industry is choked by its own blind struggles and education is still painfully mounting . . . the first rungs of its ladder. We see religion paralysed by its own inconsistencies, and administration wrapped in the swaddling clothes of indecision and mutual distrust.'

Finally he wrote: '. . . facts are still needed but the spirit of patient enquiry is abroad. . . . Every year that passes produces valuable work in this direction both official and voluntary. These considerations have reconciled me to the incompleteness of my own work. At the best speed possible to me it would have taken three more years and I suppose three more volumes to have dealt adequately with the new subjects touched upon in the preceding pages, an expectation which the limits of my readers' patience, to say nothing of my own, absolutely forbade. At this point therefore my work ends. The last word I would add is this; the object of the seventeen volumes has been to describe London as it appeared in the last decade of the 19th Century. Beyond this I have sought, however imperfectly, to show what is being done to ameliorate its conditions and have suggested some directions in which advance might be made; but this last was no part of the original design which was solely to observe and chronicle, leaving the actual living remedies to others. . . .'

The title page of this concluding volume reads: 'Life and Labour of the People in London by Charles Booth, assisted by Jesse Argyle, Ernest Aves, George E. Arkel, Arthur L. Baxter, George H. Duckworth. Final Volume.' Under the words 'Final Volume' there is a black star in a white shield.

APPENDIX F

Text of the Illuminated Address presented to
Charles Booth in the House of Commons in 1909

(see Chapter X, page 176)

'To the Right Honourable CHARLES BOOTH, Privy Councillor, Fellow of the Royal Society, Doctor of Science in the University of Cambridge, D.C.L. in the University of Oxford, LL.D. in the University of Liverpool.

We the undersigned Members and Supporters of the National Committee of Organised Labour desire to offer you our sincere congratulations on the passing of the first Old Age Pensions Act in the United Kingdom.

To you more than to any other man, this first instalment of justice to the aged is due. Ten years ago Lord Rothschild's Committee of Experts had declared all Pension Schemes impracticable, and had declined to consider the Schemes which you had advocated. Both Parties in the State appeared to acquiesce in this negative result.

Then you consented to expound your views before a series of Conferences, composed of Representatives of Trade Unions, Friendly Societies, and Co-operative Societies. Everywhere you secured a most impressive unanimity in support of your proposals. The outcome of these Conferences was the National Committee of Organised Labour, which has for the space of ten years permeated all classes with your views, and eventually succeeded in winning the Nation to your side.

The House of Commons has, either without a Division, or with overwhelming majorities endorsed the demand which we learned from you to adopt and enforce. His Majesty's Government has repeatedly declared its acceptance of your contention that Old Age Pensions should be a Civil Right, universal, non-contributory, and free from all taint of the Poor Law.

In the sphere of principle our victory is complete, and we are proud to acknowledge that our victory is yours.

227

You have supplied the ideas, the arguments, the convincing considerations, which have conquered the Nation. The half million aged persons who now draw free pensions from the State, are the first of a great multitude whose declining years will be made peaceful and honourable by your high souled initiative, and whose increasing infirmities will be sweetened and hallowed by gratitude to Almighty God for what you have done.'

The Address was signed by the following: Geo. M. Barnes (Chairman), Geo. D. Kelly (Vice-Chairman), Edward Cadbury (Treasurer), Frederick Rogers (Secretary), F. Herbert Stead (Hon. Secretary), R. Waite (Hon. Secretary), Thos. Burt, George Cadbury, John V. Stevens.

SELECT BIBLIOGRAPHY

This list is simply a guide for those who may wish to obtain more information on Charles and Mary Booth and their family, and on some others mentioned in this book. It is not meant to be a full bibliography of the Booths and their friends. Public figures such as Gladstone and Balfour will be well known to the reader and are therefore omitted. Works by Charles Booth are given first, in chronological order; then follow, in alphabetical order of authors, books giving information about the Booths and their friends.

Attention may also be drawn to the Booth manuscripts deposited by the Passfield Trustees in the British Library of Political and Economic Science (London School of Economics).

CHARLES BOOTH

1889   *Life and Labour of the People*, vol. 1.

1891   *Labour and Life of the People*,[1] vol. 2.

1892   *Pauperism: a Picture. Endowment of Old Age: an Argument.*

1892–7 *Life and Labour of the People in London*, 9 vols (second edn).

1894   *The Aged Poor in England and Wales: Condition.*

1899   *Old Age Pensions and the Aged Poor: a Proposal.*

1901   *Improved Means of Locomotion as a First Step towards the Cure for the Housing Difficulties of London* (pamphlet).

1902–3 *Life and Labour of the People in London*, 17 vols (third edn).

1910   *Poor Law Reform* (92 pp.).
       Reform of the Poor Law by the Adaptation of the Existing Poor Law Areas, and Their Administration (38 pp.).

1911   *Comments on Proposals for the Reform of the Poor Laws*, with note by Sir Arthur Downes (23 pp.).

1913   *Industrial Unrest and Trade Union Policy* (32 pp.).

All the above, with one exception, were published by Macmillan & Co.; the first edition of *Life and Labour* was published by Williams & Norgate.

[1] Original title of this volume.

Papers read before the Royal Statistical Society and printed in the Society's Journal

1886 'Occupations of the People of the United Kingdom, 1801–81' (vol. XLIX, pp. 314–435).

1887 'The Inhabitants of the Tower Hamlets (School Board Division), their Condition and Occupations' (vol. L, pp. 326–91).

1888 'The Condition and Occupations of the People of East London and Hackney, 1887' (vol. LI, pp. 276–331).

1891 'Enumeration and Classification of Paupers, and State Pensions for the Aged' (vol. LIV, pp. 600–43).

1892 Presidential Adress (on dock and wharf labour) (vol. LV, pp. 521–7).

1893 Presidential Adress: 'Life and Labour of the People in London: first results of an Inquiry based on the 1891 Census' (vol. LVI, pp. 557–93).

1894 'Statistics of Pauperism in Old Age' (vol. LVII, pp. 235–45).

OTHER AUTHORS

Beveridge, Sir William, K.C.B., 'Social insurance and allied services', report presented to Parliament, 1942 (Cmd. 6404, 6405).

Booth, Charles Zachary Macaulay, *Zachary Macaulay:* his part in the movement for the abolition of the Slave Trade. An appreciation etc. (Longman, 1934).

Booth, Mary, *Charles Booth: A Memoir* (Macmillian, 1918, reissued, with foreword by Margaret Ritchie, Farnborough, 1968).

Creswicke, Louis, *The Life of the Rt Hon. Joseph Chamberlain* etc., 4 vols (Caxton, 1904).

Crow, Duncan, *A Man of Push and Go*: The life of George Macaulay Booth (Hart-Davis, 1965).

Garvin, James Louis, *The Life of Joseph Chamberlain*, 6 vols, vols 4–6 by Julian Amery (Macmillan, 1932–69).

Holland, Margaret Jean, *The Life and Letters of Zachary Macaulay* (Edward Arnold, 1900).

Holman Hunt, Diana, *My Grandmothers and I* (Hamish Hamilton, 1960); *My Grandfather: His Wives and Loves* (Hamish Hamilton, 1969).

Hyndman, Henry Mayers, *The Record of an Adventurous Life* (Macmillan, 1911).

John, Arthur Henry, *A Liverpool Merchant House*: being the history of Alfred Booth & Company, 1863–1958 (Allen & Unwin, 1959).

Laing, Diana Whitehill, *Mistress of Herself*, the life of Mary Crowninshield Carnegie, *née* Endicott (Barre, Mass., 1965).

Mearns, Andrew, *The Bitter Cry of Outcast London* (1883, reissued by Leicester University Press, 1970, with introduction and notes by Anthony S. Wohl).

Meinertzhagen, Georgina, *From Ploughshare to Parliament*: a short memoir of the Potters of Tadcaster etc. (John Murray, 1908).

Muggeridge, Kitty, and Adam, Ruth, *Beatrice Webb. A Life. 1858–1943* (Secker & Warburg, 1967).

Phillips, Harlan B., *Felix Frankfurter Reminisces*, recorded in talks with Dr H. B. Phillips (Reynal, N.Y., 1906).

Ritchie, Margaret, *Memories and Stories* (privately printed, Farnham Common, 1963).

Rowntree, Benjamin Seebohm, *Poverty: A Study of Town Life* (Macmillan, 1901).

Simey, Thomas Spensley and Margaret Bayne, *Charles Booth: Social Scientist* (Oxford University Press, 1960).

Trevelyan, George Otto, *The Life and Letters of Lord Macaulay* (Longman, 1876).

Webb, Beatrice, *My Apprenticeship* (1926, 2nd edn 1945); *Our Partnership*, ed. Barbara Drake, Margaret Cole, etc (1948); *Diaries 1912–25* (1952); *Diaries 1924–32* (1956); Minority Report of the Royal Commission on the Poor Laws and Relief of Distress (1909); all published by Longman.

UNPUBLISHED PAPERS

Letters, papers and notebooks of Charles Booth, now in the British Library of Political and Economic Science at the London School of Economics, Houghton Street, W.C.2.

Correspondence between Charles and Mary Booth, now in the University of London Library, Senate House, W.C.1.

Correspondence between Charles Zachary Macaulay and his daughter, Mary Booth, now in the University of London Library.

The diaries of Mary Booth, now in the possession of Sir Antony Macnaghten, Bt.

Diaries and letters of Beatrice Webb, now in the British Library of Political and Economic Science at the London School of Economics.

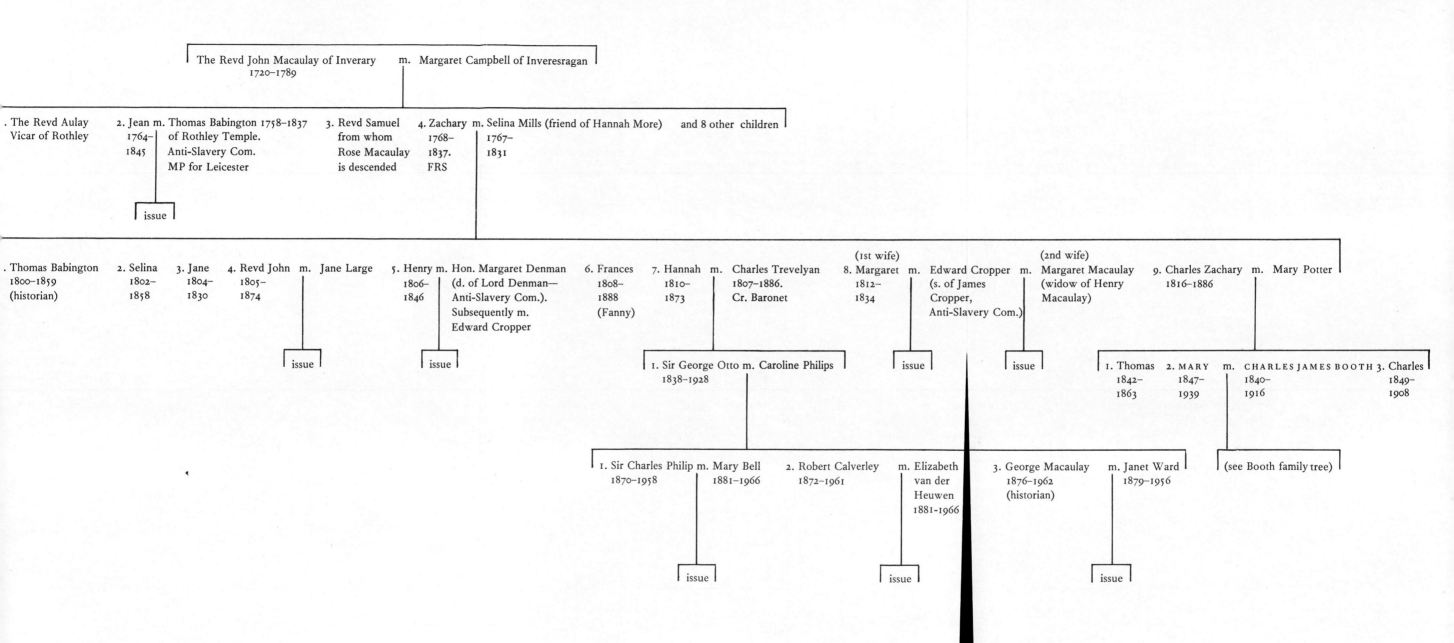

The Revd John Macaulay of Inverary m. Margaret Campbell of Inveresragan
1720–1789

. The Revd Aulay
Vicar of Rothley

2. Jean m. Thomas Babington 1758–1837
1764– of Rothley Temple.
1845 Anti-Slavery Com.
MP for Leicester

3. Revd Samuel
from whom
Rose Macaulay
is descended

4. Zachary m. Selina Mills (friend of Hannah More) and 8 other children
1768– 1767–
1837. 1831
FRS

issue

. Thomas Babington
1800–1859
(historian)

2. Selina
1802–
1858

3. Jane
1804–
1830

4. Revd John m. Jane Large
1805–
1874

5. Henry m. Hon. Margaret Denman
1806– (d. of Lord Denman—
1846 Anti-Slavery Com.).
Subsequently m.
Edward Cropper

6. Frances
1808–
1888
(Fanny)

7. Hannah m. Charles Trevelyan
1810– 1807–1886.
1873 Cr. Baronet

(1st wife)
8. Margaret m. Edward Cropper m.
1812– (s. of James
1834 Cropper,
Anti-Slavery Com.)

(2nd wife)
Margaret Macaulay
(widow of Henry
Macaulay)

9. Charles Zachary m. Mary Potter
1816–1886

issue

issue

1. Sir George Otto m. Caroline Philips
1838–1928

issue

issue

1. Thomas
1842–
1863

2. MARY m. CHARLES JAMES BOOTH
1847– 1840–
1939 1916

3. Charles
1849–
1908

(see Booth family tree)

1. Sir Charles Philip m. Mary Bell
1870–1958 1881–1966

2. Robert Calverley m. Elizabeth
1872–1961 van der
Heuwen
1881–1966

3. George Macaulay m. Janet Ward
1876–1962 1879–1956
(historian)

issue

issue

issue

Cripps,   7. Margaret m. Rt Hon.   8. Beatrice
941.   1854–   Sir Henry   1858–
rd   1921   Hobhouse   1945
r of   1854–1937

| issue—7 children |

bank

INDEX